# THE LOGIC OF
# THE PLANNED ECONOMY

# The Logic of
# The Planned Economy

## *The Seeds of the Collapse*

PAWEL H. DEMBINSKI

Translated by
KEVIN COOK

CLARENDON PRESS · OXFORD
1991

Oxford University Press, Walton Street, Oxford OX2 6DP

Oxford New York Toronto
Delhi Bombay Calcutta Madras Karachi
Petaling Jaya Singapore Hong Kong Tokyo
Nairobi Dar es Salaam Cape Town
Melbourne Auckland
and associated companies in
Berlin Ibadan

Oxford is a trade mark of Oxford University Press

Published in the United States
by Oxford University Press, New York

British Library Cataloguing in Publication Data
Dembinski, Pawel H.
The logic of the planned economy : the seeds of the
collapse.
1. Planned economies
I. Title II. Economies planifiées. English
330.124
ISBN 0-19-828686-4


Library of Congress Cataloging in Publication Data
Dembinski, Pawel H., 1955–
[Economies planifiées. English]
The logic of the planned economy : the seeds of the collapse /
Pawel H. Dembinski ; translated by Kevin Cook.
Translation of: Les economies planifiées.
Includes bibliographical references
Includes index.
1. Central planning—Europe, Eastern. 2. Europe, Eastern—
Economic policy. 3. Marxian economics. I. Title.
HC244.D37313 1990    338.947—dc20    90–7721
ISBN 0-19-828686-4


Typeset by Latimer Trend & Company Ltd, Plymouth
Printed in Great Britain by
Biddles Ltd,
Guildford & King's Lynn

*To my family*

# PREFACE TO THE
# ENGLISH EDITION

The original French edition of this book was published in early 1988, under the title *Les Économies planifiées: La Logique du système* (Planned Economies: The Logic of the System). Just two years later, we are witnessing what appears to be the complete collapse—at least in Europe—of the system of centrally planned economies (CPEs). During the second half of 1989, the political face of Poland, Hungary, Czechoslovakia, the GDR, Bulgaria, Romania, Yugoslavia, and even the USSR unexpectedly started to change. As this book goes to press, the forces behind what is already being referred to as 'the 1989 revolution' are still largely a mystery and remain in disequilibrium. Yet, whatever happens, the disintegration of Communist rule in this part of the world now seems irreversible.

In 1989, in one Communist country after another, the Communist party either withdrew from power or was forced to yield it up. This seriously weakened the foundations of the CPE system. The collapse, or near-collapse, of the CPE system is not accidental; it is a direct result of the fact that by 1989 the internal tensions inherent in the system had greatly exceeded the system's ability to withstand them. Although the implosion of the system came as a surprise not only to most observers but also to those directly involved, the *seeds of the collapse* had existed within the system from the very start.

The research and conceptual work contained in this book had a twofold objective. The first was to assess whether there were inescapable internal contradictions that threatened the system. If this were shown to be so, the second objective was to identify the critical level at which such contradictions would cause the system to collapse.

The main finding of the book is that the internal consistency of the CPE system—its overriding logic—has always been entirely derived from, and is thus totally dependent upon, Marxist Communist ideology. There was therefore no way that the system could survive, or adapt to, changes in this ideological corner-stone. Moreover, the system's orthodox ideological principles left it little room to attain the level of efficiency required in a modern economy. Paradoxical as it may seem, the poor economic performance of the CPEs appears to have been rooted in the system itself and, at the same time, to have been the main threat to the system's survival. The analysis contained in this book makes clear that—contrary to the view taken until recently by most Sovietologists—the CPE system is incapable of reform, in the sense of institutional or organizational changes leading to a marked improvement in economic performance.

The collapse of the system, as well as the way in which it has behaved and operated in the past, is easily explained in terms of the inescapable dilemma that forces the system to choose between ideological legitimacy and economic performance. Since these are fundamentally irreconcilable, the history of the system has been one long sequence of precarious compromises, half-hearted reforms, and desperate yet unsuccessful attempts to reorient its policies. By failing to deal with the basic dilemma, such delaying tactics could only postpone the ultimate and inevitable collapse of the CPE system.

The basic dilemma facing the system entirely conditioned each of its constituent parts, as well as the overall logic behind its economic functioning. Here the irresolute nature of the system expressed itself in three 'internal dilemmas', regarding the role of planning, the nature of the enterprise, and the function of money. The inability of the system to tackle these crucial economic problems squarely explains why it proved unable to offer effective resistance to pressures from its environment, in other words to escape the three 'external dilemmas', concerning its relations with society, the arms race, and trade with the West.

None of the economic problems the CPE system has had to face over the last twenty years can be properly understood without reference to the basic dilemma of ideological legitimacy versus economic performance—which can be said to have sown the seeds of the collapse. From the mid-1960s onwards, conditions were particularly conducive to the growth of these seeds into real forces that made the final collapse inevitable. These conditions included:

  major gains in efficiency forced upon the market economies by the oil crisis of the mid-1970s;

  the Western technological breakthrough in the highly sensitive fields of telecommunications and computer science, culminating in the Star Wars project;

  the dependence of Eastern Europe on the market economies through debt and import reliance, which started with *détente* and have been growing ever since;

  the inclusion of the Western concept of human rights in the Helsinki Agreement, which came to be used as a way of legitimizing popular discontent with the CPE system in Eastern Europe.

When this book was first being written in 1986–7, the system was desperately playing for time. There were two possible scenarios of collapse, though at the time neither seemed imminent: either the Communist parties would peacefully commit ideological suicide, or they would be violently overthrown by civil war or revolution. In 1989, the CPE system in Eastern Europe was not physically destroyed, but was dislocated by the sudden disappearance of its source of ideological cohesion. Whereas violent destruction eliminates the actual components of the system—its institutions, structures, mechanisms, and patterns of human behaviour—as well as the rules governing the relations between them, in the case of dislocation it is only the rules that disappear. Consequently, after the system collapses its components continue to exist but are no longer governed by the logic of the system.

Thus, even though the CPE system as such has ceased to exist in Eastern Europe, it remains present in the form of its surviving components. These components are profoundly conditioned by their political origins, by the logic and needs of the CPE system which governed them for the previous forty years. That is why the replacement of a Marxist creed by a liberal one is merely the beginning of the process of transition to a market economy system—it is not the process itself. Recasting the economic system involves shifting from overall economic logic based on central planning to logic based on the market, and transforming the

former components of the old system to make them compatible
with the new rules. This process requires time, as well as a proper
understanding of the origins and previous functions of each
component that is to be integrated into the new system.

As explained in the Introduction, the research presented in this
book sets out from a conviction that economists, both Eastern and
Western, have been using the same terminology to describe
different realities. This creates a semantic haze which, on the one
hand, prevents Western economists from understanding the CPE
system and, on the other hand, prevents Eastern economists from
fully grasping the workings of a developed market economy. This
book helps to show that the realities described by terms such as
'accounting', 'bank', 'enterprise', 'management', 'money', 'economic policy', 'exchange rate', 'State budget', etc. look very
different in developed market economies and in Eastern Europe.

Before the collapse of the CPE system, the consequences of this
semantic haze were chiefly intellectual, adding one more distorted
analysis of the problems facing Eastern European economies to the
endless rows of irrelevant literature. Yet in today's transitional
situation, where the CPE system is totally discredited and economic decisions are being made by people with only a text-book
knowledge of market economies, or else by Western advisers
whose knowledge of the CPE system is too often based on gross
misconceptions, there is a grave risk that the semantic haze may
lead to errors of policy. The author hopes that, by bridging the
semantic gap, this book will help to prevent at least some such
errors from occurring.

This translation was generously sponsored by the Wilsdorf
Foundation, Geneva.

P.H.D.

*Geneva*
*February 1990*

# CONTENTS

# LIST OF TABLES

## CENTRALLY PLANNED ECONOMIES
## AS SEEN BY THE MAN IN THE STREET

*There's no unemployment, and yet nobody works.*

*Nobody works, and yet the plan gets fulfilled.*

*The plan gets fulfilled, and yet there's never anything in the shops.*

*There's never anything in the shops, and yet every fridge is full.*

*Every fridge is full, and yet everyone complains.*

*Everyone complains, and yet the same people keep getting elected.*

# INTRODUCTION

Before jumping to the conclusion that this is just another book about the Eastern European economies, please read on.

Despite the wealth of literature on the subject, we still do not have a proper conceptual framework with which to understand the true nature and causes of the economic problems facing the centrally planned economies (CPEs). In other words, we still lack a paradigm. It is hoped that this book will go some way towards filling the gap.

Why has this never been done before? The problem is basically one of methodology. Classical economic theory either misrepresents the problems facing CPEs or else treats them as though they were not worth considering. Furthermore, while writings on the subject by experts in both parts of Europe display all the detail and technical excellence one has come to associate with serious contemporary economic theory, their essentially mechanistic approach usually prevents them from getting at the underlying phenomena. This apparently bothers non-economists more than it does economists, who seem blinkered by their training. In the words of the historian Alain Besançon:

There has been a considerable amount of academic writing on the Soviet economy. . . . Yet those . . . who have become familiar with the Soviet system through history, literature, travel or stories told by emigrants fail to recognise it when described by economists—as though there were an unbridgeable gulf between the system of the economists, recorded in terms of measurements and figures, and their own instinctive understanding of the system, without measurements or figures of any kind, based entirely on their own immediate experience.[1]

His fellow historian Norman Davis goes even further:

they [journalists] rely on the academic profession, on the army of Western Sovietologists and Slavicists, who nowadays are clearly divided between those who do not know how the Soviet world works and those who cannot explain it.

Someone at some time will have to sort out the vocabulary used to discuss Soviet affairs. People must be weaned off Western terminology when describing organs of the Leninist state that share only the name with the Western democratic institutions.[2]

Non-economists may be quicker to perceive such shortcomings in economic literature for the simple reason that the other social sciences—sociology, political science, anthropology, and ethnography—are essentially based on the notion of 'otherness'. Economic theory, on the other hand, has always considered economic problems to be universal ones; accordingly it sees itself as being quite different from the other social sciences, and economic analyses are therefore much more general, which is to say more abstract. In fact, economic theory claims to be able to dispense with the first level of abstraction, namely *conceptualization*, and move straight on to the higher level of *deductive model-building*. Jean-Pierre Dupuy believes that this claim to universality can be explained by the circumstances under which economic theory first emerged as a separate discipline:

In order to become an independent discipline, with a specific area of human affairs as its subject-matter, economics obviously had to become separate from politics, but also, less obviously, from morality. *Such a separation was made possible by the emergence of the modern individual, who had thrown off the rigid social codes that had kept traditional man trapped in a web of constraints and obligations, and was freed from subjection to any kind of all-embracing, integrating totality.*[3]

This reminder about the origins of economic theory shows that, whatever its claims, it is actually only applicable to societies in which *Homo oeconomicus* is able to function. Nevertheless, ever since the 'universal' concept of *Homo oeconomicus* was first introduced (invented?), economic theory has been busily building deductive models on the basis of a single conceptual apparatus which is assumed to apply to all economic problems, irrespective of the socio-political conditions under which they occur.

The respective status of Sismondi in economic theory and Tocqueville in contemporary sociology illustrates the differing methodologies that have come to prevail in these two fields. Sismondi (1773–1842) and Tocqueville (1805–59) were practically contemporaries. Both were inquisitive, open-minded men who travelled in order to study societies with which they were unfamiliar: Tocqueville to learn about the workings of the newly founded American republic, and Sismondi to investigate the factors that governed the circulation of goods in various countries. Today Tocqueville is acclaimed as a genius who laid the foundations of political sociology, whereas Sismondi is known to a mere handful of particularly well-read economists. And yet their approach was very similar. They both attempted to understand the mechanisms that governed the workings of society in countries that differed from their own, and both based their observations and conceptualizations on reality rather than theory. The fact that Sismondi is scarcely mentioned in economics textbooks is symptomatic of the methodology currently prevailing in economic theory, which encourages model-building at the expense of observation and conceptualization.

The purpose of this book, then, is to analyse CPEs from a 'social sciences' point of view—in other words, an attempt will be made to conceptualize the 'otherness' of such economies, instead of building models as economic theory has been wont to do. The essential premise of this book is that, contrary to popular belief, economic problems are not expressed in a universal manner. *Thus, while the subject-matter of this book may be economic, the basic theoretical approach is not* (in the sense in which Western economics understands the term).

It is not my intention to provide a structured, testable theory, but rather a paradigm which may one day form the basis for such a theory. If we are to devise a conceptual framework with which to analyse CPEs, we must look at the *essential linkages* of the Eastern European economies. An over-descriptive approach may make it harder rather than easier to grasp the underlying phenomena, since the reader may simply drown in a flood of unstructured data. There is nothing particularly new about my approach, but it has tended to be forgotten by economists in recent years. Back in 1959, André Marchal described the intermediate level of abstraction used here in the following terms:[4]

... the concepts of structure, system, and 'type of organization' appear, particularly in the writings of Akerman and Eucken, *as an essential link that makes it possible to move from historical description to theoretical analysis* [my italics], by providing the former with a frame or system of reference without which concrete research becomes random, without any goal or guiding principle. Perroux describes these concepts as 'tools of analysis and interpretation whereby historical material can be polished so as to become usable', while Eucken sees them as 'a solid link between the empirical view of historical events and the overall theoretical analysis that is necessary in order to understand the relationships concerned'.

What concepts are available to help us construct our conceptual framework? Here again, economic theory is caught in a rut, and we are forced to look elsewhere, even create new concepts. However, caution is required—for it is just as dangerous to invent entirely new terminology as it is to take traditional economic concepts and apply them to CPEs unchanged. Let us take a closer look at both alternatives.

Why not attack the problem at the root and create a new vocabulary especially for CPEs? Well, first of all, by no means all traditional economic theory is irrelevant here. Secondly, it is surely worth broadening the conceptual apparatus of economic theory so that comparisons can be made between different systems later on.

Taking the other alternative, why should we hesitate to use terms such as 'price', 'money', 'profit' and 'enterprise', since these patently exist in every Eastern European economy? The reason is that, if we are not careful, we may find ourselves using the same words to mean different things. As long as a given term actually means what those who use the term instinctively intend it to mean, there is no problem. If it does not, however, there is a serious risk of confusion. Once we move away from the familiar ground of the market economy, our conceptual spectacles cease to be reliable; a given term may suddenly mean something else altogether, and our view may thus be distorted without our realizing it.

If terms derived from a particular system are applied in a context where they do not belong, any reasoning based on them is bound to be inaccurate. Far from making it easier to understand an unfamiliar kind of reality, such terms may simply be misleading, since they will constantly throw their user back to his original frame of reference. This will continue to happen until the relationship between the new situation and the old term has been properly analysed. The literature on Eastern Europe is full of examples of authors who have fallen into terminological traps of this kind.

A good example is the term 'money'. In market economies, money functions 'naturally' as a standard of value, a means of exchange, and a diachronic store of wealth. If we simply take this term and apply it to CPEs unchanged, we are assuming that money fulfils the same functions as in market economies, whereas there is no evidence whatsoever that this is so. This example shows that before transposing any term from one system to another, we must be quite sure what it means in its new environment. In other words, we need to sharpen our conceptual tools and to cleanse them of any irrelevant connotations that link them back to the user's original frame of reference.

These problems of methodology and terminology account for the structure of this book: instead of beginning with the economic problems that face CPEs, we will conclude with them. Part I deals with the *structural and philosophical basis* of the System[5] and the essential principles that govern the way it works. Part II examines what will be referred to as the System's *internal dilemmas*: economic planning and the organizational problems it causes, the role of money, and requisitioning. Finally, Part III discusses the relationship between the System and its environment, in which actual economic problems bring the System face to face with its *external dilemmas*: the social dilemma, the military dilemma, and the dilemma of growth.

## Notes

1. Alain Besançon, *Anatomie d'un spectre: L'Économie politique du socialisme réel*, Calmann-Lévy, Paris, 1981, p. 9.
2. Norman Davis, 'Polish isn't Russian; Russia isn't America', *International Herald Tribune*, 26 Nov. 1985.
3. J.-P. Dupuy, 'L'Émancipation de l'économie: Retour sur "Das Adam Smith Problem"', paper presented at the André Gide conference, Montpellier, France, Sept. 1984 (my italics).
4. In *Systèmes et structures économiques*, Presses Universitaires de France (PUF), Paris, 1959, p. 14.
5. For a definition of this key concept, see p. 28–32.

# I

# The Essence of the System

The structure of this book, already briefly outlined in the Introduction, is as follows. Part I is divided into two chapters, the first which examines the philosophical basis of the System (from here on the CPE system will be referred to simply as 'the System'), and the second the principles that determine how it works in practice. The more specifically economic aspects of the System will be dealt with in Parts II and III.

# 1
# A Matter of Doctrine: Messianic Communism and the System

In the first part of this chapter we will be looking at the doctrine, or creed, that serves as the basis for the role of the Eastern European Communist parties, and in the second part we will examine how the System helps them to deal with the problems they encounter.

## THE PHILOSOPHICAL ESSENCE OF MESSIANIC COMMUNISM

### *Marxism, the Creed, and the Promised Society*

The Eastern European Communist parties espouse an official metaphysical world-view in which they have a specific 'historical mission', and which forms the basis for their entire social, economic, and political policy. The source of this world-view is Marxist theory, which the East European Communist parties claim that they alone have successfully put into practice. We will therefore begin by taking a look at what the Marxist world-view means in terms of the Communist parties' historical mission — in other words, their ultimate goal.

The term 'Marxism' is open to numerous interpretations. It can mean anything from the actual theories of Marx and Engels to any one of the overlapping currents of contemporary thought based on those theories, each with its own interpretation of what Marx and Engels are supposed to have meant. The range is very wide: there is a world of difference between the theoretical Marxism of a philosopher such as Althusser and the popular Marxism of *Pravda*, which in turn is a far cry from 'shop-floor' or 'bar-room' Marxism. In short, there is no universally acceptable definition of Marxism, nor even a reliable common denominator.

None the less, the Eastern European Communist parties continue to invoke the prophetic dimension of Marxism. To quote Raymond Aron:

currently, the outcome of [Marxist] prophecies is either Soviet ideo-cracy—in which various ideological themes are used to justify the party's maintenance of absolute power—or else a vague set of prejudices which together constitute a kind of vulgate.[1]

Therefore, if we are to understand the philosophical origins of CPEs and the mission they are called upon to fulfil, we need to take a closer look at the Communist party's main sources of inspiration. For the purposes of our analysis, we will refer to the kind of Marxism currently practised in Eastern Europe as 'the Creed'—a sort of basic Marxist-Leninist framework which includes all the main theses of Marx, Engels, and Lenin.[2] Let me stress at this point that my purpose is not to attempt a comprehensive analysis of Marxist theory, but simply to analyse the creed on which the Communist party's mission is based.[3] Messianic Communism and the Creed have a symbiotic relationship, held together by a number of perfectly interlocking factors on which the Communist party depends for its survival. First of all, the Creed states the essential conditions for universal happiness; it then goes on to demonstrate that these conditions will inevitably be fulfilled in the 'Promised Society'; and, finally, it shows the faithful what they must do to hasten the dawning of the new era.

## Universal happiness: the Promised Society

What, then, are the essential conditions for universal happiness? To discover this, let us look at how the Creed analyses human nature.

As a student of philosophy, Marx soon came into contact with Hegelian thought. He was in his early twenties when he first read Feuerbach's *Essence of Christianity* (1841), according to which man was oppressed by an idealized image of himself which he called God. Although this situation was alienating to man, Feuerbach saw it as a necessary stage in the development of human consciousness; this development would only be completed once man assumed the place he had temporarily abandoned to 'God'.

Soon afterwards, in *The Jewish Question* (1844), Marx parted company with Feuerbach by rejecting the inevitability of religious alienation:

Man emancipates himself *politically* from religion by expelling it from the sphere of public law to that of private law. Religion is no longer the spirit of the *state*, in which man behaves, albeit in a specific and limited way and in a particular sphere, as a generic being, in community with other men. It has become the spirit of *civil society*, of the sphere of egoism and of the *bellum omnium contra omnes*. . . . The division of man into the *public person* and the *private person*, the *displacement* of religion from the state to civil society—all this is not a stage in political emancipation but its consummation.[4]

By cutting man off from his fellows, religion helped to blind him to the fact that he was essentially a *generic being*. However, the real roots of this estrangement lay elsewhere, in socio-economic alienation:

Man, in his *most intimate* reality, in civil society, is a profane being. Here, where he appears both to himself and to others as a real individual, he is an *illusory* phenomenon. In the state, on the contrary, where he is regarded as a generic being, man is the imaginary member of an imaginary sovereignty, divested of his real, individual life, and infused with an unreal universality.[5]

Thus, according to Marx, man was a generic being who could only thrive through social contact with his fellows. The bourgeois state did not allow man to be himself, since it kept the political dimension separate from the economic dimension, thereby cutting off man's truth from man's reality. In bourgeois society, man could thrive as a generic being in the field of politics, but the economic dimension was dominated by individualism, which was at variance with human nature. Thus, said Marx, man could only thrive, and alienation truly cease, if the political dimension (truth) and the economic dimension (reality) were united in a single, indivisible social dimension:

Human emancipation will only be complete when the real individual man has absorbed into himself the abstract citizen; when as an individual man, in his everyday life, in his work, and in his relationships he has become a *generic being*; and when he has recognized and organized his own powers (*forces propres*) as social powers so that he no longer separates this social power from himself as *political* power.[6]

Unlike Hobbes, Locke, or Rousseau, to whom the state of nature was irretrievably lost in the distant past, at the dawn of human history, Marx saw it as a future state of perfect stability that would coincide with the end of history, that is, the point at which the passage of time would cease to bring about any further transformation in human society. The Promised Society would then be achieved in all its communist glory. This society would be a strictly unitarian one, permitting of no diversity, since diversity of any kind—religious, political, or economic—conflicted with the generic nature of man. Accordingly, in the Promised Society there would no longer be any need (or indeed any place) for individual freedoms, in the sense of guaranteed individual autonomy from society.[7] The convergence of human truth and human reality would eliminate the dichotomy between the individual and society, making way for a new, indestructible whole—*generic man, who would be both individual and society*.

This claim to have grasped the essence of human nature[8] is the basis for the Creed's ethical condemnation of bourgeois society. The latter is seen as essentially evil because it stifles human nature; a 'good' society, on the other hand, is a society in which human nature is able to thrive. This paramount moral ideal of universal happiness is undeniably one of the most powerful, and most misunderstood, aspects of East European Messianic Communism.[9]

## The inevitability of the Promised Society

The Creed uses the universal law of motion known as dialectic to prove the inevitability of the Promised Society. Having done so, it can then identify the forces that determine the evolution of social systems and that inevitably cause history to move ever nearer to the Promised Society. These forces are the *forces of historical materialism.*

## Dialectic motion

Up to the eighteenth century, the term 'dialectic' was merely a synonym for Aristotelian logic. Only in the nineteenth century did the works of Kant, Fichte, and Hegel give the term a totally different meaning, which was then borrowed by Marx and Engels and eventually became a corner-stone of the Creed.

The essential distinction between Hegelian dialectic and Aristotelian logic lies in the principle *tertium non datur* (also known as the principle of non-contradiction). Put very simply, in Aristotelian logic negation destroys or eliminates that which is negated, whereas in Hegelian dialectic it absorbs and, as it were, feeds on the original assertion. The consequences of this distinction are far-reaching and rather surprising. In Aristotelian logic, successive negations lead to a see-sawing motion (original assertion—negation of the assertion—negation of the negation), which effectively brings us back to where we started from. In Hegelian dialectic, on the other hand, successive negations are part of a cumulative process in which the original assertion is outweighed by the negation, which in turn is outweighed by the subsequent negation, and so on.

According to the Creed, dialectic determines the motion of all matter and thought. The Creed then goes on to state that social realities have an intrinsic and irrepressible tendency to generate their own dialectical contradiction. The resulting dialectical motion only ceases when the contradiction generates its own contradiction; at that point reality is raised to a new and qualitatively higher state, just as successive negations raise thought to ever higher levels.

It might seem that we are then simply faced with an endless succession of contradictions. However, dialectic 'proves' that the Promised Society is inevitable: Marx indicated that dialectical motion would cease of its own accord at the point where all contradictions had been resolved—in other words, at the point where the essential conditions for universal happiness had been fulfilled. Up to this point, social structures would be subject to objective laws of transformation which could be understood by man but would also act without his conscious assistance. The discovery of this universal law of motion made the coming of the Promised Society inescapably real—it could thus be seen as a prophesied society.[10]

Marx's espousal of dialectic led him to invent the concept of scientific socialism, in contrast to Utopian socialism. According to the Creed, dialectic is the only method of scientific investigation that allows history to be understood and the contradictions that obstruct its progress to be properly identified and overcome. This scientific claim is based on the premiss that whatever direction thought may take, it will inevitably discover the truth (i.e. material reality) as long as the principles of dialectic are observed. Whether thought delves into the distant past or probes the future, it can only discover what has already existed or what is bound to exist according to the laws of history. If we accept this premiss, then dialectical thought is the only means of unravelling the secrets of the future, since the future is bound by the workings of dialectic. However, dialectical thought cannot fully grasp the reality under-lying the concepts it constructs without referring to intuitive knowledge of that reality. In other words, *as an instrument of knowledge dialectic remains dependent on what already exists.*

---

### The relationship between ideology and reality, as seen by Hannah Arendt*

'. . . since the ideologies have no power to transform reality, they achieve this emancipation of thought from experience through certain methods of demonstration. Ideological thinking orders facts into an absolutely logical procedure which starts from an axiomatically accepted premise, deducing everything else from it; that is, it proceeds with a consistency that exists nowhere in the realm of reality. The deducing may proceed logically or dialectically; in either case it involves a consistent process of argumentation which, because it thinks in terms of a process, is sup-posed to be able to comprehend the movement of the suprahuman, natural, or historical processes. Comprehension is achieved by the mind's imitating, either logically or dialectically, the laws of "scientif-ically" established movements with which through the process of imitation it becomes integrated. Ideological argumentation, always a kind of logical deduction, corresponds to the two aforementioned elements of the ideological—the element of movement and of emancipation from reality and experience—first, because its thought movement does not spring from experience but is self-generated, and, secondly, because it transforms the one and only point that is taken and accepted from experienced reality into an axiomatic premise, leaving from then on the subsequent argumentation process completely untouched from any further experience. Once it has established its premise, its point of departure, experiences no longer interfere with ideological thinking, nor can it be taught by reality.'

* The Origins of Totalitarianism, Allen & Unwin, London, 1967, p. 471.

---

## Historical materialism

Dialectic makes it possible to identify the socio-economic factors whose interaction will bring about the Promised Society. It was Marx and Engels who discovered these factors by using the dialectical method to study history and to observe the world about them. For the purposes of the Creed, these factors and the laws that govern them are known as *historical materialism*, which from the Marxist point of view is not simply a theory of social evolution; rather, the inevitability of its prophecies means that, in a sense, historical materialism *is* social evolution.

Basically, historical materialism means the interaction of a number of variables, described by Marx in *The Poverty of Philosophy* (1984):[11]

Social relations are intimately bound up with productive forces. In acquiring new productive focus men change their mode of production, and in changing their mode of production, their manner of making a living, they change all their social relations. The windmill gives you society with the feudal lord; the steam mill, society with the industrial capitalist.

The same men who establish social relations in conformity with their material productivity also produce principles, ideas, and categories conforming to their social relations.

Hence these ideas, these categories are no more eternal than the relations which they express. They are *historical and transitory products*.

There is a continual movement of growth in productive forces, of destruction in social relations, and of formation in ideas; there is nothing immutable but the abstraction of the movement—*mors immortalis*.

Thus 'productive forces', 'social relations' (i.e. relations of production), and 'principles, ideas, and categories' (the super-structure) determine the course of human history. Let us look more closely at each of these concepts.

'*Productive forces*' means man's ability to transform matter at a given moment in time—in other words, the technical and techno-logical ability of society to produce new goods from existing ones. This includes both the productive capacity of existing physical capital and the technological skills that can be used in order to improve it.

'*Social relations*' means the type of social organization used by a given society in order to manage and exploit the productive forces available to it—in other words, the social organization of produc-tion, whose principal elements are the system of ownership and the division of labour.

'*Superstructure*' means those features of social organization that do not directly concern the production of goods, the main such feature being the political system. The superstructure also in-cludes prevailing forms of consciousness, religion and philosophy.

Marx described the relationship between those three variables in the following classic sentences from *Preface to a Critique of Political Economy* (1859):[12]

In the social production of their life, men enter into definite relations that are indispensable and independent of their will, relations of production which correspond to a definite stage of development of their material productive forces. The sum total of these relations of production constitutes the economic structure of society, the real foundation, on which rises a legal and political superstructure and to which correspond definite forms of social consciousness.

Thus the three factors act in an immutable order: from produc-tive forces to relations of production, and from relations of produc-tion to superstructure. Historical materialism only envisages two kinds of contradiction: the contradictions that arise between the relations of production and productive forces, and those that arise between the relations of production and the superstructure.

Productive forces evolve without being in any way determined by either the relations of production or the superstructure. However, at various times in history they come into conflict with the relations of production, which are suddenly revealed to be obsolete and are forced to adapt. When this happens, the productive forces can evolve further. The relationship between the relations of production and the superstructure is similar: in the event of a clash, the superstructure will eventually adapt so that the relations of production can evolve further.

This might appear to be an endless process. However, in the dialectical scheme of things there is a limit, namely the point at which productive forces reach their ultimate stage of development or, to put it another way, the point at which all contradictions between *Homo faber* and matter cease to exist. The forces of historical materialism will then act upon the obsolete relations of production until they adapt once and for all to the productive forces, and the superstructure will in turn adapt to the relations of production. At this point history will come to an end.

Historical materialism claims to reveal the true essence of capitalist society, whose intrinsic contradictions are bound to bring about its collapse. The Creed states that in capitalist society productive forces have reached their ultimate stage of development and that only the strait-jacket of the relations of production (with which they are in conflict) prevents them from flourishing. If this strait-jacket can be thrown off, then the way to the Promised Society[13] will lie clear and man will be able to take full advantage of the goods he is already capable of producing under capitalism.

The process of historical materialism is inexorable, and there is nothing man can do to oppose it. On the other hand, those who have awoken to its inevitability can take action to hasten the advent of the Promised Society. Awareness of the laws of historical materialism thus allows the forces that attempt in vain to oppose the onward march of history (the forces of reaction, or conservatism) to be distinguished from those that smooth the way for its triumphant passage.

The Eastern European Communist parties have answered the call of history. So what exactly does the Creed require them to do, and what problems does this cause?

## THE PRAGMATIC NATURE OF MESSIANIC COMMUNISM

### *The role of the proletariat*

According to historical materialism, the Promised Society emerges out of the final round of the class struggle, in which the proletariat finally succeeds in smashing capitalism.[14] In order to make this appointment with history, the proletariat starts to emerge as a class before capitalist society has actually crumbled. This proletarian class is a forerunner of generic man, in the sense that it grows ever more conscious of the essence of human nature and the meaning of history. As soon as the individual awakens to the truth, he loses his freedom, since his newly acquired consciousness forces him to place all his resources at the service of this revelation of things to come. Thus enlightened and spurred to action, the proletariat emerges as a class and works to create and thereby hasten the advent of the Promised Society.[15]

The Creed's call to consciousness, and thus to action, may appear hard to reconcile with the basic premiss of historical materialism that purely human action can have no effect upon history. Yet if we remember that the Creed's call is a call to speed up rather than determine the course of history, there is no real paradox. In fact, the newly enlightened have a positive moral duty to 'give history a helping hand' and work together with the laws of evolution, which have hitherto only been able to operate slowly, secretly, and without assistance.

Having answered the call of history, however, the newly enlightened are faced with the question of what to do next—for, while affording them a revelation of things to come, the Creed cannot free them from the reality that surrounds them. As long as capitalism prevails, says the Creed, the proletariat should concentrate on smashing it. But once that task has been accomplished, the proletariat is suddenly at a loss. Post-revolutionary society turns out to be very different from the Promised Society that the Creed has taught the proletariat to expect.

In the Russian Revolution the Bolsheviks succeeded in destroying the old order and defeating what they called the forces of reaction; thirty years later, the same thing happened elsewhere in Eastern Europe. By claiming to represent the proletariat, the Communist parties were able to assume a total monopoly on historical consciousness and accordingly lay claim to legitimacy in terms of the Creed. Yet despite the fact that revolution has destroyed capitalist society, post-revolutionary society turns out to be different from the Promised Society. So the question is, how do we get from here to the Promised Society? This is not a question the Communist parties expected to have to answer, but answer it they must—for the differences between post-revolutionary society and the Promised Society are very numerous indeed.

## The economic structure of the Promised Society

Perhaps on the grounds that the Promised Society is inevitable, the Creed does not bother to say much about how it is to be organized. Such pointers as it does give are in any case too vague to be of help to the Eastern European Communist parties in pursuing their economic policies.

### Socialization of the means of production

According to the Creed, the essential feature of the Promised Society is socialization of the means of production, which resolves once and for all the fatal contradiction within capitalist society between productive forces and private ownership of the means of production.[16]

We have seen repeatedly that in existing bourgeois society men are dominated by the economic conditions created by themselves, by the means of production which they themselves have produced, as if by an alien force . . . Mere knowledge, even if it went much further and deeper than that of bourgeois economic science, is not enough to bring social forces under the domination of society. What is above all necessary for this, is a social *act*. And when this act has been accomplished, when society, by taking possession of all means of production and using them on a planned basis, has freed itself and all its members from the bondage in which they are now held by these means of production which they themselves have produced but which confront them as an irresistible alien force . . .

While the concept of private ownership is well defined, the Creed fails to provide any clear definition of socialization. This is because 'socialization', as used by the Creed, is nothing more than the dialectical contradiction of private ownership—in other words it is simply the 'next stage'. This is of little practical help to those who, in the name of the Creed, wish not only to destroy private ownership but to establish social ownership in its place. In Eastern Europe, the Communist parties have certainly put an end to private ownership of the means of production, but the question remains whether they have thereby established social ownership. In questioning whether state ownership of the means of production is a form of social ownership, Wlodzimierz Brus has shown how imprecise the whole concept actually is.[17]

There are only marginal differences between the rules governing ownership in the various Eastern European countries, for the principle of socialization has been adopted in all of them. Such minor differences as do exist concern the role of the co-operatives, the ownership of agricultural and building land, the size of the private sector, and, finally, the conditions under which foreign investment is allowed to take place.[18]

## Rational management of the economy

In *Umrisse zu einer Kritik der Nationalökonomie* (1844), Engels wrote: 'If producers as such knew consumers' needs, organized production and shared it out among themselves, the fluctuations of competition and the tendency towards economic crisis would be eliminated.'[19]

Just as, for the purposes of the Creed, socialization of the means of production is simply the dialectical opposite of private ownership, rational management of the economy is nothing more than the opposite of the disorderly, erratic workings of market forces as competing producers attempt to dispose of their goods. Thus rational management of the economy involves abolishing allocation by the invisible hand of market forces and replacing it by allocation according to the 'social contract'

If we conceive society as being not capitalistic but communistic ... the question then comes down to the need of society to calculate beforehand how much labour, means of production, and means of subsistence it can invest, without detriment, in such lines of business as for instance the building of railways, which do not furnish any means of production or subsistence, nor produce any useful effect for a long time, a year or more, where they extract labour, means of production and means of subsistence from the total annual production. In capitalist society however where reason always asserts itself only *post festum* great disturbances may and must constantly occur.[20]

According to the Creed, the fatal contradiction within capitalist society between productive forces and the relations of production is evident from the way in which capitalist society determines its objectives. These are simply the sum total of individual objectives, or what contemporary economic theory calls individual preferences. Thus society exists for the benefit of the individual, and the individual takes priority over society—a view supported by political philosphers such as Hobbes, Locke, and Rousseau, who held that society existed in order to protect the individual, his safety, his freedom, or his property.

However, priority of the individual over society is incompatible with the generic nature of man. Here the Creed makes an essential distinction between the aims of the Promised Society and those of capitalist society: since the Communist party has the gift of historical consciousness, its preferences will no longer be individual but generic, in other words *social*.

Yet such reliance on the 'social contract' is not, in practice, sufficient to provide Communist parties with the guidance they need when selecting their goals. The Creed leaves the parties entirely free to decide how specific questions are to be answered— questions such as how social preferences are to be identified, and by whom. In the absence of guidance from the Creed, the response of the Communist parties has been quite simply to establish a monopoly at the first possible opportunity and impose their own preferences upon the entire economy.

## Problems with the law of value

Now that we have examined the institutional features of the Promised Society, it is time to look at one of its more specifically economic features: the law of value.

The law of value as set out in the Creed reconciles three concepts of value which, until Marx, were a serious source of controversy among economists: *value in use*, *value in exchange*, and *labour value*. The first two of these can be reconciled by equivalent exchange. However, according to the Creed, only the Promised Society provides the conditions under which *all three* are equivalent, in other words the law of value can operate unhindered; in all other types of society this is impossible.

In capitalist society it is impossible for all three values to be identical, since the chaos and uncertainty of market forces make prices essentially unstable.[21] This means that labour value can only incidentally coincide with value in exchange, since the capitalist assigns to labour a value in exchange (roughly speaking, wages) which is less than the value in exchange of the goods it produces (roughly speaking, the price of the goods concerned). Thus, instead of the entire value in exchange of the goods going to the worker who has produced them, the capitalist seizes part of it in the form of surplus value.

The Creed claims that in order to allow the law of value to operate fully, all that we need to do is *abolish surplus value and eliminate market forces*. However, as the Communist parties have discovered, even when market forces have been eliminated and private ownership of the means of production has been abolished, the law of value does not operate in post-revolutionary society the way the Creed said it would. Instead, the parties are faced with a twofold problem. Firstly, the relationship between value in use and labour value—the basis for determining prices—is subject to differing interpretations. Secondly, the problems involved in assessing labour value cause all kinds of additional complications.

*1. Value in use, labour value, and price policy.* According to the Creed, the value in exchange of a good in capitalist society depends on its value in use, in other words its ability to satisfy a need. Accordingly, there is no such thing in capitalist society as a good that has value in exchange but no value in use—either it has value in use and therefore value in exchange, or it has neither.

On the other hand, says the Creed, in the Promised Society the value in exchange of each good will be equal to its value in use *and* its labour value, since production will be directly determined by social needs. However, in order for this to be so, the economy must fulfil the following three conditions:

(*a*) since production is supposed to satisfy needs, the latter must be perfectly known before production commences;

(*b*) needs must not change between the point at which the decision is taken to produce and the point at which the good is used; and

(*c*) production must actually *succeed* in satisfying needs, in other words the user must never be disappointed.

Patently, post-revolutionary society does not always fulfil these conditions, and may therefore produce goods that have no value in use, in violation of the law of value. Faced with such shortcomings, post-revolutionary societies have had to choose between the following alternative pricing mechanisms:

(*a*) Value in exchange is not determined in advance, but is freely determined by the user on the basis of the value in use of each good—in other words, market forces are allowed to operate. This alternative makes official provision for wastage of labour (something which according to the Creed should no longer exist); such wastage occurs whenever the price paid by the consumer is less than the value of the labour involved in the production of the good.

(*b*) The user is denied the right to assign goods a value in use. Instead, all goods are deemed to have value provided that their production involves labour. Value in use then ceases to exist as an independent factor and becomes automatically synonymous with labour value. This alternative makes it possible to disguise wastage of productive effort and the resulting failure to satisfy needs; instead of being purely economic phenomena, both of these shortcomings thus become political and social issues.

The question we must now ask is which of these alternative mechanisms is most compatible both with the economic principles laid down by the Creed and with the need for efficiency within a modern economy. The fluctuating pattern of economic reform in the Eastern European countries indicates that, so far, a final choice has yet to be made.[22]

2. *How is labour value to be assessed?* In post-revolutionary society, the question of how to assess labour value has become a crucial one. Marx may well have seen the complexity of the

problem, but either he underestimated its significance or else, realizing he could offer no real solution, he decided to dodge the issue altogether.

A use-value, or useful article, therefore, has value only because human labour in the abstract has been embodied or materialised in it. How, then, is the magnitude of this value to be measured? Plainly, by the quantity of the value-creating substance, the labour, contained in the article. The quantity of labour, however, is measured by its duration, and labour-time in its turn finds its standard in weeks, days, and hours.[23]

Here Marx introduced the concept of the 'labour quantum' in order to deal with the problem inherent in the immense diversity of types of labour—skilled labour and unskilled labour, physical labour and intellectual labour, direct labour and labour that is embodied in capital goods. Marx realized that it was not enough simply to add up the time taken by each job, in the absence of a common denominator that would bridge the diversity of the types of labour involved. This was where the 'labour quantum' came in. However, as Henri Denis points out:

Marx explains that the formation of abstract labour implies three separate operations: first, the various unskilled types of labour must be reduced to 'productive exercise of the brain, the muscles, the nerves, the human . . . hand'; second, complex types of labour must be reduced to simple labour; and third, socially unnecessary concrete labour must be eliminated. But now (in *Capital*, Part I) he states that these operations are an abstraction whose nature is not real.[24]

Leaving aside the issue of whether or not Marx is inconsistent with himself, it is a fact that the Creed fails to indicate how the law of value is to be applied in practice. Hence the helplessness of the Communist parties when faced with the duty of assessing labour value in post-revolutionary society.

A similar problem is whether the same good has the same value when produced in one hour as when produced in an hour and a half. Here again, Marx's solution is of no practical relevance: 'Every individual effort of labour is equal to every other in that it is, and operates as, an average social force, in other words it uses only the average working time needed—the *working time that is socially necessary*—in order to produce a good.'[25]

It is this 'average' solution that has been applied in Eastern

Europe. However, its distorting effects have been considerable, particularly since it discourages marginal productivity gains.[26]

## Scarcity versus abundance

According to the Creed, the proletarian revolution establishes new relations of production and a new superstructure in keeping with the current stage of development of productive forces, which are thus able to flourish. Under capitalism, says the Creed, productive forces have reached their ultimate stage of development.[27] Revolution, by freeing them from the strait-jacket of capitalist relations of production, will ensure the satisfaction of all material needs in post-revolutionary society—in other words, it will usher in an age of *abundance*.

Yet, despite the elimination of capitalist relations of production, post-revolutionary societies continue to be plagued by a scarcity of both consumer and capital goods. In fact, shortage has become so characteristic of CPEs that a major work on the subject by the eminent Hungarian economist Janos Kornai is quite simply entitled *Economics of Shortage*.[28]

The Communist parties have had to face up to the fact that 'rational management of the economy' cannot provide all the answers. If 'rational management' of economic activity is to work in times of scarcity, there needs to be a suitable procedure for comparing the benefits of potential resource allocations. Accordingly, the meaning of the term 'planning' will vary according to whether the prevailing climate is one of scarcity or abundance. In a climate of scarcity, planning means choosing the best out of a number of possible allocations, whereas in a climate of abundance it means organizing activities to take account of technological constraints.

Such crucial distinctions are overlooked by the Creed, which simply takes abundance for granted and relies entirely on planning as the way to run the economy in the Promised Society. After inducing the Communist parties to dismantle the mechanism of allocation by market forces, the Creed has left them totally unprepared to deal with the scarcity that prevails in post-revolutionary society. Planning has turned out to be incapable of providing an objective basis for economic decisions, and is thus, from the economic point of view, a totally unreliable means of allocating resources. The proletariat, unprepared to deal with scarcity, can only watch helplessly as it takes hold and turns into chronic shortage.

## The role of money

The Creed states that money is an indispensable part of capitalism, which uses it to realize surplus value. Money turns labour into a commodity like any other, and exchange becomes the sole social nexus:

Through this alien mediation (money) man regards his will, his activity, and his relationship to others as a power independent of himself and of them—instead of man himself being the mediator for man. His slavery thus reaches a climax. It is clear that this mediator becomes an actual god, for the mediator is the actual power over that which he mediates to me. His worship becomes an end in itself.[29]

Therefore, says the Creed, when capitalism is abolished money will be abolished with it. The Promised Society, in which all alienating factors have vanished and money no longer holds sway, will then emerge from the ruins.

This vision of the Promised Society stands in stark contrast to the reality of post-revolutionary society, in which money not only definitely exists but is apparently ineradicable—as witness the unsuccessful attempt by the USSR to abolish it between 1918 and 1922.[30] Quite clearly, then, the Promised Society is still a long way off.

How, indeed, can society manage without money? The Creed does not say.

## THE SYSTEM

We have seen that there are considerable economic differences between post-revolutionary society and the Promised Society. Thus, even though capitalism has been eliminated from Eastern Europe, the task assigned to the Communist parties by the Creed is by no means over.

The discrepancy between the two types of society raises serious doubts about proletarian consciousness. What if the revolutionary proletariat, even though acting in accordance with the laws of history, has somehow gone astray? What if the Creed itself is wrong? Does this mean that the Communist parties have set themselves an impossible task?

The Communist parties have never questioned the truth of the Creed, for their actions can only be justified by their claim to possess the gift of historical consciousness. Since this claim is entirely based upon the Creed, questioning the Creed would be tantamount to suicide. At various periods the unity of Communism has been shaken by revisionists, who have dared to question parts of the Creed; yet none of them has ever challenged the Creed in its entirety.

How, despite the differences between the Promised Society and post-revolutionary society, have the Communist parties managed to uphold the Creed and keep their actions consistent with it? The answer to this question must be a matter of conjecture, but the following explanation is surely a plausible one. If we simply assume that the time-scale used by the Creed to record the various stages of social evolution is different from the time-scale used to record the movements of history, then the Creed can be reconciled with post-revolutionary society. According to this theory, the Creed records social evolution in *ordinal* time, while historical reality is recorded in *cardinal* time. The Creed sees time in ordinal terms because the various stages of society occur in a set order: primitive society is followed by slavery, which gives way to feudalism, which evolves into capitalism, which finally collapses to make way for the Promised Society. As far as the Creed is concerned, the order of the various stages of society is the only scale by which time can be measured. Historical time, on the other hand, can be considered objective and linear, since it is measured solely according to the sequence of days, weeks, months, and years, each of these units having an objective length which can never change. Since this time-scale is not dependent on human history, historical reality is measured in cardinal time. Thus when the Creed states that the Promised Society will follow on the heels of capitalist society, this only tells us something about the *order* of historical events, not how long each of them will take.[31]

The Eastern European Communist parties have used this theory to justify their mission. By claiming that it is impossible to convert the ordinal time of the Creed directly into the cardinal time of historical reality, they are able to explain away the discrepancy between post-revolutionary society and the Promised Society. Thus the *transitional period* between capitalist society and the Promised Society can extend over decades or even centuries without the Creed being called into question or the Communist parties risking being denounced as impostors.

In this way, not only is the Communist party confirmed in its historical mission as spelt out by the Creed, but it is also empowered to transform the present in the light of its own awareness of current contingencies and of its special role. The legitimacy enjoyed by the party is thus extended beyond the destruction of capitalism to include the next period of ordinal time, namely the transitional period between capitalism and the Promised Society. This 'transitional period'[32] is an ingenious device which is used again and again. Indeed, it even turns up in the constitutions of the various Eastern European countries, none of which speaks of the Promised Society in the present tense or claims that Communism has already arrived.[33]

While the transitional period accounts for the gap between revolutionary action—which was supposed to usher in the Promised Society—and the social transformations embarked upon by the Communist party, it does not give the party any guide as to how to proceed while the transition is in progress. The transitional period having brought history to a grinding halt, the Communist party is forced to change its tactics. Instead of violent, destructive action, the watchword is now long-term and—hopefully—constructive action. The party must now decide what means it will use to bring about the desired transformation. In order to fulfil their mission according to the Creed, the Eastern European Communist parties have turned to the System, which enables them to keep control of the societies they are bent on perfecting. In other words, the centrally planned economy needs to be seen and analysed as an instrument devised by the Communist party to create the Promised Society after the revolution has put an end to capitalism.

## Successive Soviet constitutions: Stages on the journey through the transitional period

*1. Extracts from the report by Leonid Brezhnev to the Plenary Assembly of the Central Committee of the Communist Party of the Soviet Union which adopted the new Constitution,* Pravda, 5 June 1977*

'While the Party saw the Constitution as enshrining the conquests of revolution, it also conceived of it as proclaiming the main goals, the major tasks involved in building socialism. Such was the first Constitution of the RSFSR in 1918, which enshrined the October conquests and defined the class nature of the Soviet state: a dictatorship of the proletariat. Such also was the Basic Law of 1924, which embodied the constitutive principles of the federal socialist state. The 1936 Constitution provided a legal basis for the establishment in the USSR of socialist social relations, to which all administrative, political and electoral authorities conform. . . .

'Why a new Constitution? Because for forty years profound changes have been taking place in our country and in our society. Effectively, when the 1936 Constitution was adopted, we had just laid the foundations of socialism. . . . The legacy of the pre-revolutionary era was still evident in many fields.

'Now, on the other hand, the Soviet Union is a socialist, developed, mature society. Fundamental and major changes have affected every aspect of social life. . . .

'Fortified by what has been achieved, the Soviet people, under the leadership of the Party, are now embarking on new tasks: establishing the infrastructure of Communism, gradually changing socialist social relations into Communist ones, and educating people in the spirit of Communist awareness.'

*2. Preamble to the Constitution of the USSR, dated 7 October 1977†*

'The Great October Socialist Revolution, carried out by the workers and peasants of Russia under the leadership of the Communist party headed by V. I. Lenin, overthrew the power of the capitalists and landowners, broke the fetters of oppression, *established the dictatorship of the proletariat* and created the Soviet State—a new type of state and the basic instrument for the defense of revolutionary gains and the construction of socialism and communism. *Mankind's world-historic turn from capitalism to socialism began.* . . .

'The supreme goal of the Soviet state is the building of a classless communist society *in which public communist self-government will receive development.* The principal tasks of the *socialist* state of *all the people* are: creating the material and technical base of communism,

improving socialist social relations and transforming them into communist relations, rearing the man of communist society, raising the
working people's material and cultural living standard, safeguarding the
country's security and helping to strengthen peace and to develop
international cooperation.'

* *The Current Digest of the Soviet Press,* 29. 21 (22 June 1977), 1–5.
† Ibid. 29. 41 (9 Nov. 1977), 1.

---

The Eastern European CPEs, which arose out of the clash
between the revolutionary action of the Communist parties and
the profound forces that the revolution failed to destroy, symbolize
the change of tactics by the Communist parties. The fact that they
arose spontaneously explains why there are both similarities and
differences between individual Eastern European CPEs. The
similarities derive from their common origins in Messianic Communism, while the differences lie in the fact that in each country
the revolution ran into different forces to which it has had to adapt.
However, since Messianic Communism is firmly rooted in the
Creed, such differences as do exist can only be superficial ones.
Therefore, since the purpose of this study is to grasp the essential
principles that govern the economic functioning of the societies
concerned, the use of 'the System' as a generic term to describe
them all is perfectly justified. Since national differences are purely
incidental, they can be ignored, and we can concentrate on the
basic features common to all CPEs.

The System is designed to fill the gap between the ordinal time-
scale and the cardinal time-scale, which for the time being are still
totally separate. The purpose of the System is clear—namely, to
transform post-revolutionary society into the Promised Society, a
task for which the gifts of revelation and of historical consciousness have made the Communist party especially well fitted.
However, the position of the Communist party in relation to its
guide (the Creed) on the one hand and its instrument (the System)
on the other remains an ambiguous one. At the risk of overstress-
ing the recursive nature of the System, it may be said that through
the System the Communist party becomes the instrument of the
proletariat, while at the same time the revelations contained in the
Creed enable the party to embody the proletariat.

The close relationship between the System and the Creed

underscores the most essential and profound difference between CPEs and market economies. The System is essentially an instrument devised by a demiurge in order to achieve goals that transcend the System[34]—that is, it has been adopted by the Communist party in pursuance of its Messianic mission as dictated by the Creed, and in order to increase its control over society. Market economies, by contrast, create their own ends and hence can manage without transcendental ones. Thus, to borrow a term from Jean-Pierre Dupuy, market economies have the power to 'self-create', whereas CPEs are created by a force that surpasses them. That force is the Creed, of which the System is merely the passive instrument.

Taking Dupuy's analogy further, the System can be analysed as a cybernetic system that adapts its behaviour to changes in its environment, while at all times maintaining the unalterable course set by the Creed. In the next chapter we will be examining the means the System uses to carry out this unusual mission.

## Notes

1. R. Aron, *Plaidoyer pour l'Europe décadente*, Laffont, Paris, 1977, p. 34.
2. See I. M. Bochenski, *The Soviet Russian Dialectical Materialism*, Reidel, Dordrecht, 1969.
3. The term 'creed' could be replaced here by 'ideological premises', as used by Hannah Arendt in *The Origins of Totalitarianism*, Allen & Unwin, London, 1967 (repr. Deutsch, 1986). I use 'creed' simply in order to avoid any misunderstanding about the term 'ideology' (defined by Arendt as 'the logic of an idea').
4. Karl Marx, *The Jewish Question*, trans. T. B. Bottomore, London, 1963, p. 15. All quotations from Marx are adapted from Bottomore's translation. In the remainder of the book I will therefore merely quote the title of the original work and the volume of the edition in which the extract appears.
5. Ibid., p. 13.
6. Ibid., p. 31.
7. 'A single sense of the term "freedom" is advanced in Soviet philosophical literature. Freedom is defined in every philosophical text and reference work as consisting in "the recognition of necessity"—the acknowledgement of, and the acquiescence in, the objective inevitabilities that structure the world around us' (James P. Scanlan, 'Doublethink in the USSR', *Problems of Communism*, Jan.–Feb. 1985, p. 71). Seen in this light, the very notion of human rights takes on an unexpected new meaning; see Leszek Kolakowski, 'Marxism and Human Rights', *Daedalus*, Autumn 1983, pp. 81–91.

8. The Creed's claim to have 'objectivized' good and evil is based on the conviction that it has revealed the eternal truth about human nature. However, it would have to abandon this claim if it were to acknowledge that, far from *revealing* the truth about human nature, it has merely made certain assumptions about it.

9. Somewhat extreme views on this subject have been expressed by Milovan Djilas in his *Ecrits politiques*, Belfond, Paris, 1982, p. 28: 'By combining revolution and sociology, Marx made it possible for extremely broad strata of society to acquire economic knowledge ... the purpose of such persistent research was not to ascertain the laws that govern society in general or capitalism in particular. Rather, Marx was seeking a justification for his youthful belief in the inevitable advent of Communist society, in a new, spontaneous, active, talented—in short, dis-alienated—kind of human being.'

10. Bronislaw Baczko (*Les Imaginaires sociaux: Mémoires et espoirs collectifs*, Payot, Paris, 1984, p. 23): 'Marx saw his own theory—expressing as it did the true interests of the proletariat—not as an ideology but as a *criticism of ideologies*. Accordingly, he believed, his theory *transformed into science* the hitherto Utopian dreams of socialists, which only expressed the aspirations of the proletariat on the ideological plane.'

11. Trans. Loyd D. Easton and Kurt H. Guddat, New York, 1967, pp. 480–1.

12. K. Marx, *Preface to a Critique of Political Economy* (1859), trans. and ed. David McLellan, OUP, Oxford, 1977, p. 389.

13. In *USSR in Crisis: The Failure of an Economic System* (W. W. Norton & Co., New York and London, 1983, pp. 5–6), Michael Goldman writes: 'The purpose of the revolution, therefore, would be to change the distribution process. . . . It was intended . . . that the new revolutionary government would not have to concern itself with industrial development—the bourgeoisie had already seen to that.'

14. According to Baczko (*Imaginaires sociaux*, p. 23): 'Marx, in introducing the image of the proletariat (a class required to be totally transparent to itself), actually interprets it as a non-image, a mere observation of fact.'

15. 'In order for a society to exist and maintain itself, in order for it to achieve a minimum of cohesion, if not a consensus, social agents must believe that the social is superior to the individual, in other words they must develop a "collective consciousness", a system of beliefs and practices which unites all those who adhere to them in a single community, the supreme moral arbiter' Baczko, ibid., p. 24).

16. Friedrich Engels, *Anti-Dühring*, Lawrence & Wishart, London, 1969, pp. 357–8.

17. Wlodzimierz Brus, *Socialist Ownership and Political System*, Routledge & Kegan Paul, London, 1975.

18. See Ch. 4, which deals with the dilemma of methods.

19. *Werke*, 1, Deitz Verlag, Berlin (East), 1957, p. 514.

20. K. Marx, *Capital*, Lawrence & Wishart, London, 1957, 2, pp. 314–15.

21. According to Marx, value in exchange in capitalist economies is not the

market price at a given moment in time, but the average price over a long
period.

22. See Chs. 4 and 6.
23. K. Marx, *Capital*, Lawrence & Wishart, London, 1955, 1. 1., p. 38.
24. H. Denis, *L'Économie de Marx: L'Histoire d'un échec*, PUF, Paris, 1980,
    p. 167.
25. Ibid., p. 566.
26. See Ch. 6, and in particular the discussion of microeconomic terms of trade.
27. '. . . naïve progressivism and the powerful charge of extreme Utopian and
    millenarian fantasy have been essential to Marxism as a mass political creed,
    and this was derived, though usually inexplicitly, from the underlying
    eschatological fantasies regarding the economic Utopia which was just
    around the next corner' (T. W. Hutchinson, 'Friedrich Engels and Marxist
    Economic Theory', *Journal of Political Economy*, 86. 2 (1978), 313. On the
    subject of expected and promised abundance, see also Alec Nove, *Economics
    of Feasible Socialism*, Allen & Unwin, London, 1982.
28. North-Holland Publishing Company, Amsterdam, New York, and Oxford,
    1980.
29. K.Marx, 'Money and Alienated Man' from *Writings of the Young Marx on
    Philosophy and Society*, edited by L. D. Easton and K. H. Gudaal,
    Doubleday, New York, 1967, p. 266.
30. See the now classic work by A. Z. Arnold, entitled *Banks, Credit and Money
    in Soviet Russia*, Columbia University Press, New York, 1937.
31. However, the Communist parties have not always succeeded in resisting the
    temptation to convert the ordinal time of the Creed into cardinal (i.e. real)
    time. An example of this can be found in the programme that Khrushchev
    encouraged the Communist Party of the Soviet Union to adopt in 1961. Here
    it was boldly announced that communism would be achieved some time
    during the 1980s. In comparison, the 1985 programme is extremely circum-
    spect and avoids specifying when exactly communist society will come about
    in the USSR; see 'It's a Long Way to Communism under Gorbachev', *The
    Economist*, 2 Nov. 1985, pp. 61–2.
32. 'the illusions of childhood . . . are consumed and vanish without a trace . . .',
    wrote Bukharin and Preobrazhensky in *ABC of Communism*, first published
    in Russian in 1919 (University of Michigan Press, Ann Arbor, 1966).
33. The term 'advanced socialist society' was used by Brezhnev to describe the
    stage the USSR had reached on the way to 'building communism'. See M.
    Lavigne, 'La société socialiste advancée', *Économie politique de la planification
    en système socialiste*, Economica, Paris, 1978, pp. 300–8, and 'The Decline
    and Fall of "Developed Socialism" ', *Radio Liberty Research Bulletin*, 27
    Sept. 1986 (RL 314/86).
34. These terms have been borrowed from J.-P. Dupuy, *Ordre et désordre:
    Recherche d'un nouveau paradigme*, Le Seuil, Paris, 1982, p. 225.

# 2
# How the System Works

In the previous chapter we saw that the System is the instrument with which the Communist parties implement the Creed. In this chapter, we will be taking a closer look at the essential characteristics of the System. This new perspective involves examining not only the System's eschatological mission, but also the environment in which it attempts to fulfil this mission. The way in which the System performs its duties needs to be analysed on two essentially interrelated levels:

(a) *legitimacy*, in other words how the System manages never to deviate from the Creed; and

(b) *efficiency*, in other words how the System copes with its social, economic, and international environment.

In this chapter we will be looking at the means the System uses in order to carry out its historical mission. The term *survival mechanism* will be used to refer to all such means; however, the reader should beware of seeing evidence of a mechanistic approach in this choice of terminology, which is used purely for reasons of convenience.

How, then, does the System manage to survive and to withstand the battering it receives from its environment? How does it maintain its legitimacy? In order to answer these questions, we need to examine the basic principles that have kept the System going for over seventy years.

This chapter is divided into three sections. The first of these examines in turn the three components of the survival mechanism and their respective limitations; the second discusses how the mechanism operates, that is, how the three components interact;

and the third goes on to assess how the System copes with the economic problems that arise when it attempts to carry out its mission.

## THE COMPONENTS OF THE SURVIVAL MECHANISM

The survival mechanism of the System has enabled it to survive in two essential respects:

(a) *physically*, by enabling the System to withstand a hostile environment for more than seventy years;

(b) *philosophically*, by keeping the System faithful to its Messianic mission in terms of the Creed and thereby allowing it to claim legitimacy.

The existence of the survival mechanism and its importance to the survival of the System mean that the System differs from all other socio-economic systems in at least one fundamental way.

The survival mechanism has three recognizable components which, however, interact so closely that they are difficult to analyse separately. They are the System's *self-justifying ability*, its *self-targeting ability*, and its *self-organizing ability*. The term 'ability' has been used in place of 'function' in order to emphasize that there is nothing automatic or deterministic about the way in which the survival mechanism is used by the Communist party.

## *Self-justification*

Although the Creed justifies the existence of the System, it does not directly justify everything that it requires the System to do during the transitional period. The System is therefore obliged not only to choose what it is going to do, but also to justify it. The Creed provides the System with the necessary means of discernment and justification, which we will refer to as the System's self-justifying ability. This is the key to the entire survival mechanism, for it guides everything the System does and makes sure that, one way or another, it is justified in terms of the Creed.

The two basic features of this ability are (*a*) its frame of reference, and (*b*) its method of operation.

## The frame of reference

On its own, the Creed is neither solid nor consistent enough to serve as a means of discernment or basis for justification. For this reason, the System justifies itself by returning directly to the original sources of the Creed—the writings of the 'founding fathers'—which will be referred to below as 'the Scriptures'.

In order for such writings to serve as a frame of reference, a certain amount of restructuring and commentary must take place beforehand. In this way the Scriptures are transformed into a sort of ideological grammar, which is operational, explicit, and codified but remains sufficiently flexible to encompass an unlimited number of situations. This painstaking process is the prerogative of the Communist parties, which can thereby strengthen their position as the sole interpreters of the Scriptures. For this reason, Raymond Aron referred to the System some years ago as an 'ideocracy'.[1] However, Aron's disciple Alain Besançon[2] used the same premises to reach the conclusion that the System was a 'logocracy'. Is there an essential difference here?

Both Aron and Besançon agree that the frame of reference used by the System to justify itself has two components: (*a*) the Scriptures; and (*b*) the restructuring that is required in order to turn them into a frame of reference. Aron and Besançon only differ as to the relative importance of the two components. According to Aron, the 'idea' remains unchangeable and cannot therefore be significantly distorted by structuring. Besançon claims just the opposite, namely, that in the interests of self-justification the original 'idea' can be twisted or watered down by means of appropriate restructuring, or even abandoned altogether. Thus the argument turns on the amount of room for manœuvre that is available (in the form of restructuring) and, to a lesser extent, the ways in which the Communist parties of Eastern Europe make use of this.

If the frame of reference becomes too elastic, a twofold problem will arise: on the one hand, the discernment supposedly embodied in the frame of reference will appear less sound and, on the other, the System's external credibility will be undermined, since the justifications it produces will be less convincing. This shows that the logocracy theory has its limits, but that does not mean that the ideocracy theory is right either. The true situation appears to be that, although the System is fairly free to restructure its frame of reference, it still takes care never actually to diverge from the Creed. In other words, even a purely economic analysis of the System must always take account of its need to obey the Creed.[3]

However, while the Creed is always obeyed, the specifics of the frame of reference are continually changing as a result of restructuring. This entails fairly constant updating, which is carried out by the party's ideological watchdogs. Outside observers can keep track of this by noting the frequency and type of references to the Scriptures in official speeches and the party media. Minor alterations of this kind serve not so much to justify the previous behaviour of the System as to mark out the path for its future behaviour—for, under the System more than any other socio-economic arrangement, *the present is (at least in theory) determined by the future*, rather than the other way around.

On the other hand, any major alteration to the frame of reference is a moment of truth as far as the System is concerned, and such alterations are consequently rather rare. Mostly they serve to endorse changes at the top of the political hierarchy, though occasionally they pave the way for them. The most recent alteration of this type occurred in China in the autumn of 1984, when Chinese leaders officially acknowledged that there were limits to the relevance of the works of Marx.[4] Such recasting of the frame of reference was apparently necessary in order for the System to justify the innovations being introduced at the time.

The fact that each Communist country has its own party means that no single party is free to establish its own basis for self-justification; instead, the supranational community of Communist parties must decide. The spirit of the Creed requires those Communist parties that recognize one another as 'brother parties' to make sure that, in the interests of proletarian internationalism, any major alterations to the frame of reference are undertaken in unison. Minor alterations to the basis for self-justification may be undertaken by the local party in each country, but must be ratified at the supranational level.

However, it is not always clear whether alterations are minor or major, and the term 'national road to socialism' is hard to define with any accuracy. As recent history shows, what may look like attempts to find a 'national road to socialism' are likely to be firmly squashed if the results are not to the liking of the brother parties. Soviet intervention in Hungary in 1956, the Warsaw Pact invasion of Czechoslovakia in 1968, and the military takeover in Poland in 1981 all show how fragile this concept is. When it comes to the crunch, it is the supranational community that decides—frequently after the event—whether a given alteration to the frame of reference is minor (i.e. acceptable) or major (i.e. unacceptable). Hence the importance attached in Communist countries to the presence of delegates from brother parties at national ideological conferences, and the need for unanimous decisions at international meetings of Communist parties. This is, of course, one area where the Comintern and more recently the Cominform have had a vital role to play.[5]

Eurocommunism first arose out of the difference of opinion between three Western Communist parties and the parties of Eastern Europe as to the right of the former to adopt their own *ad hoc* frame of reference.[6] In this connection, the statements made in January 1985 by the general secretary of the Italian Communist Party, Alessandro Natta, and subsequent Eastern European responses are clear indications of a continuing rift.[7]

Thus we have seen that the frame of reference is amenable to change, but major upheavals are relatively uncommon. Now let us examine how the frame of reference is used for purposes of self-justification.

## How self-justification works

In Eastern Europe, the System's self-justifying ability has resulted in the development by the ruling Communist parties of a specific kind of logic whereby concrete situations can be linked back to the frame of reference. This entails first of all analysing the concrete situation in terms of the frame of reference, so that the System can establish a basis for its own conduct. Interpretation of the present, which is an essential part of both self-justification and discernment, is based on the 'scientific method', in other words, dialectical analysis.[8] Accordingly, the parties' self-justification has two sources: 'scientific' analysis of reality, and the linking of such analysis back to the frame of reference.

These two sources correspond to two separate stages in the self-justification process: the stage at which the scientific analysis is carried out, and the stage at which it is officially approved or 'passes the orthodoxy test'. In the course of these two stages, which in practice tend to overlap, dialectical analysis of the present is converted into self-justification for use by the System.

In order for 'scientific analysis' to have any chance of being officially approved as orthodox self-justification it must conform to the Creed, that is, it must be based on the dialectical method. The Creed claims that this method—a scientific method if ever there was one—is infallible, since it reveals 'historical necessity' and its findings are of direct practical relevance. But how are we to tell whether or not a given analysis has been carried out in accordance with the dialectical method? The answer given by the Creed is that a correct analysis will identify *essential* contradictions, whereas a faulty analysis will stop at *superficial* ones. In practice, there is no firm criterion for telling which is which. Contrary to what the Creed would have us believe, the fact that a given analysis has been carried out according to the dialectical method tells us nothing whatever about its scientific value, but merely proves that it is semantically orthodox.

To be officially approved, analysis not only must be dialectical, but must also pass the orthodoxy test. The power to bring this about lies with the aforementioned ideological watchdogs which, as and when needed, convert certain analyses into self-justification for use in guiding the operation of the System. These guardians of party orthodoxy thus have considerable power to influence the workings of the System.

It is clear, then, that the Communist party not only creates its own frame of reference for self-justification, but also determines which analyses will be officially adopted as self-justification. We must then ask ourselves whether changes in the frame of reference precede dialectical analysis of concrete situations, or vice versa.

Systems analysis cannot provide us with a clear answer, since in practice it is the party that officially approves both the changes in the frame of reference and the corresponding self-justification. This means that a well-placed individual with a strong following inside the party apparatus is more likely to see his own analyses prevail than someone in a less advantageous position. In times of transition, when the authorities are wavering and the political succession is uncertain, the power of the ideological watchdogs will paradoxically increase, since the orthodoxy test will ultimately decide between the rival factions. In the name of the Creed—but with due respect for the balance of power—the watchdogs will accordingly brand certain factions as 'revisionist', 'deviationist', 'counter-revolutionary', and so forth, while hailing others as the true heirs of orthodoxy.

The System's self-justification[9] (and the process whereby it is developed) serves as a means of communication within the party and at the same time conveys information to the outside world. Within the party, it identifies current 'historical necessities' and lays down guidelines for the System, which makes it an important factor in maintaining the unity of the party apparatus. Outside the party, on the other hand, it works by appealing to common sense and objective reasoning rather than the frame of reference embodied in the Creed. In normal times, this outside function remains a secondary one; it is in time of crisis—when the very survival of the System is at stake—that this function comes into its own.

---

### The Fundamental importance of the System's self-justifying ability, as expressed by Mikhail Suslov (member of the Politburo and Marxist-Leninist theoretician)*

'The dialectical unity of real socialism, profoundly imbued as it is with the vital energy and the scientific doctrine on which it is based, and the unity of Marxist-Leninist teachings and socio-political practice lend revolutionary force and an invincible will to workers in the socialist countries, and to the entire international working class. . . .

'The multiplicity of national and historical peculiarities, which require each Communist party *to adapt and to develop Marxist-Leninist doctrine*, to carry out a concrete and relevant analysis, and to take account of specific circumstances, results in a variety of roads leading to socialism. . . . Parties that fail to take account of specific, concrete national circumstances and of trends in the balance of world power cannot be said to be acting positively. However, as life shows, the variety of ways of struggling to achieve socialism, and of socialist methods of transformation, raises the *question of the general principles of Marxism-Leninism*, in terms of both doctrine and practice, *and of the general laws governing socialist revolution and the building of socialism*. Such laws are not a code of 'abstract' rules, but a set of scientifically established and effectively verified reference points. . . . If it remains unaware of these general rules governing socialist revolution and the establishment of a socialist regime, the Party is doomed to go astray. . . .

'At the present stage of the revolutionary movement, the relationship between the national and the international is becoming more flexible. While the role of national principles in overall world development is undeniably growing, it is equally true that the importance of the international unity of all liberating forces is becoming established.'

---

* 'Marxism-Leninism and revolutionary renewal', *Kommunist*, Moscow, 14 (Sept. 1977), from the *Current Digest of the Soviet Press*, 29. 45 (7 Dec. 1977).

---

## The System's 'active' abilities

### The consistency of the survival mechanism

The System's self-justifying ability enables it to prove that it never deviates from its eschatological mission. Given the crucial importance of doctrine, this self-justifying ability may well be considered the centrepiece of the survival mechanism. However, beside this ability to maintain its legitimacy, the System also has various means at its disposal with which to control its environment. We are referring here to the other two components of the System's survival mechanism—its self-targeting ability and its self-organizing ability. These 'active' abilities enable the System to affect reality and to change it or, at the very least, influence the changes in it and thereby withstand the pressures from its environment.

The System's active abilities are directed and/or protected by the self-justification described above. Indeed, were the System to act in a manner that it could not justify, or were it to prove incapable of withstanding environmental pressures, it would fail in its mission. The survival mechanism makes sure that nothing of the kind ever happens. Thus the System's self-justifying ability paves the way for its self-targeting and self-organizing abilities by laying down the limits of what is justifiable in the future. It also legitimizes the present state of affairs, even if this is the result of unjustifiable action by the System's active abilities—that is, if reality has forced the active abilities to do something that the self-justifying ability would not normally countenance. Ultimately, therefore, there is no fixed order of precedence among the three abilities that make up the survival mechanism, but an apportionment of tasks: the System's self-justifying ability prevents the System from conflicting with the Creed, while its self-targeting and self-organizing abilities help it to withstand the pressures from its environment. This interdependence means that the System must make sure it uses its three abilities consistently, or at least not inconsistently. We will return to this problem in a moment. First, however, let us take a closer look at the two active abilities.

## Self-targeting

'Self-targeting' is the term we will use to describe the way in which the System enables the party to determine its economic objectives. However, this ability is restricted on the one hand by the System's self-justification and on the other hand by reality.

In the name of the Creed, the System's self-justification limits the choice of objectives, since it prescribes that the long-term objective of the System is to create the Promised Society. Short-term objectives selected by the System's self-targeting ability must not conflict with this long-term objective. However, this restriction is no great hindrance, since the Promised Society is to emerge in ordinal time, whereas the System's self-targeting ability operates in cardinal time and can thus take advantage of the ambiguities inherent in the 'transitional period'.[10] In practice, the range of short-term objectives compatible with the System's Messianic mission is very wide, and the System's self-targeting ability is thus only marginally restricted by the Creed.

Nevertheless, from the point of view of the Creed the importance of the long-term objective is such as to dictate certain *formal* requirements (as opposed to material ones). In the first place, every objective adopted by the System must be officially based on 'social preferences', which only the Communist party is in a position to ascertain. Secondly, all such objectives must, like the long-term objective, apply to the whole of society and profoundly influence its structure. We shall be returning to these very real restrictions in the next chapter, which deals with the planning dilemma. Before doing so, however, we need to look at the third component of the survival mechanism: the System's self-organizing ability.

*Self-organization*

Although the System's self-justifying ability and its self-targeting ability function quite differently within the survival mechanism, they both result in a non-material end product: self-justification in the former case, and planning in the latter. The System's self-organizing ability, on the other hand, directly concerns material reality: it is the instrument the Communist parties use to organize and administer the societies they control.

The Creed imposes narrower restrictions on the System's self-organizing ability than on its self-targeting ability, for the limits of what is justifiable are more clearly marked out. As we saw in the previous chapter, the Creed is fairly explicit about the organizational structure of the Promised Society.[11] Thus, for example, the self-justifying frame of reference can never be extended so far as to endorse private ownership or market forces.

In addition to the doctrinal restrictions just mentioned, the room for manœuvre available to the System's self-organizing ability also depends on how hostile its environment is. The System is merely a tool used by each Communist party to adapt the domestic economy to its own ends; it therefore constantly encounters resistance from other parts of the economy, so that the party's control over economic performance can never be total.

This is a useful point at which to examine the internal structure of CPEs. There are three levels. The first of these is *material reality*, which is shaped by the people and includes such things as economic performance, products and raw materials, the physical environment, etc. The second level is the complex network of human relationships, the *socio-economic tissue* (referred to in the remainder of the book as 'the tissue').[12] At the top of the pyramid we find the third level—the secular instrument of metaphysical revelation referred to as the *System*. This System, or more specifically its self-organizing ability, is used by the Communist party to help it overcome resistance from the economic tissue, and thus transform material reality—which it cannot directly control—into the Promised Society. The System's attempt to dominate man in order to improve its control over things exposes its self-organizing ability to resistance from the tissue, which it is not always able to overcome.

Jean-Louis Le Moigne[13] has defined 'organization' as 'the arrangement of activity', consisting of three primary components: *structures*, *mechanisms*, and *behaviour*. In order for us to identify the ways in which the tissue resists the System's attempts at self-organization, we need to know to what extent each of these three components of the economic system succeeds in eluding the grasp of the System's self-organizing ability.

Let us take *structures* first. These provide an economy with a stable foundation for the establishment and expansion of its activity. A modern society contains various such structures: the institutional structure, which allocates powers; the administrative structure, which enables those powers to be exercised; and the legal structure, which supervises the operation of the entire system. The Communist parties' monopoly on political power enables them to exercise complete control over the formal economic and political structures of society. In this area, therefore, the tissue cannot seriously restrict the System's self-organizing ability in any way.

Secondly, *mechanisms* ensure that the various structures interact reliably and, at the same time, provide the flexibility the System needs in order to adapt to changes in its environment. Their special function is to ensure, again and again, that a given microeconomic decision will always produce the same effect. Thus mechanisms act as an interface between structures and the individual behaviour that makes up the tissue.

There are two kinds of mechanism: those based on customary practice, and those based on regulation. In addition to controlling the political and economic structures of the CPEs, the System's self-organizing ability also controls the mechanisms that are rooted in those structures. At the same time, however, mechanisms can only function in relation to behaviour, which is part of the tissue and therefore beyond the System's control. In other words, the System's self-organizing ability is incapable of ensuring the total control over mechanisms that the System requires in order to adapt socio-economic reality to its own needs.

The third component is *behaviour*, a term covering billions of individual actions that interweave to form a dense, impenetrable socio-economic tissue. Although individuals are restricted in their behaviour by the structures dictated by the System and their decisions are to some extent circumscribed by the mechanisms that the System has a hand in creating, their freedom of manœuvre nevertheless remains quite considerable. Using his prior knowledge of the mechanisms, each individual exercises his freedom so as to behave in a way which he believes will come closest to fulfilling his aims. Try as it might, the System's self-organizing ability has never succeeded in gaining complete control over behaviour, which ultimately remains the prerogative of the individual. Efforts to dictate individual behaviour by manipulating structures, adjusting mechanisms, or even attempting to gain control of the individual's conscience have all been in vain. Behaviour—in other words, the tissue—essentially remains beyond the System's control.[14]

Behaviour is thus the most successful of the three components at eluding the grasp of the System's self-organizing ability, and ultimately it also has a direct influence upon material reality. In fact, individual behaviour thwarts the System's self-organizing ability to such an extent that it may be wondered what, if anything, the System has the ability to organize. In practice, its self-organizing ability does not extend beyond the confines of the System; while it exercises complete control over structures, it can influence mechanisms only to a limited extent, and its effect upon behaviour (the tissue) is purely incidental and uncontrollable.

### *Homo systemicus*—corner-stone of the CPE

Sociological analyses of contemporary Eastern European societies have led many Western sovietologists to see them all as being essentially

divided into two quite separate social groups: 'the privileged bureau-
cracy' (a.k.a. 'the ruling class' or 'the *nomenklatura'*) and 'the people'
(alias '(civil) society' or 'the proletariat').

Yet, for all their scholarliness, such analyses fail to reflect the reality of
Eastern Europe. In actual fact, the privileged and the proletariat both
quite plainly exist throughout society, a fact that is bound to confuse
both sociologists and travellers. How can the System and the tissue both
be everywhere at once?

The sociological approach assumes the indivisibility of man, which
means that no individual can simultaneously belong to more than one
social class, stratum, or group. In CPEs, however, the dividing lines do
not run in between individuals, but right through the middle of them.
Each individual is, in one way or another, part of the System and
performs various functions accordingly; but he is never entirely part of it,
and therefore also functions intermittently as part of the tissue.

This analysis is the exact converse of Marx's analysis of the individual
in bourgeois society. Marx depicts him as a schizophrenic, two-faced
creature, torn between the public sphere (in which capitalist relations of
production force him to behave selfishly) and the private sphere (in
which his generic instincts can flourish). Similar schizophrenia occurs in
CPEs, only here the contents of the public and private spheres are the
other way round. Where the individual is forced to function as a mere
cog in the System, the System will determine his behaviour; but
whenever he succeeds in eluding the System's grasp, he will use that
freedom to his own advantage, usually at the System's expense. Such
schizophrenic behaviour is a kind of psychological shield used by the
people of Eastern Europe to protect themselves against the System. The
result of this clash of interests is a new type of individual who is
fundamentally different from generic man. This new individual, *Homo
systemicus*, is equipped with all the necessary instincts for material and
mental survival in a people's democracy.

Without ever having been specifically identified, *Homo systemicus* has
already been the subject of much study. Though non-economic in
approach, the most accurate portrait of *Homo systemicus* has been
provided by Alexander Zinoviev in various relevant passages of *Radiant
Future* and *Homo sovieticus.**

*Homo systemicus* is the cornerstone of the CPE, since he forms the
essential link between the tissue and the System. Were *Homo systemicus*
to be replaced in Eastern Europe by *Homo oeconomicus* (the discovery
of whom led to the emergence of economic theory), it would mean the
end of the System. On the other hand, were he to be replaced by generic
man, the tissue and the System would merge.

The schizophrenia typified by *Homo systemicus* affects the entire population of Eastern Europe, though it affects each individual to varying degrees. A handful succeed in avoiding it altogether: a monk is perhaps the best example of an individual who lives entirely outside the public sphere, while at the other end of the scale we find senior political figures who live in the public sphere far more than the private sphere and, in extreme cases, are quite unaware that the private sphere exists. However, since the number of individuals that manage to avoid the prevailing schizophrenia in this way is very small, we can legitimately disregard them here.

* A. Zinoviev, *Radiant Future*, Bodley Head, London, 1974, and *Homo sovieticus*, Victor Gollancz, London, 1978.

The System tends to ignore the limitations that behaviour imposes on its self-organizing ability, and to act as though it had complete control over the tissue. Thus for forty years the System has persisted in introducing economic reforms, all of them disappointing and therefore short-lived. Yet, despite such persistent failures, the limitations on the System's self-organizing ability have continued to be ignored.

## HOW THE SURVIVAL MECHANISM WORKS

Up to now, the legitimacy of the System and its efficiency have been discussed on a more or less equal footing. Now, however, it is time to see how the System needs to perform economically if it is to keep its environment under control. The survival of the System depends on both how consistently it uses the three components of the survival mechanism and how efficiently it can adapt its environment, or adapt itself to it. These factors are analysed below.

### *Internal consistency: Balancing ends and means*

The System's survival depends on its using the three abilities described above in such a way that they do not conflict. In other words, the System needs to achieve a balance between the means provided by its self-organizing ability and the ends selected by its self-targeting ability. These are essential factors in assessing the efficiency—particularly the economic efficiency—of the System. At first, this may strike economists as strange, since economic theory has taught them to restrict their analyses to the choice of means, in accordance with the now classic definition by Lionel Robbins.[15]

In defining economics, Robbins also defined the role of the economist as that of helping society to use available means in such a way as to satisfy the greatest possible number of needs. The effect of this approach, which has become part of contemporary economic theory, is to exclude the choice of ends from the field of economics and to assume that ends are not specific to each socio-economic system, but are universal. If we accept the epistemological assumption that ends are external to and independent of economic factors, then there is by definition no possible feedback between ends and means. Yet in CPEs such feedback does occur, since—subject to the limitations described earlier—the System's survival mechanism guides its choice of both means and ends.

The fact that the System's self-organizing and self-targeting abilities are both part of the same survival mechanism makes it clear that analytical tools based on Robbins's definition are not appropriate to economic systems other than market economies. Since the System can both determine its objectives and provide the means needed in order to achieve them, it can adjust either the means to the ends or vice versa so as to obtain the best possible balance. Whereas Robbins calls upon economists to decide how best to satisfy needs, the question that faces the System is how to keep ends and means consistent.

For this purpose we require an indicator that will allow us to classify the various scenarios. There are three possible kinds of indicator:

(a) one that operates in relation to a given objective by indicating the amount of resources required in order to achieve it;

(b) one based on a given level of use of resources, so that the extent to which ends are achieved varies from scenario to scenario (only this indicator is recognized in economic theory);

(*c*) a complex indicator or 'meta-standard', which will indicate both the level of use of resources and the extent to
which ends are achieved; this is a purely hypothetical
indicator, and is mentioned here only for the sake of
completeness.

What kind of indicator does the System apply in order to ensure
that it uses its two active abilities consistently? Does it adjust the
ends to the means or vice versa, or does it perhaps have a meta-
standard which provides it with an algorithm for the maximization
of consistency?

The recent history of the CPEs has been marked by drastic
reversals of policy and major reorganizations of economic activity.
Ever since the end of the Stalin era, the CPEs have been uncertain
as to how best to allocate the fruits of material production, and
priority has alternated between investment and consumption.
Reversals of policy from year to year or from one five-year plan to
the next are evidence of considerable uncertainty as to objectives.
As for means, reorganizations of economic activity ('economic
reforms') have been frequent ever since the mid-fifties: such
reforms were carried out in the USSR in 1962 and 1964, in the
GDR in 1963, in Poland in 1967–8 and 1982–5, in Hungary in
1968, 1973, and 1985, and in Czechoslovakia in 1968.

Thus, according to circumstances, the System determines either
the ends or the means in advance and adjusts the other one
accordingly. Such varying behaviour suggests that there is nothing
that can prevent the System from being inconsistent in its use of
the survival mechanism. At best, the Communist party possesses
an appropriate meta-standard, in other words a degree of discernment that enables it to determine whether the combination of ends
and means it intends to adopt is not inconsistent. Thus, when the
party leadership rejects a draft economic plan[16] or approves a
reform measure, we may assume that its decision is based, if not on
an algorithm of maximum consistency, at least on an intuitive
awareness of the point at which inconsistency will become critical.
This is probably where the System's self-justifying ability comes
into its own.

It is thus apparent that the Communist party has no way of
guaranteeing maximum consistency in its use of the survival

mechanism. We must then ask ourselves under what circumstances the System resorts to its self-justifying ability. Janusz Zielinski provides a clue:

It is a historical fact that a given economic system can accommodate quite a *broad range* of economic policies. It is also clear by now that this range of economic policies is a *finite* one. A given economic system can serve— not always with equal effectiveness to be sure—a quite diverse set of priorities (anti- and pro-consumer, autarchic- and open-development strategies, anti- and pro-family farming, etc.). At the same time— whatever the priorities pursued—it has *inherent limitations* which do not change with different economic policies.[17]

Here Zielinski is merely elaborating upon an idea originally expressed by Michal Kalecki,[18] namely, that the efficiency of an organization (Zielinski uses the term 'system') has its limits, rather like a tool that is only able to perform a finite number of tasks (achieve a finite number of objectives). According to this theory, the need for efficiency forces the System to change the way it is organized in the light of new objectives. However, there is no indication whatsoever that such changes occur automatically in CPEs. On the contrary, the sluggishness of the System's responses means that pressures from its environment may threaten its very survival.

## The survival mechanism versus the environment

If the System cannot succeed in using its self-targeting and self-organizing abilities with even a minimum of consistency, it may be wondered how it survives at all.

The answer to this question depends upon whether the problem is looked at from inside the System (in which case the degree of consistency required is already determined by the System's self-justifying logic), or with reference to its environment (in which case actual economic performance must be taken into account). In the former case the degree of consistency can be determined in advance, whereas in the latter case the answer depends on subsequent economic performance—the sole indicator of whether given choices are efficient, i.e. consistent. However, the System cannot afford to leave its survival at the mercy of subsequent performance, since it is then too late to do anything about it. The survival mechanism must therefore ensure that even if economic performance proves disappointing, the System can continue to survive amid a hostile environment. Accordingly, the survival mechanism must enable the System to shape material reality in such a way that none of the following three constraints ever gets the upper hand:[19]

1. *On the domestic front*, people are not prepared to let their living standards take second place to purely hypothetical ideas about generic man or the Promised Society. The survival mechanism must therefore prevent the discrepancy between aspirations and actual living standards from becoming so great that social discontent reaches boiling-point. By a judicious combination of repression and economic concessions, the System can prevent this latent friction from degenerating into the kind of open confrontation that has occasionally marked recent Eastern European history. The unsatisfied aspirations of the people are a veritable sword of Damocles; in order to keep it from falling, the System must either adjust its objectives or change the way in which the economy is organized. Toleration of the private sector is an example of a concession by the System's self-organizing ability, while an increase in the proportion of national revenue allocated to consumption is a typical self-targeting concession.

2. *In the field of international relations* the predominant factor for the last forty years has been the East–West power struggle, in which cold war has alternated with *détente* and the arms race has continued unabated. Keeping up in the arms race is a duty that the System considers essential to its survival. The survival mechanism must ensure that the economic cost of this remains bearable, and accordingly the System relinquishes some of its self-targeting powers in order to ensure that the economies it controls will provide the necessary military resources. However, this is not the whole price that must be paid for competing in the arms race, for the System must also relinquish some of its self-organizing powers. Such sparse information as is available concerning the military sector indicates that it differs significantly from the rest of

the Soviet economy. Such differences[20] are made necessary by the arms race.

3. *In the field of international trade*, the System must avoid becoming too dependent upon the West and running up excessive foreign currency debts. Since trade necessitates the System remaining solvent, there are limits to the use it can make of its self-organizing and self-targeting abilities.

Thus the System is exposed to constant pressure from its environment, which conditions its economic performance. This state of affairs to some extent restricts the System's ability to select its objectives, and likewise limits the resources it can allocate in the short term to building the Promised Society. To ease the pressure, the System must use its survival mechanism as consistently as possible, in other words with the greatest possible degree of economic efficiency.

The above description of environmental constraints on the System will have made it clearer what its historical mission actually entails—namely, short-term survival in order to keep alive its long-term chances of building the Promised Society. Yet these two objectives may well be incompatible. Can the System survive and still fulfil its Messianic mission? Can it remain true to its principles without collapsing altogether?

## THE SYSTEM: FOREVER IN A DILEMMA

How has the System succeeded for seventy years in a turbulent and often hostile environment and, at the same time, managed to maintain its legitimacy in terms of the Creed? There are two alternative explanations:

1. The System survives because it is thoroughly *pragmatic* and totally hypocritical in the way it justifies its actions. According to this explanation, the System is extremely shrewd and clear-sighted, and does not let ideological principles get in its way. The System can thus always use its survival mechanism with the utmost consistency and achieve a level of economic performance

that will shield it against the environmental pressures to which it is exposed.

2. The System remains in thrall to the Creed, which limits the use it can make of its active abilities and results in a level of economic performance that is barely adequate to withstand environmental pressures. In this scenario, the System is caught in a never-ending struggle to maintain a sufficient level of economic performance. It is constantly forced to adapt its organization and its objectives so as to comply with the Creed and at the same time cope with whichever of the three economic constraints currently looks the most threatening. To put it another way, the System is trapped in a *looking-glass world* in which it has to keep running as fast as it can just to stay in one place.

According to the *pragmatic* theory, the System puts all its energy into coping with its environment, and automatically justifies every action *ex post* as being a historical necessity. The active abilities of the survival mechanism are totally unhindered by the System's self-justifying ability. For all its simplicity, this hypothesis is hard to sustain as an explanation of how the survival mechanism operates, since it is based on a particularly unrealistic assumption—namely, that the Communist parties are capable of making a dispassionate analysis of the situations facing the System and then hypocritically using the System's self-justifying ability to dress this up as a scientific analysis. This would mean crediting the Communist parties with quite exceptional powers of doublespeak and doublethink; in effect, it would mean assuming that the Communist leadership possesses a literally superhuman degree of intelligence, historical awareness, and manipulative genius. Since this is unrealistic, the pragmatic hypothesis must be rejected.

Unlike the pragmatic hypothesis, the *looking-glass* hypothesis does not involve supernatural powers; on the contrary, it asserts that the System's perception of possible choices is essentially limited by the terms of the Creed. In other words, the System survives as best it can by obeying the Creed and keeping the degree of inconsistency between ends and means below a critical threshold. This could also be termed the *stopgap* hypothesis.[21] The System adapts either its objectives or its method of organization whenever a new threat appears or an old one becomes more pronounced, but never deviates from the Creed as interpreted by its self-justifying logic.

Given the serious and persistent nature of the environmental constraints to which it is exposed, the System would endanger its own survival if it were to redefine its objectives or its organization too abruptly; for, if the results proved disappointing and the degree of consistency between ends and means grew smaller rather than larger, the economic situation would worsen and the pressure of external constraints would increase. The System dislikes taking risks and prefers gradual, limited action to major upheavals. This leads to constant hesitation, experimentation, and reforms of earlier reforms, all of which are quite simply reversals of policy in disguise. In this way the System attempts to bring about a gradual improvement in the efficiency of its survival mechanism without at the same time threatening the status quo.

In this continual process of trial and error, new organizational arrangements are simply grafted onto existing ones. Thus, in the course of time, economic structures and mechanisms grow more numerous and more complex. Since the System has no clear criteria with which to assess the economic efficiency of its organizational arrangements, it is hesitant to abandon those that have become obsolete, and instead allows them to subsist alongside the new arrangements. This lack of criteria makes it even harder to find appropriate organizational means of dealing with economic constraints, since the weight of bureaucratic inertia is increased and may even interfere with the operation of the survival mechanism.

*Since the System is unwilling (i.e. unable) to let its self-justifying and self-targeting abilities make clear choices, it eventually gets bogged down in a succession of unresolved dilemmas.* As time goes on, the number of these increases, and the System's self-justifying and self-targeting abilities find themselves with even less room for manœuvre. At the same time, new measures introduced in an effort to lighten the economic burden of environmental constraints are bound to be less and less effective.

Thus the System is constantly faced with economic choices it is poorly equipped to make. It responds by trying to keep all its options open, which ultimately prevents it from functioning properly and does nothing to improve its economic performance.

It is now time to look at each of the dilemmas in turn and to examine the factors that prevent the System from making the necessary choices in each case. This is an unusual approach, but one that will give us an insight into the essential workings of the System. Basically, the dilemmas that the System has to cope with are of two kinds: *internal dilemmas*, which essentially concern organizational arrangements; and *external dilemmas*, which concern the (potential) relationship between the System and its environment.

## Notes

1. R. Aron, *Paix et guerre entre les nations*, Calmann-Lévy, Paris, 1962.
2. A. Besançon, *Court traité de soviétologie*, Hachette, Paris, 1976.
3. In 'Contradictions in Soviet Socialism', *Problems of Communism*, Nov.–Dec. 1984, p. 7), E. Kux writes: 'Thus, a crisis of ideology is for Soviet leaders potentially much more serious than even acute crisis in the economic sphere, because it chips away at the cornerstone of the system.'
4. In a statement made in October 1984, Deng Xiaoping extended the scope of economic reform, and ordered the works of Marx to be given less emphasis. For an excellent commentary on this, see 'China Notes that Marx is Dead', *The Economist*, 22 Dec. 1984, pp. 54–5.
5. For a review of the major ideological schisms and rifts that have occurred within the Communist world, see François Fejtö, *Histoire des démocraties populaires*, 2 vols., Le Seuil, Paris, 1978, and *Chine–URSS, de l'alliance au conflit (1950–1977)*, Le Seuil, Paris, 1978.
6. Le *'Nouveau Communisme': Étude sur l'eurocommunisme et l'Europe de l'Est*, supervised by M. Molnar and H. Kapur, Études et Travaux HEI, Geneva, 1978.
7. *L'Unità*, 27 Jan. 1985; for an analysis of the Eastern European response, see *Radio Free Europe Research Bulletin*, Munich, 10. 7 (15 Feb. 1985).
8. See Ch. 1.
9. It has become customary to dismiss the System's self-justifying logic as cliché-ridden propaganda, but as my analysis shows it is more flexible than this. A similar view is expressed in an article by Roger Bautier and Barbara Rogulska, entitled 'La Communication sociale: Langue de bois ou langue de caoutchouc?' ('Social communication: More than just clichés?'), *Économie et humanisme*, July–Aug. 1984, pp. 21–31.
10. See Ch. 1.
11. See Ch. 1.
12. This term was first introduced by Jan Drewnowski in 'The Anatomy of Economic Failure in Soviet-type Systems' (Jan Drewnowski, ed., *Crisis in the East European Economy*, Croom Helm, London, 1982).
13. J.-L. Le Moigne, *La Théorie du système général, théorie de la modélisation*, PUF, Paris, 1984.

14. See Ch. 3, particularly the section dealing with the effectiveness of the various ways in which the System exercises power.
15. In his *Essay on the Nature and Significance of Economic Science* (Macmillan, London, 1932), Robbins wrote: '. . . when time and the means for achieving ends are limited *and* capable of alternative application, *and* the ends are capable of being distinguished in order of importance, then behaviour necessarily assumes the form of choice. Every act which involves time and scarce means for the achievement of one end involves the relinquishment of their use for the achievement of another. It has an economic aspect.'
16. See Gorbachev's rejection in June 1985 of the proposed Soviet 1986–90 five-year plan (*Wall Street Journal*, 12 June 1985).
17. 'On System Remodelling in Poland: A Pragmatic Approach', *Soviet Studies*, 30. 1 (Jan. 1978), 3–38, at p. 4.
18. 'Political Aspects of Full Employment', *Political Quarterly*, 10. 4 (1943).
19. The last three chapters of this book contain a detailed discussion of how these constraints influence the workings of the System.
20. This issue is discussed in Ch. 7. Raymond Aron (*Plaidoyer pour l'Europe décadente*) actually claims that capitalism can challenge the System in every economic field; the military sector is then merely a sublimated form, and accordingly the most hazardous as far as CPEs are concerned. If this assessment is to be believed, then the System must relinquish even more powers than I have indicated.
21. In an interview in the *Journal de Genève* (18 Nov. 1985) regarding his book *Condemned to Co-exist: Road Maps to the Future* (Pergamon Press, Oxford, 1980), Bohdan Hawrylyshyn said: '. . . a senior Soviet official I was speaking to recently admitted: "The reforms you suggest are attractive, only if we were to adopt them it would mean abandoning Marxism . . ." This is the basic dilemma facing a ruling class which knows what needs to be done but cannot do it without endangering the system which keeps it in power.'

Hawrylyshyn's position lies half-way between the pragmatic theory and the looking-glass theory. It is similar to the pragmatic theory in crediting Communist leaders with the power to make a clear-sighted analysis of Marxism, but it comes closer to the looking-glass theory in stressing that there are definite limits to what can be justified. Ultimately, Hawrylyshyn rejects the pragmatic theory, so only the looking-glass theory remains.

# II

# Internal Dilemmas

The Creed's occasional pointers regarding the organization and functioning of the Promised Society (see Chapter 1) are *ideological constraints* which the System cannot ignore if it is to remain credible in terms of the Creed (although they can be somewhat toned down in the interests of self-justification). At the same time, the System has to cope with constraints arising out of *its relationship with its environment*.

If the System were unable to cope with its social and international environment, the very political and economic survival of the Eastern European regimes would be at stake. On the other hand, if the System failed to take account of the various ideological constraints, its credibility in terms of the Creed would be threatened. Although these two kinds of constraint are essentially quite different, they are interrelated. The credibility of the System in terms of the Creed depends not only on astute self-justification but also on its choice of economic organization and objectives. The material survival of the System depends entirely on how effectively that choice enables the System to withstand its hostile environment.

The System is simultaneously confronted with two sets of problems. First of all, its choice of organization and objectives must both be credible in terms of the Creed and ensure maximum efficiency. Here the System is faced with what will be referred to as *internal* (or *organizational*) *dilemmas*. At the same time, the everyday relationship between the System and its environment is continually testing the economic efficiency of the System's choice of organization and objectives. The dilemmas that face the System at this point will be referred to as *external* (or *environmental*) *dilemmas*.

Part II is divided into three chapters, dealing respectively with the three internal dilemmas: the planning dilemma, the dilemma of methods, and the money dilemma. The three external dilemmas—the social dilemma, the military dilemma, and the dilemma of growth—will be discussed in Part III.

# 3

# The Planning Dilemma: Legitimacy versus Efficiency

Each organizational dilemma needs to be examined from two points of view, since it arises out of the clash between the need for legitimacy in terms of the Creed and the need for economic efficiency. This is particularly true of planning, which is the end product of both the System's self-organizing ability and its self-targeting ability. The nature of the problem is reflected in the structure of this chapter. In the first section we will be looking at planning from the point of view of the Creed, i.e. in terms of its credibility, while the second part will examine the relationship between planning and economic reality. Finally, the third section will analyse the planning dilemma and examine both how the System responds to it and the effect of its response in terms of both the Creed and the economic situation.

## PLANNING AND CREDIBILITY

According to the Creed, the Communist party (and thus the System) is the sole guardian of proletarian consciousness, which means that no one is entitled to question its legitimacy. However, it is not enough simply to be aware of social preferences; in order to be credible, the System must *act* in accordance with both the spirit and the letter of the Creed, in other words the society it controls must move as quickly as possible towards Communism. For this purpose the System possesses its own special methods, discussed in the previous chapter, which—at least in theory—enable it to bring about material changes in society. The System's use of planning must satisfy the Creed in two ways: firstly, it must be oriented towards long-term objectives, and secondly, it must be economically credible.

## The need for long-term objectives

### The concept of planning

A plan is an ordered sequence of operations designed to achieve a given goal.[1] It indicates the actions that must be carried out in order to attain a predetermined future state of affairs, and specifies the stages in the transformation of the present that are necessary in order for the future to turn out as intended. Three elements are thus involved: the present state of affairs, the intended future state of affairs, and the series of actions that are needed in order to turn the former into the latter.

Unlike a forecast or a project, a plan extends well beyond the speculative sphere in which it is first conceived, since the action it generates helps to determine reality. Although forecasts, projects, and plans are all directed towards the future, they differ in other ways. A forecast merely extrapolates trends on the basis of the previous dynamics of certain factors that are independent of the observer, while a project envisages certain actions by the observer, subject to certain conditions. A plan, on the other hand, is based on a commitment by the subject to act in a predetermined, co-ordinated manner, in order to achieve a set goal. A plan is thus an instrument that a conscious individual uses as a means of controlling reality through predetermined action.

Thus defined, planning differs from mere rational decision-making[2] in the extent of the initial commitment, which comprises an entire series of actions to be carried out over a predetermined period. Whereas rational decision-making leaves the subject free to reconsider each separate action as and when new information becomes available, planning commits him to carry out an entire series of actions and thereby excludes the possibility of reconsidering each separate action until the plan has been completed.

From the point of view of the Creed, economic planning is a technical method used by the System to ensure that the essential logic behind all economic activity is the notion of society's progress towards Communism. Thus, at least in theory, it is an extremely effective means of controlling the tissue.

## Left in the lurch

After endowing the System with the ability to plan, and asserting that planning is an economically efficient means of building Communism, the Creed fails to say how exactly the System is to use its planning ability. The dialectical method, which as we have seen is unable to describe the inevitable, explains this failing but cannot do anything about it. Communist parties therefore have no idea which path will lead to the Promised Society. Radical American economists, using the same dialectical method, have run into similar problems:

why are there such discordant radical tones on these issues [the transition to socialism—PD]? Under the best of circumstances, these are difficult problems, and one should expect sharp differences of opinion. But the basic reason for disarray, it seems to us, is that radicals do not have a useful theory of long-term, global socialist development that informs them of the characteristics of socialist societies in their early, middle and latter stages of development. Radicals do have such a theory about capitalist development . . .[3]

Left in the lurch by the Creed, Communist parties are forced to work out for themselves—in other words to invent—the economic specifics of the new reality they hope planning will bring about. If the System does not have a clear, detailed view of its objective, it runs the serious risk of losing its way, of straying from the true path. Moreover, the need to transplant the Promised Society from the ordinal time-scale of the Creed to the cardinal time-scale of history means that Communist parties must not only invent the specifics of the new reality, but also the various intermediate stages on the way. Only after it has successfully performed this dual feat of imagination and analysis is planning in a position to channel the energies of the economy towards its chosen objective.

In order to remain credible in terms of the Creed, the System must therefore plan on the basis of a clear, long-term objective.

Although this is not at first sight a difficult requirement, the material problems of drawing up very long-term (or perspective) plans make it almost impossible to satisfy this requirement in practice.

## The time-scale of planning

Materially speaking, a plan is a document covering a period of cardinal time with a specified beginning and end. The longer the period, the greater the scope of the potential changes, and thus the greater the difference between the state of society at the beginning and at the end of the plan.

The System generally uses three different types of plan at once: short-term plans (one-year or even shorter plans), medium-term plans (five-year or occasionally three-year plans), and long-term plans (plans lasting between ten and twenty years). In theory, there are several ways of combining these various types of plan into a single structure,[4] although the extent to which the System requires a clear vision of the Promised Society differs considerably from case to case. This is illustrated by the following three scenarios.

1. Here the long-term plan is the frame of reference, on the basis of which the successively more detailed medium-term and short-term plans are drawn up. The long-term plan is central to this scenario, for the entire exercise starts again as each long-term plan comes to an end. Furthermore, the long-term objective is presumed to determine all economic activity throughout the period concerned.

2. Here, the medium-term plan is central. As in the first scenario, it forms the basis for the more detailed short-term plans, but at the same time it acts as the basis for the long-term plan, which extrapolates over the long term the trends contained in the medium-term plan. In this scenario, long-term plans are never completed, since they are reformulated whenever a medium-term plan comes to an end. By using this scenario, the System can dispense with a clear vision of the ultimate objective and thus has more scope for improvisation than it does in the first scenario.

3. Here the short-term plan is crucial. In this scenario both long-term and medium-term plans are really only projects, since

they are reformulated whenever a short-term plan comes to an end and thus, by definition, can never be completed. This scenario provides planners with greater room for manœuvre than either of the other two scenarios.

In addition to these three scenarios, it is possible to imagine a situation in which the System only plans in the very short term; if taken to extremes, this results in 'open planning', in other words, planning that never gets beyond the project stage.[5]

---

### The planning principle*

'Among the principles of economic law . . . the *planning principle* deserves particular mention. The fact that our entire economy is based upon national economic planning is specifically acknowledged as a systematic principle in the Constitution.

'The literature stresses that "planning that is not based upon a comprehensive social strategy and social preferences, but that simply consists of adding up the plans drawn up by enterprises, households and consumers, is . . . *passive planning*. Ultimately, such planning is the result of processes in which spontaneous forces manifest themselves." It is clear that such planning is fundamentally at variance with socialist economics. *Planning must be active*, and must represent the conscious, targeted direction of socioeconomic development processes.

'. . . The problem is that, if socioeconomic plans are to be anything more than mere administrative documents, they need to be translated into orders, directives and executive decisions; in a word, they need to be converted into legislative terms. The weakness of our longer-term plans lies in our failure to do this; instead, such plans are considered merely as guidelines for use when drawing up medium-term [five-year] plans, which do have legal status. However, since plans approved by parliament have a definite legal character, the planning principle must be considered as a principle of economic law . . . It becomes a fundamental principle, one which permeates every institution of economic law.

'. . . It is obvious that, above all, the principles of civil law, which govern relations between *distinct* subjects pursuing *distinct* interests, cannot be applied in the same way to relations between subjects of social ownership which, by definition, are supposed to pursue *identical* social interests . . . The consequences of this are particularly evident with regard to the principle of freedom of contract. This principle undoubtedly applies to trade in consumer goods, since it guarantees households freedom of choice, which is the best means of ensuring that their needs are satisfied. On the other hand, it cannot apply to transactions involving intermediate goods, let alone investment goods, which are rooted in the socialized sphere. Here planning decisions enable resources to be concentrated on activities that are socially useful and desirable and are therefore encouraged.'

* Marek Madey and Andrzej Stelmachowski, *Zarys prawa gospodarczego* (Outline of economic law), PWN, Warsaw, 1980, pp. 22–7.

A number of comments can be made at this point:

1. There is less need for a clear vision of the long-term objective in the second scenario than in the first, while in the third such a vision can be dispensed with almost entirely. This suggests that the Creed's failure to provide a clear vision of the Promised Society can best be accommodated by the third scenario.

2. The amount of resources required for planning purposes increases with each successive scenario. This is because considerable effort goes into drawing up long-term or medium-term plans, and the amount of resources involved will differ according to whether such plans are drawn up once a year or once every five years.

3. The above scenarios are based on the implicit assumption that all plans are completed, in other words, that no adjustments are made half-way. However, the adverse effects upon the planning structure of failing to complete a given short-term plan decrease with each successive scenario.

4. The technical difficulties involved in creating a planning structure are greater in those scenarios in which longer-term planning is central.

Taken literally, the requirement that the System be credible in terms of the Creed means that all planning should be based upon long-term objectives. However, since from the technical point of view this happens to be the most difficult method of planning, the System prefers planning based on the second or third scenarios, at the risk of forgoing a certain amount of credibility; just how much depends upon how easily the System is able to come up with self-justification to suit the occasion.[6]

In addition to the requirement that planning be based on long-term objectives, the Creed requires the System to use planning in an economically credible manner. Let us take a closer look at this requirement.

## The need for economic credibility

### The economic virtues of planning

The System's self-justification uses the term 'planning' to describe its method of allocating and managing the circulation of goods throughout the economy. The System claims that planning is more efficient at doing this than market forces. Let us examine this claim in more detail.

For at least two centuries market forces have been the central concept in economic theory. If allowed to operate perfectly, it is claimed, market forces will ensure *optimal allocation of resources* within the economy. In order for market forces to operate perfectly, a large number of conditions need to be fulfilled, but for the purposes of this study only two need be mentioned: prices must be free from distortion of any kind; and economic agents, assisted by economic calculus, must display the perfectly rational behaviour of *Homo oeconomicus*.

In the opening decades of this century the question of whether planning is a more efficient allocating mechanism than market forces produced one of the most prolonged controversies in the history of economic theory, between Enrico Barone, Friedrich von Hayek, and Ludwig von Mises on the one hand, and Oskar Lange, Maurice Dobb, and Fred Taylor on the other.[7] The latter claimed to have proved once and for all that planning was perfectly capable of ensuring a price structure that was free from distortion, and that accordingly economic calculus was as efficient and practicable in a planned economy as it was in a market economy—i.e. that planning was capable of allocating resources at least as efficiently as market forces.

As the terms of this controversy show, the advocates of planning were out to prove that planning could beat market forces on their own ground—in other words, they were prepared to see planning judged by exactly the same criteria as market forces. In contrast, the System's self-justification—and indeed the Creed itself—

rejects such a comparison, arguing that the criteria which planning uses to allocate resources are not the same as those used by market forces.

Economic theory assesses the quality of allocation by the extent to which it satisfies individual needs. According to Pareto's classic definition, allocation is optimal (i.e. Pareto-efficient) if an individual's utility cannot be increased without reducing another individual's utility by at least as much. This criterion is based upon the assumption that man is an essentially selfish creature, quite unlike generic man in the Promised Society. For this reason the Creed categorically rejects Pareto's definition of optimal allocation in favour of a definition based upon the satisfaction of social preferences. However, since social preferences can only be identified by the Communist party, which refuses to disclose exactly what they are, the question of whether or not planning is a more efficient allocating mechanism than market forces must remain unanswered for lack of criteria for comparison.

Since, then, there is no way to prove the superiority of planning as a method of allocation, the System's self-justification resorts to a number of selective arguments, the most important of which are the wastage of value inherent in the operation of market forces, the ability of planning to control externalities, and, last but not least, the absence of economic fluctuations.

*Wastage of value.* This argument, which demonstrates the shortcomings of market forces rather than the advantages of planning, is based on Marx's labour theory of value, According to this theory, a good acquires labour value when it is produced: in other words, before it is sold. This means it has an intrinsic value that does not depend on the price the market eventually pays for it. Since in a market economy the price of a good is determined by supply and demand, it may well turn out to be lower than the labour value of the good, in which case the difference between the price and the labour value is wasted. In order to prevent such wastage of value, said Marx, all we need to do is make the price equivalent to the labour value of the good—which is what the System attempts to do. According to the System's self-justification, all labour thus acquires a social value. However, the way planning prevents wastage is by determining supply and demand in advance, which means that demand no longer has any independent economic function.

*Control of externalities.* Any economic activity by an economic agent can directly or indirectly affect the utility of other agents who are not involved in that activity. If the result is an increase in the utility of the other agents, the externalities are said to be positive; in the case of a decrease in utility, they are negative.

Left to their own devices, market forces do not take full account of all externalities when setting the price for a given activity, and therefore cannot force the responsible agent to compensate society in full. Here the superiority of planning is obvious, since prices are not dependent on either supply or demand. The planner is in theory perfectly free, when setting prices, to take account of the indirect costs of the activity to society, and thus to internalize the externalities.[8] On this extremely hypothetical basis, the System's self-justification claims that planning entirely eliminates distortions in price structure and, at the same time, makes it possible to allocate resources in a socially optimal manner.

*Absence of economic fluctuations.* Even the opponents of planning grudgingly concede that it does have one virtue—freedom from cyclical fluctuations. This is reflected in the fact that CPEs have almost no unemployment or inflation and that, at least in the short term, their growth rates remain fairly stable. This, however, is not so much an intrinsic virtue of planning as a logical consequence of market forces having been eliminated. Planning determines the quantity and price of each good that is produced, adjusts the amount of resources to the available labour, and fixes the level of investment so as to ensure the highest possible rate of growth. Not surprisingly, there is little room for fluctuation.[9]

Unfortunately, not only are the above three arguments economically biased, but they are based entirely on a theoretical view of the virtues of planning, rather than on how it operates in practice. Accordingly, they overlook its potential drawbacks, which are in fact the mirror image of its theoretical advantages. Apart from outdoing market forces—something the Creed considers self-evident—the need for economic credibility means that planning must also satisfy a number of formal economic criteria.

## The limits of comprehensive planning

Since the Creed considers planning as the most reliable and quickest means of establishing communism, the only policy open to the System is that of 'comprehensive planning'. Comprehensive planning ensures that changes are brought about as rapidly as possible and that they extend to even the remotest corners of society. If any area of economic activity were to remain beyond the reach of planning, says the Creed, the productive resources in question would be diverted from their one legitimate objective— the building of Communism. Accordingly, the System must endeavour to reduce such diversion of resources to a minimum. Thus, from the point of view of the Creed, comprehensive planning is a perfectly legitimate aim, and finds its logical expression in the ambitious kind of planning known as 'voluntarist' or 'taut' planning.

Unfortunately, comprehensive planning soon founders on the rock of unforeseen circumstances, which by definition cannot be planned for. Three readily identifiable sources of unforeseen circumstances are the weather, international trade, and individual behaviour.

Both the quantity and quality of agricultural produce are entirely dependent upon the weather. Planning can respond to this situation by always predicting average harvests; however, it then runs the risk of being either less than comprehensive (if the harvest is good and there is a surplus) or over-ambitious (if the harvest is poor and predicted needs are not satisfied). Besides agriculture, the weather can also upset planning in other economic sectors such as fuel consumption and transport. As with agriculture, the System can do one of two things—either make cautious forecasts so as to reduce the risk of the plan not being fulfilled, or else be ambitious and hope for a mild winter.

The second source of unforeseen circumstances is the unpredictability of world markets. None of the Eastern European countries is autarkic; all of them have both imports and exports and must therefore ultimately remain solvent, despite any temporary relief provided by international loans. They cannot predict with any accuracy how much they will get for their exports or how much they will have to pay for their imports. Such uncertainty, which is part and parcel of international trade, is something CPEs are particularly ill-equipped to deal with. Traditionally, the quantity of goods made available for export has been planned on the basis of import requirements; yet, since both import and export prices are unpredictable, there is no guarantee that a given quantity of exports will earn a given amount of foreign currency. As with the weather, the System must choose between a pessimistic and an optimistic approach.[10]

The third source of unforeseen circumstances is that the System's self-organizing ability cannot entirely eliminate individual freedom of action. If comprehensive planning is to be achieved without economic agents being required to perform tasks for which they do not possess the material resources, the System needs to have a perfect understanding of their behaviour. In order to acquire this, the System examines each agent's productive potential and input requirements, using what are known as 'technical coefficients'. These are used by planners to work out such things as the exact quantity of steel required to produce a rail and the exact number of rails required to build a given section of railway track. Such technical coefficients indicate the amount of technology embodied in the physical capital that exists at a given moment in time, and the productive potential made possible by the state of organization of production at that moment. However, since the state of technology and organization are constantly improving, such static instruments are bound to cause planners serious problems. Once again, the choice is between two alternative attitudes. Either plans can be drawn up on the basis of the status quo, which reduces to a minimum the risk of the plans not being fulfilled, but at the same time acts as a brake upon technological progress and encourages under-use of production capacity and over-consumption of inputs; or else they can be drawn up on the basis of forecasts, which increases the risk of their not being fulfilled.

## The limits of planning in kind

The task which the Creed assigns to planning influences its terminology. Since planning is an instrument whereby physical reality is transformed, planning objectives must be drawn up in suitable terms, namely, physical units. As far as the Creed is concerned, plans should ideally be formulated entirely in physical units, without any expression of value.

The essential economic constraint on planning is limited availability of goods (especially raw materials) and of factors of production. In order to take account of this constraint and make sure that planned uses do not exceed available quantities, planning uses what is known as the *method of material balances*. This method requires a balance to be drawn up in respect of each good, with available quantities on the credit side and uses on the debit side. Planned production and immediately available stocks are then entered on the credit side, and the needs to be satisfied during the period of the plan on the debit side. Every item in such a balance is expressed in physical units, that is, tons in the case of raw materials and semi-finished goods, and simple units in the case of finished goods. Let us look at the advantages and disadvantages of this method.

First of all, it is particularly suitable as a means of registering changes in the environment, since the physical units it uses make it impossible for value to disguise reality. The method of material balances is thus particularly suited to the aims of the System and the way in which it uses planning. However, the problems associated with this method are more serious than might appear at first sight. Two such problems deserve separate mention.

First of all, quantification in physical units only makes sense if the good concerned is *perfectly homogeneous*. Yet how are we to tell if this is so? For instance, is all coal to be considered identical in quality provided it is black, or do we need to take account of factors such as the amount of heat provided?

Secondly, application of this method throughout the economy is extremely cumbersome owing to the huge number of material balances involved. How many of these can the planning apparatus actually handle? In the Soviet Union, for example, the economy produces at least 20 million different goods. Can planning cope with 20 million material balances, and if so, how much time is likely to be involved?

In CPEs, needs should theoretically also be expressed in physical units. This would be the best way to make planning consistent, since the method of material balances would then apply to all goods throughout the economy. However, in a medium-sized economy this would involve drawing up several million material balances (and as many as 20 million in the case of a large-scale economy such as the Soviet Union), and the resulting technical and terminological problems would be immense. In order to be consistent and cover the entire economy, such a plan would need to take the form of a mammoth input–output table reflecting every historical, geographical, and structural facet of all economic activity throughout the country. Such a plan is beyond the scope of current technology, and consequently none of the CPEs has one.

This brief survey of the basic requirements for economically credible planning makes it clear what an awkward and unrewarding task the Creed requires the System to perform. Indeed, it might almost seem that the System can never use planning in a manner that is credible in terms of the Creed.

However, we have been reckoning without the System's self-justifying ability. By judicious use of this ability, the System is able to achieve credibility in terms of the Creed without needing to use planning in a way that satisfies the Creed's conditions for economic credibility. The System's self-justifying ability allows it to continue drawing up plans even if it thereby strays from the path leading to the Promised Society, and even if its plans do not strictly satisfy the criteria laid down in the Creed.

But is planning then nothing more than an ingenious pretence that invariably leads to wastage of technical and human resources? In order to answer this fundamental question, we need to consider how plans are implemented, and more specifically the constraints on the System when it attempts to put its plans into effect, and the problems that then arise.


## DEALING WITH THE ENVIRONMENT

Do plans actually need to be implemented? In order for the System to remain credible in terms of the Creed, it is sufficient if plans are merely drawn up. However, there are at least two reasons why the System needs to implement its plans. One is that the System can justify itself more easily if it achieves its objectives than if it does not, even if those objectives are not entirely in accordance with the requirements of the Creed. Secondly, the System badly needs economic resources (in other words, its economic performance must be satisfactory) if the three environmental constraints (social discontent, the need to remain solvent, and the pressures of international politics) are not to get out of hand.

Thus, irrespective of the relative importance of these reasons, the System must implement its plans and, furthermore, make sure that the economy for which it is responsible functions properly. How, then, does the System go about ensuring that the tissue will implement its plans?

## The principle of active planning

Our analysis of the principles governing the organization of CPE societies has shown that the System has considerable control over the tissue. This control is based on the principle of 'active planning', whereby the System can induce economic agents to carry out certain tasks, if necessary against their will. In the literature, such planning is also referred to as 'directive planning' (or 'command planning'), in contrast to French-style 'indicative planning' (also known as 'passive planning'). The two kinds of planning are similar in name only: whereas 'active planning' conforms to the dictionary definition of planning,[11] 'passive planning' is merely a macroeconomic projection of plans submitted by individual enterprises, and is thus not binding in any way. Passive planning, whose function is purely informative, was the basis for French economic policy for almost forty years up to 1986, when it was seriously challenged and effectively abandoned.[12]

Thus the principle of active planning is a codification of the System's control over all economic activity. However, such control is by no means as complete as might at first appear; instead, the System's economic power[13] is limited by various obstacles which even the System finds hard to overcome.

## The System's control over the tissue[14]

Since the tissue directly shapes material reality, it regularly finds itself on the receiving end of the System's self-organizing ability. The System uses its control of political and administrative structures to establish mechanisms designed to induce agents to behave in certain ways rather than others. Such mechanisms are a blend of the proverbial stick and the equally proverbial carrot. The System's self-organizing ability enables it to use any one of three different kinds of power in order to obtain the economic performance it desires. Galbraith refers to these kinds of power as *condign power*, *compensatory power*, and *conditioned power*.[15] Each of these influences and controls individual economic behaviour in different ways; and each has its advantages and its limitations as regards the implementation of planning.

*Condign power* is dissuasive power, based upon *penalties*. It is characteristic of military organizations, in which orders determine behaviour. A general uses condign power when ordering his troops to attack. However, if the troops are killed or flee in terror, condign power becomes useless, since there is no longer any meaningful penalty that the general can impose. This shows that, assuming the existence of appropriate penalties, condign power can make agents behave in a certain way, but will be less effective at getting them to produce results.

The System, a past master in the use of condign power, controls economic agents in much the same way as a general controls his troops. However, there are limits to the effectiveness of such power, since results are more important in economics than behaviour, and especially since a given type of behaviour is by no means certain to produce given results; this largely depends on how committed the agent is, a factor that cannot always be influenced by threats. Thus condign power is not an ideal way of implementing plans, for the following main reasons:

- (*a*) even a motivated individual may encounter obstacles that prevent the desired objectives from being achieved; and
- (*b*) an unmotivated individual, who is not amenable to condign power, will not behave as the planner intended.

The logic behind *compensatory power* is precisely the opposite. Here, penalties are replaced by *rewards*, which are granted if particular results are achieved. Agents who fail to obtain the desired results are penalized, but only in relative terms. Unlike condign power, compensatory power merely establishes mechanisms that will encourage the agent to produce the desired results, and leaves him free in his choice of behaviour. Since a specific reward is tied to a measurable result, compensatory power would seem to be more suitable than condign power for use in the economic sphere. However, it is still not an ideal way of getting the tissue to implement the System's plans, since the use of compensatory power makes sense only if the ultimate results are not entirely set in advance. This, of course, is incompatible with comprehensive planning, which specifies its objectives in kind rather than in terms of value.

*Conditioned power* is not based on either penalties or rewards, but on *commitment*. Unlike condign and compensatory power, conditioned power can manage without material support of any kind, since it is not dependent on the will of its user (in this case, the System) but on the willingness of its object (in this case, the tissue) to submit to it. In order for conditioned power to be applied, the individual must first of all freely acknowledge the System's authority and agree to act in accordance with it. The System can attempt to obtain such allegiance by various means, but ultimately it depends upon an act of free will by the individual. The effectiveness of conditioned power depends entirely upon commitment by an individual who agrees in advance to submit to it.

In order for the System to use conditioned power, individuals must freely acknowledge its authority, identify with it, and be convinced that planning is in accordance with their well-considered interests, whereupon plans will be received with open arms instead of having to be enforced. In fact, the System has little control over the effectiveness of conditioned power; essentially this is determined by the tissue, whose decision in the matter is final. By shifting the emphasis to the individual's conscience, conditioned power avoids the problems involved in transmitting information between the System and the individual. It would therefore be a most efficient instrument for implementing plans — if only the System could count on the individual.

### The limits to conditioned power: Wajda's film 'Man of Marble' (1977)

*Man of Marble* was released in Poland in early 1977, and reached the West in 1978. Quite apart from its undeniable artistic qualities and the political stir it caused, the film provided a dispassionate, critical analysis of how the System mobilizes the people and persuades them to help reconstruct society.

The film, set in the 1970s, tells how a young film-maker attempts to find out what has become of a former hero of socialist labour called Birkut. She gradually discovers how, back in the 1950s, this public-spirited building-worker who wanted to increase his productivity (i.e. the number of bricks he could lay in one day) was turned into a Stakhanovite by the official media. Birkut became a veritable national monument (hence the title of the film), but one day one of his assistants dropped a white-hot brick on his hands, so that he was unable to work and thus unable to raise the norms any further. The assistant, a friend of Birkut's, was promptly seized and, at a show trial so typical of the 1950s, condemned as an 'enemy of the people'.

Birkut, appalled at what he believed to be a miscarriage of justice, attempted to prove his friend's innocence. He then discovered that truth was irrelevant, and that the System had used both him and his friend to get the people to work harder and 'prove' that only the System's vigilance could prevent the enemies of the people from sabotaging their efforts. Wajda shows what has happened to the main characters (the police officer, the radio and television producers, and Birkut's own wife) in the period between the 1950s and the 1970s—how they have become cynical cogs in a machine which, in return, guarantees them material comfort. He also shows the initial enthusiasm of the working class gives way to an 'I'm-all-right-Jack' attitude, and how in 1970 the resulting bitterness leads to rioting in the Baltic ports.

The release of the film presented the System with a twofold challenge: it had to make sure the media it had always used to maintain its conditioned power were not discredited, and at the same time it had to refurbish the image of generic man. Accordingly, at the seventh plenary session of the Central Committee of the Polish United Workers' Party, the following view was reaffirmed by various delegates:

All literary works must be politically evaluated. It is quite a different matter whether a book is published in a socialist state or in a capitalist state. There it is a private matter between the publisher and the author, here it is a matter between the author and the state. There should therefore be no mitigating circumstances for authors of politically dangerous works.

We consistently instil [into the young] the fundamental truth that the only criterion of one's worth as a human being is one's labour and one's civic attitude, one's ability to tie in one's personal aspirations with the interests of society . . . Contemporary youth admires our heroes of labour for their burning enthusiasm and constant willingness to work. Their example appeals directly to the imagination. Attempts by certain films to misinterpret the endeavours of earlier generations can only provoke a natural sense of revulsion.*

A hero of socialist labour from the 1950s was allowed to speak in defence of the ideal worker:

In fact, when we started working back in those days we had no idea of becoming 'men of marble' . . . Admittedly, we were ambitious, but a worker's ambition does not involve the pursuit of glory . . . A worker's only weapon is his work; if he wants to change, to revolutionize the world, to create a new order, he must start with himself and revolutionize his labour.†

* See the proceedings of the 7th plenary session, *Trybuna Ludu*, 15 Apr. 1977.
† 'Wydobyc ciezar przezycia . . .' (The full weight of experience), *Trybuna Ludu*, 17 Mar. 1977.

---

Since the System is unable to rely upon conditioned power to implement its plans, it has to resort to a combination of condign and compensatory power. At the same time, it can attempt to persuade the people that its aims are genuine and vital, as the Soviet Union did during the war and all the Eastern European countries did during the period of post-war reconstruction. Ever since this golden age, however, the confidence of the people has been constantly diminishing, and now all that is left is a pitiful remnant.[16] By means of propaganda and education, backed up by censorship, the System keeps trying to arouse the enthusiasm of the masses and win them over to its economic policies. These attempts are usually a failure and only serve to show that *in Eastern Europe there is still no such thing as generic man.*

There is thus a considerable discrepancy between the theoretical principle of active planning and the System's actual control over the tissue. This discrepancy is aggravated by two strange phenomena that are liable to occur whenever information circulates within a hierarchical structure.

## The inversion of economic power

In order to remain efficient, the System needs to be well informed about the capabilities of the tissue. For this purpose it uses the flow of information provided—ultimately—by economic agents. However, since agents are only too aware that the System can use its condign and compensatory power against them, they tend to provide distorted information so as to get the greatest possible advantage out of the situation. Such distortion considerably reduces the System's control over material reality.

Since the agent is the sole source of information, his power over the System is quite considerable. He is able to anticipate the orders he will receive, and also to provide information that is likely to result in the kind of orders he likes and can easily carry out.[17] In this way he can avoid penalties, and thus helps to undermine the System's condign power, whose operation is limited by the information available. Thus condign power does not mean that the System is in complete control of the tissue; instead, there is a symbiotic relationship between the two.

Distortion of information has an even greater effect on the System's compensatory power, since here the agent has more freedom to determine his own behaviour and is nudged in the desired direction by means of rewards. Distortion of information causes the System either to underestimate or to overestimate the size of the rewards needed in order to make the agent change his behaviour. Either way, the tissue will not be behaving as the System would like.

To make matters worse, the System's economic control over the tissue is subject to semantic distortion.[18] This is because the same words can be used to describe a wide range of different situations. Since there is no one-to-one correspondence between reality and the various ways in which it can be described, however detailed, there are bound to be limits to planning in physical terms. Such are the constraints upon the System that it must obtain from the tissue a certain number of quite specific physical results: a volume of weapons of such-and-such a quality, a volume of goods of sufficient quality for export, a volume and range of consumer goods that can satisfy the people's most essential needs. In order to achieve such results, the System must communicate its objectives to producers with the help of language, and is thus exposed to the risk of semantic distortion. Merely issuing instructions to produce is not enough to guarantee the production of wearable (let alone comfortable) shoes, or fridges that work properly, or sturdy tanks, or exports that foreign customers will want to buy. *Like the distortion of information, semantic distortion undermines the System's condign and compensatory power and reduces the extent to which they can be used to implement planning.*

Neither type of distortion affects the System's conditioned power, which is based upon a relationship of trust between the System and the tissue. However, the System remains largely powerless to establish such a relationship.

Thus the System appears to have no reliable way of implementing its economic plans. What does this imply?

## THE PLANNING DILEMMA

There are two reasons why the System must do its best to implement its plans. One is that it must remain credible in terms of the Creed, and the other is that it must be able to withstand the pressures from its environment. These two reasons are closely related, but in the interests of clarity we will look at them separately.

## *Credibility*

In order to remain credible in terms of the Creed, the System must endeavour to ensure that planning and reality do not conflict. Either reality must conform to planning, or planning must conform to reality. Earlier in this chapter we have seen that the System has only a very limited number of ways of making reality conform to planning. In view of the pitfalls involved, the System is almost bound to opt for the alternative approach—*making planning conform to reality.*

The System regularly modifies its plans half-way so as to take account of new data. Modification of this kind is frequently carried out in Eastern Europe, in order to take account of (*a*) unforeseen circumstances or (*b*) revised objectives. The System's self-justification makes a distinction between the two: in the former case the modification is referred to as revision of an existing plan, while in the latter case it is seen as the formulation of a new plan. Revision is thus the elimination of a discrepancy between planning and reality, whereby the System implicitly acknowledges that such a discrepancy exists.

Revision enables the System to save face in terms of the Creed, even if its initial plans have to be thrown overboard. The System is thus able to respond to changes in the weather, fluctuations on the world market, or even its own mistakes. No matter if its objectives are revealed as over-cautious or over-ambitious, or the very basis of its planning turns out to be faulty, or its planning is shown to be inconsistent or incomplete—what matters is that the planner can reverse earlier decisions and thereby reduce the discrepancy between objectives and reality. By suitable recourse to revision, the System increases the chances that objectives and reality will not be in conflict when the planning period ends. The shorter the interval that remains until the end of the planning period, the more effective revision will be. If the interval is especially short, *the revised plan may even appear to be a response* ex post *rather than an adjustment* ex ante.

The secrecy that surrounds planning in Eastern Europe makes it impossible for the outside observer to follow the revision process. However, a recent study indicates that, at least in the past, revision has been a continuous rather than an intermittent process,[19] making planning almost infinitely flexible and therefore difficult to pin down in terms of exact dates. This is particularly true of short-term microeconomic planning. Overt revision of medium-term (five-year) macroeconomic plans has been less frequent, since the general nature of such plans leaves plenty of scope for interpretation and the information published about them is so sparse that they can be made to conform to any one of a wide range of realities.

There is thus nothing to stop the System revising a plan shortly before it is completed, so as to include in the final version anything omitted from the original plan. This enables the System to achieve a far greater degree of conformity between objectives and actual results than was possible in any earlier plan, and it can thus greatly enhance its credibility in terms of the Creed. This ability of the System to revise its plans half-way shields it from the theoretical risks to its credibility if objectives and actual results failed to match.

However, while revision may be an ideal way of ensuring credibility, it is of considerably less help in achieving concrete results, which the System needs in order (among other things) to survive in a hostile environment.

## Getting results

The only thing the System can do to achieve the economic results it needs in order to survive is to extend its control over the tissue. There are only two ways it can do this—either by learning from its mistakes and trying to perfect the workings of the System,[20] or by quite simply tightening its grip on the economy (a method referred to below as 'priority management').

If it is to learn from its mistakes, the System must be prepared to admit that planning has failed, to analyse the failure, and to identify the causes.[21] However, this method is so lengthy, tiresome, and above all embarrassing to the System that other approaches are preferred. Of all the Eastern European countries, only Hungary appears to have made up its mind to try this method which, far from merely 'perfecting the System', may well result in *genuine* economic reform—in contrast to what usually passes for such in Eastern Europe.

The System may attempt to improve its management of the economy by penalizing enterprises 'responsible' for the failure of the plan. What kinds of pressure can the System bring to bear upon such enterprises? Until very recently, closing them down was out of the question, since that would have involved wastage of factors of production and hence a loss to society as a whole; and, while closing down enterprises is no longer taboo, there remains the question of what criteria are to be used when making such decisions. Taxing enterprises is not much better, since the additional tax burden would have to be taken into account in the next plan. Keeping them under closer supervision would mean resorting to condign power, which penalizes employees rather than the actual enterprise. Possible penalties in this line would be the dismissal, transfer, or even prosecution of the managers concerned,[22] or alternatively reduction of the wages of some or all of the workers.[23]

To what extent can condign or compensatory power lead to an improvement in the implementation of planning? This depends on how realistic the objectives are. If they are beyond human capability, not even the harshest penalties will have any effect. If greater effort is required on the part of workers, the results may also be disappointing. But if the failure of planning is genuinely due to incompetent management, then replacing those responsible may improve things.

Instead of embarking on a process of self-criticism, the System may be tempted to look for scapegoats. The System's self-justification can then denounce the 'evil geniuses' who have deliberately sabotaged the plan. The usual culprits are 'international capitalism', 'freemasonry', 'the Zionist conspiracy', 'imperialist agents', and other 'counter-revolutionary', 'deviationist', or 'revisionist' elements. Such scapegoats make easy targets, and accordingly the histories of the CPE countries have been marked by campaigns of varying severity, ranging from full-scale purges to harassment of individuals or groups that are harming—or said to be harming—the public interest.[24]

The method of learning from one's mistakes starts to produce results only after a certain amount of time has gone by. Unfortunately, the environment does not always have the necessary patience, and the System is then forced to switch over to the alternative method, namely *priority management*.

If the System finds itself forced to achieve specific results as quickly as possible, merely in order to survive, it draws up a kind of 'super-plan' for the purpose. This super-plan is more binding on the tissue than any other kind of plan, but is limited to priority activities or projects which must be carried out at any cost. Despite the limitations of condign and compensatory power, they are very effective as a means of obtaining selective results of this kind. The System manufactures a false situation of abundance that is limited to the priority sector, and ensures that this sector receives all the resources it needs in order to achieve the objectives set out in the super-plan.[25] In this way, the System generally manages to achieve its priorities, but usually at the expense of other planning objectives, which are implicitly given lower priority or simply dropped altogether.

In any case, wholesale priority management is by no means a magic formula that will guarantee the System respite from environmental pressures. Its effectiveness depends upon the proportion of national economic resources devoted to achieving the priorities concerned. As long as this proportion remains low, priorities can simply be achieved at the expense of the rest of the economy. However, as the proportion of resources involved increases, there is less and less room for manœuvre, and sooner or later the System has to establish an order of priority among its priorities. In view of these limitations, priority management cannot be seen as the cure for all the System's woes.

## Making choices

Our analysis of the factors involved in planning has shown that the number of alternatives available to the System is limited. Basically, there are four theoretical possibilities, based on various combinations of the two main aspects of planning—*formulation* and *implementation*. The formulation of plans is subject to the need for credibility in terms of the Creed, so there are only two possibilities: either the plan is credible, or it is not. Implementation, on the other hand, involves not only credibility but also the ability to cope with environmental constraints. Here again, there are only two possibilities: either the plan is effective, or it is not. If we combine the above criteria, we can envisage four possible situations, set out in Table 1.

In the light of what has gone before, these situations may be analysed as follows:

1. The ideal situation. The plan is credible as regards both formulation and implementation, and planning is so efficient that the System can obtain whatever resources it needs in order to cope with environmental constraints. However, in view of the theoretical requirements involved and the inadequacy of available methods of implementation, the chances of this situation ever occurring are minimal.

TABLE 1. *Planning: the four possible situations*

| Formulation Implementation | Yes | No |
|---|---|---|
| Yes | 1. Ideal situation (legitimacy and survival) | 2. Survival by priority management |
| No | 3. Planning and revision (i.e. retrospective planning) | 4. Total political and economic collapse |

2. In this situation the System extracts from the tissue whatever it needs in order to survive, either by improving the System, by reform, or—the most likely solution—by priority management. If the System finds itself in this situation, it will give credibility less priority and rely on its self-justifying ability to carry it through.

3. Here the System achieves credibility by formulating economically credible plans in the first place, and by revising them sufficiently often to ensure that it can claim success despite the inadequacy of the available methods of implementation.

4. The worst-case scenario. The System is doomed, having failed either to achieve credibility or to withstand the pressures from its environment.

Situation 1 is unattainable and situation 4 is unsustainable, so both can be disregarded. The System must therefore choose between situations 2 and 3, which essentially means choosing between *centralized management* and what we may refer to as *retrospective planning*. Usually these alternatives will overlap, since retrospective planning involves a continual process of revision which is often centralized management in disguise.

The System thus gets round the planning dilemma with the help of its self-justifying ability. Without this ability, retrospective planning would not be credible and situation 3 could not be made to work. Credibility in terms of the Creed would then involve the System making a serious attempt to improve or even openly reform its economic machinery.

In practice, the System's self-justifying ability automatically ensures credibility in terms of the Creed, and the System is thus free to plan on the basis of situation 3. The real planning issue is therefore economic efficiency: in other words, the ability of retrospective planning to make the tissue provide the goods the System needs in order to deal with its environmental constraints.

Neither condign nor compensatory power can ensure that the tissue will implement the System's plans. But for environmental constraints, the System could rely for its economic needs on the spontaneous activity of the tissue, since its survival would then solely depend upon its credibility in terms of the Creed, which it could achieve by revising its plans at appropriate intervals. However, as we have seen, the situation is otherwise, and there are limits to the economic efficiency of planning. The System, which is torn between the demands of the Creed and the limited practical potential of planning, and must also cope with environmental constraints, is forced to rely on priority management and to put up with the inefficiency and costs that this involves. This it can do without much trouble, since it is perfectly entitled to seize everything the tissue produces and use it for whatever purposes it likes. Even allowing for local differences, the System thus has almost unlimited powers to use, distribute, and allocate the national product. Such *requisitioning powers* are essential to the physical survival of the System, for—given the failings of planning—the System has no other means of obtaining the goods it needs in order to survive. Though imperfect, requisitioning helps to compensate for the relative inefficiency of planning.

However, the way the System uses its requisitioning powers raises a number of additional problems, which will be discussed in the next chapter.

## Notes

1. This definition is taken from the French *Petit Robert* dictionary.
2. This is the opposite of the view expressed by Giovanni Sartori in *Democratic Theory*, Greenwood Press, London, 1973.
3. K. Griffin and J. Gurley, 'Radical Analyses of Imperialism, the Third World, and the Transition to Socialism: A Survey Article', *Journal of Economic Literature*, Sept. 1985, p. 1136.
4. Józef Pajestka, 'Institutionalization of National Development Planning', *Organizational Systems for National Planning*, United Nations, New York, 1979 (ST/ESA/SER.E/18).
5. 'Open planning' was officially introduced in Poland at the end of the 1970s.

6. See Ch. 2.

7. A splendid analysis of this controversy can be found in Martin Feucht's *Theorie des Konkurrenzsozialismus*, G. Fischer, Stuttgart, 1983.

8. However, the state of the environment in Eastern Europe and the way in which the effects of a disaster such as Chernobyl are dealt with indicate that Eastern European planners may have a rather different view of externalities than is usual in the West. In fact, the System's power to fix prices leaves planners completely free to internalize whichever externalities they wish, and ignore the rest.

9. János Kornai, 'Resource-Constrained vs. Demand-Constrained Systems', *Econometrica*, 47 (July 1979), 801–19.

10. See Ch. 7.

11. See the beginning of this chapter.

12. See P. Bauchet, 'L'Avenir des plans nationaux', *Revue d'économie politique*, 97. 2 (Mar.–Apr. 1987), 135–55.

13. Here I use the word 'power' as defined by Robert Dahl in *Modern Political Analysis* (Prentice-Hall, Englewood Cliffs, NJ, 1984, pp. 19–37); in essence, Dahl defines power as the ability of an agent to influence another agent's behaviour.

14. The term '(economic) tissue' was introduced in Ch. 2.

15. See Galbraith's *The Anatomy of Power*, Hamish Hamilton, London, 1984, pp. 30–50.

16. This subject, which is only rarely mentioned in economic literature, is discussed by Karoly Soos in *Informal Pressures, Mobilization and Campaigns in the Management of Centrally Planned Economies*, EUI Working Papers, 86/246, Florence, 1986.

    It is quite striking how often the new Soviet leadership resorts to conditioned power; scarcely a month goes by without an appeal by Gorbachev or other Soviet dignitaries to their fellow citizens' conscience or discipline—in other words, their sense of ethics.

17. The poor quality of Soviet statistics has recently been acknowledged by Soviet leaders: see 'Gorbachev Needs Data', *International Herald Tribune*, 13 Apr. 1987.

18. The semantic aspects of this issue were realized quite some time ago, by Wittgenstein among others. However, their effects on the way CPEs function have only recently been understood (see P. Pelikan, 'Language as a Limiting Factor for Centralization', *American Economic Review*, Sept. 1969, pp. 625–31, and A. Brender, *Socialisme et cybernétique*, Calmann-Lévy, Paris, 1977).

19. In *La Planification stalinienne: Croissance et fluctuations économiques en URSS (1933–1953)* (Economica, Paris, 1984, p. 615). Eugène Zaleski writes: 'This study shows that any idea of there being a perfect, coherent plan which is distributed and implemented at every level is simply a *myth*. As in any State-controlled economy, what we are really seeing are innumerable different plans which are constantly changing, and which are finally co-ordinated only in retrospect, after they have been implemented.'

20. See Tamás Bauer, *Reforming or Perfecting the Economic Mechanism in Eastern Europe*, EUI Working Papers, 86/247, Florence, 1986.
21. In *The Origins of Totalitarianism* (London, 1967), Hannah Arendt suggests that Lenin had a natural preference for this approach: 'Without the instincts of a mass leader—he was no orator and had a passion for public admission and analysis of his own errors, which is against the rules of even ordinary demagogy'.
22. In the CPE countries, 'economic crimes' are a significant feature of the legal system. In a number of such countries, those found guilty of economic crimes are put to death; for example, the article entitled 'L'Ancien Directeur d'un magasin d'alimentation a été exécuté' (Former grocery manager executed), *Le Monde*, 17 Apr. 1984.
23. In October 1985, for example, the Romanian leader Ceausescu *halved* the wages of workers in those sectors of industry that had failed to fulfil their export quotas: see *International Herald Tribune*, 30 Oct. 1985.
24. Hence, in order to create its own logic, the System's self-justifying ability needs to be able to control the way in which history is recorded. In this way the survival mechanism is able to influence collective memory, and obliterate knowledge of events which might otherwise tend to suggest that history repeats itself.
25. Classic examples of priority management are arms manufacture (see Ch. 7) and export production (see Ch. 8).

# 4

# The Dilemma of Methods: Efficiency versus Requisitioning

In the previous chapter we saw that the extent to which planning can control the economic tissue is only partial. As a result, the System is forced to seek credibility through retrospective planning and, at the same time, to secure the resources it needs by means of requisitioning. The System's planning ability, as provided for by the Creed, is in practice nothing more than the power to requisition goods and services from the tissue. Having reduced planning to an empty shell, the System can only survive by using its requisitioning powers to deprive households of a considerable proportion of the fruits of their labour and reallocating these so as to ensure its own survival and help build the Promised Society.

The term 'requisitioning' indicates that, in accordance with its own self-justification, the System does not actually appropriate available resources, but merely claims the right to use them for what it believes to be the greater good of society.

In this chapter we will be looking in turn at the limits to the System's requisitioning powers, the difficulties involved in measuring the extent of requisitioning, and the economic role of the enterprise and its influence on the way in which requisitioning is carried out. The System's dilemma with regard to choice of methods will then become apparent.

## REQUISITIONING AND ITS LIMITS

Basically, the Creed enables the System to requisition both goods and factors of production. Nevertheless, such requisitioning is subject to a certain number of external limitations.

## Geographical and natural limits to requisitioning

First of all, requisitioning is limited by national frontiers, beyond which the System has no control over either economic agents or goods. If the System wishes to acquire goods from abroad, it must therefore do so by means of trade negotiated on equal terms. Unlike requisitioning, trade involves two equal and independent agents, neither of whom can dictate to the other. The terms of trade[1] are a compromise between the valuations made by each of the partners.

In order to cope with such an unfamiliar situation, the System has traditionally created specialized agencies that are responsible for valuing the goods to be traded and for negotiating with foreign partners. We will come back to the problems this entails in Part III, specifically in the chapter dealing with the dilemma of growth.

Inside its geographical frontiers, the System's requisitioning powers are further limited by ecological factors, since the exploitation of natural resources depends on the state of the physical environment.

The System has always shown scant regard for the environment in the way it manages the economy. However, after forty years of neglect, pollution has now reached such proportions that the environmental devastation which requisitioning has helped to cause can no longer be ignored. The same applies to the management of non-renewable resources, which have traditionally been treated as though they were inexhaustible. Here again, the System is now coming down to earth with a resounding bump.[2]

## Self-limitation

Geography and ecology are not the only limitations, however. In establishing almost total social ownership of the means of production, the System has permanently confiscated most of the means of production throughout Eastern Europe. However, even within national frontiers, the powers of the System in this area are by no means unlimited. Eastern European legislation makes quite specific provision for private ownership of certain means of production. Since the System is the final arbiter of its own legislation, such restrictions on its requisitioning powers must be seen as a form of self-limitation.

*Agriculture.* Nowhere in Eastern Europe has the State seized all agricultural land. This means that land, and produce, are everywhere to some extent in private hands.[3]

*Private enterprise.* This is tolerated in most of Eastern Europe, chiefly in the crafts, services, and distribution sectors. However, in order to control the size of the private economy, the maximum size and capital of such enterprises are strictly limited. For this reason, the number, nature, and survival rate of private enterprises varies from country to country and according to whether the economic policy of the moment is to let the private sector expand or, on the contrary, to eliminate it by expropriation or prohibitive taxation, which may even be backdated.[4]

*Co-operatives.* Co-operatives are justified ideologically as (in theory) a transitional form of ownership. There is considerable variation among countries as to the size of the co-operative sector and as to the areas of the economy (apart from agriculture) in which it operates—mostly crafts, services, and small-scale labour-intensive production of consumer goods. The proportion of factors of production lost to requisitioning through the existence of the co-operatives is thus fairly small. Moreover, such limitations need only be short-term ones, for the System is perfectly free to dismantle co-operatives and take over their means of production whenever it wishes.

*Direct foreign investment.* Chiefly in the form of joint ventures, this began to develop during the 1970s everywhere except in the USSR, which only began to toy with the idea in early 1987. Conditions vary from country to country as to the sectors concerned, the volume of physical means of production involved, the permitted share of foreign capital, and, finally, the possibility of exporting profits. Whatever form direct investment takes, it is bound to have a more permanent limiting effect on requisitioning than any other form of private ownership. This is because any subsequent decision by the state to expropriate the foreign investor is tantamount to nationalization and may entail international liability on the part of the state—unless the foreign partner is compensated in hard currency, in which case we are talking about acquisition rather than requisition of the means of production.[5]

However, such a variety of legal private ownership should not be allowed to disguise the fact that, even if it cannot seize the actual means of production, the System has plenty of legal tools at its disposal for appropriating the goods that the means of production help to produce.

Like other households, owners of the means of production need consumer goods in order to survive. They can choose between being employed by the System under conditions determined by the latter, or carrying on private economic activities. In order to be attractive, the latter alternative must ensure them access to a greater volume of consumer goods than the former.

The relationship between the System and private enterprise can be seen in terms of two scenarios. In the first scenario, the System is the sole purchaser of the goods produced by private enterprise, and can thus fix prices unilaterally as a monopsonist.[6] By using this power to adjust the income differential between private and non-private households, the System can determine whether the private sector expands or shrinks. In the second scenario, the private producer is free to sell his products directly and to negotiate prices, while the System influences his income indirectly through taxation.

Ultimately, owners of the means of production are in a highly vulnerable position, since the System can always change the law and use its economic power to influence their income. Accordingly the term 'economic agents', in the sense in which it is used in economic theory, cannot properly be used in a CPE context to describe either private enterprises, or co-operatives, or even households, since none of these can force the System to abide by the rules of equivalent exchange.

Now that we have seen how the System deals with private enterprise, it is time to examine how it goes about requisitioning labour.

## Requisitioning labour

Labour is essential to production. If the System were only able to requisition capital goods or land, it could do nothing whatsoever with them. It therefore has to make sure it also has the necessary labour, and to do this it has two alternatives—it can either *purchase* labour or it can *requisition* it.[7]

Since in Eastern Europe the System has an almost total monopoly on the supply of goods produced, households have no choice but to sell their labour to the System in exchange for the goods they need in order to survive. Households and the System are therefore dependent on one another—the System depends on households to operate the means of production it controls, while households depend on the System for the satisfaction of their essential needs (if we disregard for a moment the private or unofficial sector).

According to economic theory, the answer to this problem is equivalent exchange, in which both partners obtain maximum, equitable satisfaction. However, there is no chance of equivalent exchange occurring naturally between the System and the individual, since it can only take place if neither of the partners is able to dictate to the other. What, then, are the terms of such forced trading as does occur? Since neoclassical theory cannot conceive of such a situation, it is of no help to us. Let us see why.

Let us assume an hourly wage set at a quantity of consumer goods $X$. This wage will induce households to supply their labour and obtain from wage $Z$ a level of marginal utility that exceeds the disutility entailed by working for one more hour. The entire volume of labour supplied by households will then be employed by the System, provided that:

1. its marginal physical productivity is not less than $X$; and
2. the utility to the System of employing an additional unit of labour is not less than its marginal productivity.

If the above conditions are not fulfilled, wage $Z$ will be adjusted until equilibrium is achieved, in accordance with the following equation:

> Wage $Z$ = marginal physical productivity of labour
> = marginal social utility
> = marginal private utility of the wage
> = marginal disutility entailed by working

However, neoclassical theory only applies here by way of illustration, for even in a market economy households often have no option but to supply more of their labour if their wages are not enough to live on. In CPEs the situation is distorted even further by the System's power to dictate to households, and the use of neoclassical theory to explain the terms under which labour is traded for consumer goods becomes absurd.

Contrary to what economic theory suggests—and as Marx realized back in the nineteenth century—labour and capital must eventually come to terms. The terms of trade will thus be determined by negotiation and/or pressure brought to bear by either of the partners, rather than by equations of marginal productivity. The only contribution economic theory can make is to try and predict the range within which the terms of trade will lie. Therefore, since economic theory is unable to pinpoint the equitable terms of trade, there is no reliable way of telling whether requisitioning of labour actually occurs in CPEs, let alone to what extent. In theory, the range of possible terms of trade is extremely wide: from a situation in which the wage equals the entire value of the product and the System gets nothing, to one in which the wage provides the household with no more than the bare essentials for survival and the System can do what it likes with whatever is left.[8]

In order to determine how much, if any, of the labour supplied by households is seized by the System, we must discard neoclassical theory and instead attempt to answer the following questions:

1. What is the value of what labour produces, and how does this relate to the wage received?
2. What is the return on other factors of production?

## MEASURING THE EXTENT OF REQUISITIONING

The power the System wields over households means that the relationship between them can never be based on equivalent exchange. Since the Creed has declared individual preferences to be irrelevant, the System denies households the right to negotiate the value of either the labour they supply or the consumer goods they use (though this does not mean that the volume of labour supplied by households is insensitive to the level of wages offered by the System). The System dictates its own valuation to the tissue on the basis of social preferences, to which the System has the only key, provided by the Creed.

What, then, is the source of value under the conditions provided by the System? The source of value is an issue that has continued to absorb economists ever since economics first emerged as a separate discipline, two centuries ago. There are basically two schools of thought. The neoclassical school claims that the value of a good is determined by the needs it satisfies, and is therefore determined by the user or purchaser. According to the labour theory of value, on the other hand, a good acquires value as soon as it is produced, through the labour embodied in its production.

In CPEs, product users are divided into two categories: households (which use consumer goods) and the System (which uses all other products). However, the position of the two categories is by no means comparable. The System can force households to accept such terms of trade between labour and consumer goods as it sees fit. Furthermore, the System is able to obtain the goods it needs directly, through centralized management, without having to resort to the market. Instead of having to signal its valuation by means of prices, it can simply make an *ex ante* valuation in kind. According to neoclassical theory, it is clear that if the System assesses the value of the goods it uses in terms of their value in use, its instructions to produce will be based on this assessment, which accordingly does not need to be further quantified.[9] This approach, which can be compared to natural consumption in primitive societies, enables the System to requisition goods and services without needing to measure the value of what is requisitioned. The difficulty is thus that any attempt to measure the value of what is requisitioned by the System means nothing in economic terms, since requisitioning takes place directly, without involving market forces. The whole procedure takes place in physical terms that are independent of the accounting value involved, even if the latter is measurable.

However, in the previous chapter we saw that, much as the Creed would like the economy to be administered entirely in physical units, the System cannot do so. In order to compensate for the inadequacy of its instruments, *the System is forced to keep accounts*. This means that while in theory the System can manage without prices, in practice it has no option but to introduce them, if only for accounting purposes. The value of what is requisitioned thereby becomes measurable; however, the value thus measured does not reflect the value to the System of what it has requisitioned, but is based entirely upon the accounting method. We are thus talking about accounting value, not economic value.[10]

Theoretically, the System is in a position to reconcile the two sources of value. It can start by converting the (social) value in use of every good into a price, and then make sure that production costs do not exceed this price. In order to do this, the System needs to keep accounts. However, in order to keep such accounts, the System must be able to specify production costs accurately, which means adopting a standard accounting method. This is because of the need for a uniform method of recording the return on factors of production. To illustrate this, let us compare a situation in which the only costs recorded are wages with one in which costs also include the return on physical capital. Clearly, the production costs for a given good will be less in the former situation than in the latter, and the purchasing power of labour expressed in terms of goods produced will also be very different in each case.

Consequently, we can measure the extent to which requisitioning of labour takes place only if the *accounting method* is known. The basic principles of cost accounting in CPEs are contained in the Creed and have already been mentioned in our discussion of the labour theory of value.[11] According to Marx, the only possible source of value is labour; in effect, says Marx, the notion of return on capital is merely a pretext used by capitalists to rob the workers of part of their labour, in the form of surplus value.

Hence the basic principles of *socialist accounting*: labour is the only source of value, and prices are simply thresholds that serve to prevent labour being wasted on production that has no social value. In such a situation, what is the accounting value of requisitioned labour? The answer is quite simple. If prices equal costs, and if the only cost is wages, the value of what is requisitioned will be zero, since the total value of production will be returned to households in the form of wages. This, however, leaves the System in a paradoxical situation: having set the price of goods in accordance with its own preferences, it does not have access to the goods it needs, since the purchasing power of households is sufficient to buy up everything produced. Although this situation is the logical consequence of the Marxian theory of value, it conflicts with the System's mission, which is to build the Promised Society. In order to fulfil this mission and to cope with the pressures from its environment, the System needs unrestricted access to part of what is produced, something it cannot be sure of achieving by means of taxation (the method used in market economies).

In other words, the System's need to survive and to remain true to the Creed mean that, in macroeconomic terms, *total wages must be less than the value of production as calculated strictly according to the labour theory of value.* The difference is the accounting value of what is requisitioned or, as Oskar Lange puts it, the 'price the consumer has to pay for living in a socialist society'.[12]

From the technical point of view, there are at least two ways in which the System can make requisitioning feasible in accounting terms. Either it can alter the accounting method by including more items under costs, or it can alter the method of pricing consumer goods. For practical requisitioning purposes there is no difference between the two methods; both entail a difference between the accounting value of total production and the accounting value of consumer goods made available to households in return for their labour.

*Altering the accounting method.* In this case, the return on labour needs to be split into two components: one paid to the worker in the form of wages, and one which theoretically also belongs to the worker but which the System appropriates in order to help build the Promised Society. For accounting purposes, this second component is referred to indiscriminately as depreciation accruals, return on capital, interest payments, or normalized profit.

By altering the accounting method in this way, the System reserves part of what is produced in accounting terms, and can thus be sure of balancing its accounts with households, since the wages paid to the latter will automatically give them purchasing power equal to the value (i.e. costs) of the consumer goods produced. However, this solution does not altogether satisfy the System, since it is then forced to compete with households for access to the physical goods it needs (in a market economy, taxation proceeds force the government to compete in a similar way). In fact, this method of requisitioning is strangely reminiscent of the way in which Marx claims surplus value is seized from the workers in a capitalist economy.[13]

*Two-tier pricing.* The System can make sure that households do not buy up everything that is produced, and can at the same time maintain an accounting method based on the labour theory of value, simply by setting the prices of consumer goods above their labour value. In this way, the System can make a profit out of its transactions with households, equal to the difference between the income from the sale of consumer goods and the cost of producing them. This difference will indicate the value of requisitioned labour, that is, the accounting value of the goods that remain available to the System. Two-tier pricing enables the System to specify in advance which goods will be available to households by assigning them a retail price; all other goods are then reserved for sole use by socialized enterprises. The disadvantage of this method is that total wages are not automatically adjusted to the value of the goods available for consumption. The System must therefore constantly manipulate retail prices to ensure that total wages and salaries (including the social security benefits paid to households) remain equal to the total value of consumer goods as expressed in retail prices.

The complex economic problems that now face the CPEs are forcing the System to resort to a combination of both methods, in order to secure access to the goods it needs and at the same time balance its accounts with households.[14]

## REQUISITIONING IN PRACTICE

We will now look at the microeconomic problems that arise when the System attempts to requisition what it needs in order to fulfil its allotted mission and/or survive. The ambiguous function of enterprises in CPEs will now become apparent. First we will briefly analyse enterprises in their capacity as production units, legal entities, and economic agents respectively. We will then examine what is meant by the term 'economic agent', and show

how the System's power to determine the physical composition of what is requisitioned would be seriously reduced if true economic agents were allowed to operate.

## The three aspects of the enterprise

An enterprise can be defined from at least three different aspects— technological, legal, and economic. In market economies, the term 'enterprise' evokes all three aspects at once. To what extent is this true of CPEs?

*Enterprises as production units.* From a technical point of view, 'enterprises' means factories, i.e. places where matter is transformed by a specific process involving a combination of available means of production and labour. Technologically speaking, enterprises can be defined in terms of technical coefficients that describe the transformation processes occurring within them. However, besides material transformation, there is also an accounting process; and while material transformations may be identical from system to system, transformations of value will vary according to the accounting method used, and thus according to the economic system under which they occur. Enterprises are thus not merely places where goods and services are produced, but also—and perhaps above all—places where *value is created.*

*Enterprises as legal entities.* Each enterprise has a separate legal identity and is marked off from its environment by means of a book-keeping boundary between what takes place inside and outside the enterprise. In market economies, the enterprise is seen as a legal entity which is independent of its environment, and as such it has a number of specified legal obligations. The following is a definition of a market-economy enterprise: 'a legal fiction which serves as a nexus for contract relationships and which is also characterized by the existence of divisible residual claims on the assets and cash flows of the organization which can generally be sold without permission of the other contracting individuals'.[15]

In market economies, then, the following three conditions must be satisfied in order for an enterprise to function as an independent legal entity:

1. the legal system must recognize it as such;

2. the necessary means of production (or financial resources) must be available; and

3. the owners of the latter must give their consent, since it will be their task to manage the enterprise in such a way that it will fulfil its obligations towards its environment.

From the strictly legal point of view, the same conditions apply in CPEs. However, the System is based upon social ownership of the means of production, over which it has complete control. The System is therefore responsible for providing the enterprise with the necessary means of production or starting capital. The System likewise specifies the duties of the enterprise (either by legislation or simply by means of internal regulations), and can redefine them whenever it wishes. Finally, the System controls the way the enterprise is run, since it is both the organizer of production and the ultimate recipient of the goods produced. The enterprise is thus organizationally dependent upon the System in every sense.

In both market economies and CPEs, the primary duty of enterprises is to do their owners' bidding. However, in a market economy this duty is limited by contracts drawn up between the enterprise and its environment, as well as its obligations under the law. In a CPE, on the other hand, there are no such limitations: contracts only involve one party—the owner—who can therefore break them at will, and the same owner makes the law and can change it to suit his own purposes.[16]

*Enterprises as economic agents.* In market economies, enterprises can only survive if they succeed in ensuring that their receipts ultimately exceed their expenditure. Their function as economic agents derives from their function as legal entities possessing the necessary resources to honour their agreements expressed in terms of value.

Since in CPEs every enterprise belongs to the same owner, it is impossible to draw a clear dividing line between an individual enterprise and its environment. Moreover, the single owner is the ultimate purchaser of a large proportion of the goods produced. It is therefore debatable whether, in CPEs, enterprises can function as economic agents in the market-economy sense of the term.

However, if we consider the entire socialized sector as a single enterprise whose environment is made up of households plus domestic and foreign private companies, the answer to this question is yes. As with enterprises in a market economy, the socialized sector can only survive economically in that environment if the value of goods produced ultimately exceeds costs. We have already seen that the socialized sector's receipts will, at most, be equal to its costs (wages and miscellaneous benefits paid to households). The System is thus in a position to make a macro-economic profit—the equivalent in accounting terms of requisitioning ('natural consumption' by the socialized sector of the economy), which is accomplished simply by dictating to households and the private economy the terms on which labour is to be traded for consumer goods.

## The ambiguous function of enterprises[17]

We have seen how the System attempts to organize production in such a way as to ensure that the quantity and the quality of the goods it keeps for natural consumption are sufficient and that the accounting value of consumer goods corresponds to total wages. If every production unit were automatically to fulfil its norms both in terms of value and in terms of quantity and quality, the System would have no trouble in getting its plans implemented by the tissue. However, since in practice this is not the case, the System has to choose between the following alternatives: either it must allow enterprises to act as economic agents (in which case they have no option but to balance their accounts), or else it must subject them to the strictest possible control (in which case balancing accounts becomes a secondary issue). Let us look at the relative merits of these alternatives.

*If the enterprise is to act as an economic agent*, i.e. is forced to balance its accounts, two conditions must first be fulfilled:

1. the System must abstain from intervening in the running of the enterprise, in other words, it must allow the enterprise's contractual obligations to prevail over its own rights as the owner of all enterprises; and
2. the enterprise must not be able to influence prices, nor must there be any overall guarantee that its products will be sold.

Clearly, if the System were to fulfil both conditions, it would lose control over the physical composition of production and could thus no longer be certain that its own consumption requirements would be met. It would also have to allow unprofitable enterprises to go out of business, which would mean establishing a mechanism whereby labour and capital assets were transferred from bankrupt enterprises to profitable ones. Such an automatic mechanism would, however, be incompatible with the System's need to supervise the allocation of the means of production. Allowing enterprises to act as economic agents would thus interfere with the System's requisitioning powers in two ways:

1. the concept of social ownership of the means of production would become meaningless; and
2. the System would lose control over the means of production.

On the other hand, this approach would enable the System to control production costs more effectively, and thus to reduce the value of the inputs required in order to achieve the same output. It would thus guarantee more efficient functioning of the economy (as envisaged by classic economic theory) and would ensure that the socialized sector balanced its accounts with households.

However, the System can retain far greater control over prices and product range and their use if the function of enterprises is restricted to that of 'pseudo-economic agents'. In this case requisitioning will be more effective, since there will be nothing to prevent the System from continually intervening in the running of enterprises. However, while this approach has definite advantages as regards credibility in terms of the Creed and the survival of the System, it does require the System to keep a constant watch on its dealings with households, and also involves the risk that the economy will be inefficient—for, as we saw in the previous chapter, efficiency can be seriously undermined by deliberate distortion of information as well as semantic distortion.

### Directors: The main obstacle to economic reform

In the summer of 1984, after two years of 'serious economic reform' in Poland, the Public Opinion Research Centre in Warsaw asked over one hundred directors of enterprises what they thought of the reforms, the economy, and their own role. The interviews essentially turned on the issue of whether the reforms heralded an entirely new economic system, or simply interfered with the running of the existing one.

The Polish reforms of 1982 were claimed to be founded on three unshakable principles: *autonomy*, *self-financing*, and *self-management*. Directors had the following to say:

Self-financing is a burdensome, uncomfortable state of affairs, and autonomy is seen chiefly in terms of autonomy for directors rather than for enterprises. Many directors still cannot believe in the idea of autonomous enterprises; they see it as an administrative fiction that is not backed up by opportunities to make economic decisions, i.e. decisions regarding what and how much to produce, where to sell it, where to get one's supplies, and what production methods to use.

Directors are uncertain about their professional position. Their status, role and responsibilities are not clear . . . Directors have external autonomy, which means that they do not need to submit their decisions for approval by the economic authorities. Nevertheless, they *are* answerable to the authorities for the consequences of their decisions, and they do not know what criteria are used by the funding agency to assess their work . . . *It is therefore debatable how autonomous directors actually are.* They may find themselves transferred as a result of what are often radical decisions by the self-management authority, which bears no responsibility for such decisions, or by the economic authorities acting in their own interests.

. . . directors do not perceive or analyse their environment in terms of the interests of the enterprise. In a sense they remain on the outside, and do not identify with the enterprise which they direct. They see the enterprise as simply one component of a larger whole, in which they are mere managers rather than autonomous individuals . . . *As directors see it, enterprises and their employees are at no risk whatsoever, whereas directors are exposed to numerous hazards.* They may be transferred for all kinds of reasons—political, economic, or purely personal—and, worst of all, they will never discover the real reason for their transfer. They are completely in the dark as to what their status is and how their work is assessed.

. . . since directors are all agreed that reform cannot offer them new opportunities, there is little chance of their changing their behaviour. The mere existence of such a coherent group with such a uniform attitude to reform is sufficient to make sure that the new rules of the game are not accepted.*

* 'Dyrektorzy o reformie: Na przeczekanil' (Directors and reform: Sitting it out), *Polityka*, 12 Jan. 1985.

The advantages of treating enterprises as pseudo-economic agents—who, although required to keep accounts concerning their receipts and expenditures, can make losses with impunity—are the exact converse of those of the previous approach. Provided that the economy is able to produce the quantity of goods the System needs to requisition, the System will therefore opt for this second alternative, which leaves it considerably more room for manœuvre and direct intervention. However, requisitioning is dependent upon the level of production, and there is always the risk that sooner or later the level of production will prove inadequate.[18] The System will then be faced with the serious dilemma of whether it should aim for an efficient economy (which involves treating enterprises as economic agents) or instead make sure that it can requisition what it needs, if necessary by reducing its requirements (in which case enterprises will be treated as pseudo-economic agents).

Nothing if not unadventurous, the System dodges the issue as usual, and instead desperately seeks a compromise which will somehow enable it to run the economy efficiently and at the same time requisition what it needs. Its efforts to find such a compromise revolve around the issue of *centralization versus decentralization*, which will be the subject of the remainder of this chapter.

## CENTRALIZATION VERSUS DECENTRALIZATION

Ever since the early 1950s, the relative merits of centralization and decentralization have been the central issue in the economic organization of the CPEs.[19] Before examining to what extent a compromise between efficiency and requisitioning is possible, we must therefore look at the various sides to this debate.

### Basic assumptions

In the first two chapters we saw how the System's self-organizing ability enables it to control the tissue. This self-organizing ability is ultimately one of the tools the Creed makes available to the System in order to build the Promised Society. Total decentralization would require the System to relinquish its self-organizing ability, which it can never do if it wishes to claim legitimacy in terms of the Creed. This means that the problem of centralization versus decentralization will last as long as the System.

The Communist party's analysis of the merits and drawbacks of centralization and its attempts at decentralization are therefore bound by a number of basic assumptions:

1. the party's attitude to centralization must not conflict with its use of the other abilities that make up its survival mechanism;

2. since the System's requisitioning powers are an essential part of its economic arrangements, enterprises can never become economic agents in the full sense of the term and there are therefore limits to how far the economy can be decentralized; and

3. given the fact that enterprises cannot become economic agents, the only way in which centralization or decentralization can influence them is by altering their legal status.

It is thus vital to find out exactly what is involved in centralization and decentralization—in other words, to discover what kind of unit will be designated as a legal entity and what its characteristics will be.

## Types of decentralization

Regardless of the extent of centralization or decentralization, the System will always include two specific elements: the central authority (embodying the overall interests of the economy) and the factory (the smallest possible technical unit).[20] The only organizational room for manœuvre available to the System is thus the power to determine the size of the unit it designates as a legal entity—which may be an association of enterprises, a sector, or even the entire field of jurisdiction of a particular ministry.

In CPE countries, the number of economic ministries is traditionally large and extremely variable. This is because their function within the System is rather ambiguous: either they are part of the central authority and thereby responsible for managing a group of production units, or they represent a particular production sector in its dealings with the central authority. This distinction, which is a subtle one, focuses on whether the ministry requires the enterprises under its control to act in accordance with the interests of the central authority, or instead defends their interests against those of the central authority.

In the former case, the ministry is responsible for attaining the objectives assigned to it by the central authority and is designated as a legal entity for this purpose. Accordingly, production units controlled by the ministry have only one duty, which is to carry out its instructions.

If, on the other hand, the ministry represents a given sector in its dealings with the central authority, it supervises the work of the production units under its control, but is not directly responsible for their performance and is not a legal entity. Legal status is then assigned either to associations of production units (in which case the individual production units are treated as mere departments), or to individual enterprises. In the latter case, the ministries and associations are simply representative—or, to put it another way, corporatist—bodies, and responsibility for implementing the directives of the central authority rests entirely with the individual enterprises.

In order to appreciate how these various organizational alternatives influence the System's attempts to strike a balance between efficiency and requisitioning, we need to look more closely at the implications of assigning legal status to any particular unit or body rather than any other.

The unit or body concerned automatically incurs responsibility for implementing the plan and is treated as an accounting unit. The pressures the System brings to bear to make the tissue implement its plans were discussed in the previous chapter. We will now look at the role played by the accounting unit within the System.

The *khozraschet* (literally 'economic accounting') principle was first introduced in the USSR during the 1930s.[21] Units subject to the *khozraschet* system must keep comprehensive accounts of their production costs, using the approved accounting method, and must make sure their receipts exceed their costs. However, since the approved accounting method treats government grants and other forms of subsidy as normal income, accounting units can easily be prevented from making a loss. Moreover, while the microeconomic effects of *khozraschet* will vary according to whether it is applied to each individual enterprise or to associations of enterprises,[22] its macroeconomic effects will be the same. This is why it is quite normal for the *khozraschet* system to be applied to differing kinds of organizational units within a single country; in one sector it will be applied solely to associations of enterprises, while in another it will be applied to individual production units.

However, the *khozraschet* system is purely an accounting method; it does not presuppose either decision-making powers, or responsibility, or even efficiency.

## Decision-making powers and responsibility

Whenever an organizational change takes place, decision-making powers are transferred in accordance with the change in legal status. Yet however great the powers transferred to subordinate units, they can only be identified in terms of what they are not, since the System—being the controller of the means of production and also the maker of the law—will not relinquish even part of its self-organizing ability for any length of time. Subordinate units are therefore only free to make decisions in areas where their masters do not intervene; the extent to which they can exercise such freedom is highly variable and, indeed, changes far more frequently than legal status. Given such a chronically unstable situation, there is little point in studying the distribution of economic decision-making powers, since it is by definition impermanent. On the other hand, the rules that govern the allocation of decision-making powers are well worth examining.

In a market economy, there is a clear link between the decision-making powers of an enterprise and its responsibility. The enterprise is constantly required by its environment to answer the following three questions simultaneously: what should it produce, how should it produce, and for whom should it produce? These three questions indicate the extent of the decision-making powers of the enterprise, which is responsible for ensuring its own survival. In a market economy, it must rely on its decision-making powers for this purpose.

In CPEs, on the other hand, no single economic unit has such clearly defined responsibilities. How, then, are economic units to use the decision-making powers the System allows them with regard to such matters as choice of product range, technological methods, and customers? Or, to put it another way, how can the System be sure that an enterprise's use of new decision-making powers will not result in wastage of resources, but will genuinely help to satisfy the System's needs?

Since decisions taken by pseudo-economic agents do not put their means of production at risk, their decision-making powers are not counterbalanced by direct economic responsibility of any kind. Since an enterprise is not threatened with automatic extinction if it fails to balance its accounts, the System must bear the risk of any decisions the enterprise takes, but the only possible penalties are criminal or disciplinary proceedings against the *individuals* responsible for the decisions.

*Decentralized irresponsibility.* Responsibility at each administrative or organizational level can only be clearly defined if rules for assigning such responsibility have been laid down in advance. Failing this, responsibility becomes vague and difficult to pin down, and is eventually submerged in the System's broad responsibility for fulfilling its historical mission. The response of the System, backed up by the Creed, is to appeal to the judgement of history—as interpreted by its own self-justifying ability.

Any hopes that the System may have of using decentralization to achieve a more efficient economy will thus always be dashed as long as decentralization means delegating decision-making powers but not the responsibility that goes with them. By refusing to delegate responsibility, the System can continue to assess each decision according to *ad hoc* criteria and recover at the drop of a hat the powers it has delegated. *The battle between centralization and decentralization is thus kept going by the System's inability to decentralize responsibility without reducing its requisitioning powers.*

*Corruption and unofficial economic activity.* Far from encouraging decision-makers to take their responsibilities more seriously, the absence of clearly defined responsibilities makes them think chiefly in terms of protecting themselves against subsequent charges of having abused their powers. Since this threat may come from any of a number of quarters, the precautions taken need to be fairly involved.

They range from outright fraud, whereby economic performance can be brought into line with the System's predictions and
wishes, to the creation of entire networks of individuals who will
protect one another in times of need. Some swap their political or
economic influence for goods or services to which others have
access through their work; those in plum jobs feather their nests
while the going is good, since there is always the risk that they will
be transferred elsewhere without warning.

Such behaviour, which we will be looking at more closely in
Chapter 6, is the tissue's way of evading the System's clutches.
Not only are energy and resources diverted away from the pursuit
of efficiency but, what is worse, they are actually used to interfere
with requisitioning. The resulting dysfunction is at times so
serious that, in order to recover its requisitioning powers and
indeed simply survive, the System must resort to condign power
and purge those in charge of the economy. However, this is an
extreme and highly unusual measure, partly because there are not
enough experts to replace those purged, and also because the
ruling class (or *nomenklatura*)[23] is only too aware of the ever-
present risks of dismissal or transfer, and protects itself accordingly.

We have now seen why the System does not delegate specific
responsibilities that could counterbalance the decision-making
powers granted to various units. However, by restricting its
potential use of decision-making tools, this exposes it to the risk of
being economically inefficient.

## The scope for microeconomic decision-making

In what areas can the System delegate decision-making powers in
the hope of achieving a more efficient economy, without at the
same time impairing its requisitioning powers? The three questions mentioned earlier—what to produce, how to produce, and
for whom to produce?—are bound to arise in any economic
environment. The System's response, however, is highly characteristic.

*What to produce?* This question concerns the range of products
available both for individual consumption and for requisitioning.

Since the physical content of what is requisitioned is vitally important, the System will naturally be most reluctant to delegate decisions concerning the range of products. However, even with centralized decision-making powers, the System cannot entirely determine what will be produced by the economy. Its solution is to make it illegal for enterprises to change from one field of operation to another and to maintain a tight grip on investment and/or financing, so as to restrict the amount of freedom that enterprises might otherwise surreptitiously acquire.[24]

*How to produce?* This question concerns the range of available techniques and technologies. The answer depends on the means of production belonging to the enterprise, the quality of the labour and know-how available to it, and, finally, the manner in which it uses its means of production. The enterprise is clearly the best judge of its own technical and technological potential, and it also has an almost total monopoly on the information it supplies to the central authority. Thus, even if the central authority claims to retain full decision-making powers concerning choice of technology, in practice the enterprise will always have some room for manœuvre, if only because distortion of information and semantic distortion can never be eliminated.

*For whom to produce?* The answer to this question is largely determined by the way in which decision-making powers concerning choice of product range and technology are allocated within the System. There are two possible situations:

1. The product range is determined by the central authority, which keeps control over all investments, and the choice of technology is enforced by means of technical coefficients. Nevertheless, by modifying quality and production techniques, the enterprise retains its usual room for manœuvre. If the entire economy operates in this way, the answer to our question 'For whom to produce?' will be provided—if only indirectly—by the central authority. In such a situation, even if the central authority officially leaves enterprises free to choose their customers, such freedom is bound to be illusory.

2. The central authority does not intervene in the choice of either product range or technology, but restricts itself to controlling the allocation of goods and, above all, investment. However,

such control over the physical allocation of what is produced substantially restricts the freedom of enterprises to determine their product range or technology; since the System decides who the customers will be, it also indirectly determines what will be produced.

However, the limits the tissue places on the System's self-organizing ability prevent the System from ever fully controlling product range or technology. The central authority's control over technology and outlets will thus never be so thorough that it can dispense with controlling distribution. Conversely, since the System is unable to control distribution entirely, it must maintain its control over product range, investment, and technology. In practice, therefore, every kind of control is necessary, since none can ever be complete.

Whatever the formal distribution of powers between the central authority and the enterprise, the latter will thus always retain a decision-making margin which the System must attempt to restrict or else to exploit for its own purposes. To do this, the System can resort to a number of instruments whose advantages and disadvantages we have now seen. Together, these instruments can be seen as two feedback loops between the central authority and the enterprise.[25]

The central authority uses the *macroeconomic loop* to transmit its orders or wishes to the enterprise (condign power), and to receive information on the enterprise's results and operations. In addition to this macro-loop, the enterprise is locked into a *microeconomic feedback loop* which essentially links it to the central authority by means of the reward mechanisms (compensatory power) the System has set up.

If both loops signal the same decision to the enterprise, that decision will be taken. The enterprise, while pursuing its own interests, will then unwittingly have used its room for manœuvre to the System's advantage and will thereby have helped to achieve both a more efficient economy and more effective requisitioning. If, on the other hand, the loops send out conflicting signals, the enterprise is very likely to use its room for manœuvre to frustrate the System, for instance by reducing the quality of its products or by choosing the type of technology that involves the most inputs.

In that case, the economy will be less efficient and/or requisition-ing will be less effective. Therefore, in order to achieve as efficient an economy as possible and to requisition goods and services as effectively as possible, both loops must send out the same signals.

---

## The behaviour of enterprises in CPEs

Since the late 1960s a team of researchers at the Warsaw Higher College of Planning, led by Janusz Beksiak, has been trying to explain the rational basis for the behaviour of enterprises. The methods used include questionnaires and also repeated extensive interviews with directors of enterprises included in the sample (which not only is representative of the economic structure but also reflects geographical distribution). The results of this research into decision-making procedures give some indication of what it is that makes enterprises in CPEs behave as they do. Between 1976 and 1980 the Polish economy was operating fairly normally—the upheavals of 1980 were still to come—and there is therefore no serious reason to think that the behaviour of the enterprises concerned was different from that of enterprises in other countries controlled by the System.

As in previous studies, the stated objectives of decisions by enterprises were divided into categories according to their 'orientation', which was determined by analysing the frequency of various 'clusters' of stated objectives.

The distribution of the various orientations throughout the population showed that decisions by enterprises were very often determined by their own interests (46.2% of the decisions covered in the survey), as measured in terms of both financial effects and smoother, more effective functioning of the enterprise. Another frequent orientation was fulfilment of government requirements. Signi-ficantly, fulfilment of the expectations of consumers or one's own employees was very low on the list of orientations.

The extent to which objectives were achieved was assessed from two points of view: firstly, from the point of view of the enterprises themselves (i.e. the extent to which the chosen objectives were attained), and secondly, in relation to social and macroeconomic objectives.

In 60.7% of cases, enterprises fully achieved the objectives they had set themselves, with partial success in a further 22.4% of cases . . . The researchers also discovered that these objectives fully coincided with macroeconomic object-ives only in 46.3% of cases, and partially coincided with them in a further 14.9% of cases. In 8.2% of cases, the behaviour of enterprises was found to have had adverse social or macroeconomic effects. Additional data showed that in 23.2% of cases the objectives were contradictory, in other words the achievement of the kind of objective reduced the possibility of achieving another kind of objective.

. . . The economic choices made by the enterprises in the survey were characterized by three variables: available information, the number of alternatives considered, and decision-making procedures. The data showed that enterprises were well-informed: in 75.6% of cases the information available could be described as comprehensive. At the same time, surprisingly, in 68.7% of cases only one possible choice was considered, or else a simple choice was made between doing something or not doing it. In only 31% of cases was a choice made between two or more alternative kinds of positive action. This may be due to two causes at once. The first is the imperative system of management, which does not encourage enterprises to examine alternative choices carefully; the second is the fact that, since there is a seller's market, no special effort is required on the part of enterprises when making economic choices.

This is confirmed by the data concerned with decision-making procedures. The distribution of alternative within this variable was as follows:

| economic calculus | 5.4% | habit | 41.4% |
| informal analysis | 19.7% | intuition | 33.3%* |

* Janusz Beksiak and Barbara Czarniawska, *Sposoby reagowania przedsiebiorstw w Polsce* (How Polish enterprises respond), *Ekonomista* (1982), Nos. 3–4, pp. 401–19.

## The terms of the dilemma

There is no obvious compromise between centralization and decentralization whereby the System could avoid the dilemma of requisitioning versus efficiency. The economic virtues of such a compromise should in any case not be overstated, owing to the limitations inherent in both condign and compensatory power. However, since neither complete centralization nor complete decentralization will do, the System has no option but to compromise. It cannot survive without requisitioning, but nor can it keep on requisitioning without at the same time trying to improve the efficiency of the economy.

The System is thus pursuing two aims, neither of which it is capable of achieving—a situation which can be traced back to the ambiguous economic role of the enterprise. Neither compensatory power (which is more likely to lead to an efficient economy) nor condign power (which ensures effective requisitioning) can provide the answer unless the System does something forbidden by the Creed, namely, relinquish part of its self-organizing ability. The System can avoid such self-mutilation as long as the lack of efficiency does not make effective requisitioning impossible. But when that point is reached, the System can only survive by using its self-organizing ability to set enterprises free.[26]

The System's failure to decide between requisitioning and efficiency leads it to see-saw back and forth between centralization and decentralization, a problem aggravated by the ambiguous role of money within the System. Is money a flexible tool used by the System to achieve more effective requisitioning? Or, on the other hand, does it encourage efficiency? To put it another way, has money been corrupted by the System, or is the System now being corrupted by money? This third internal dilemma is the subject of the next chapter.

## Notes

1. In economic literature it is axiomatic that all relationships involve equivalent exchange; economic theory thus cannot recognize, still less analyse, phenomena such as grants, requisitioning, transfers, etc.

    However, these phenomena have been touched on indirectly in two specific areas of research: the history of medieval economic thought, and grant economics. For an example of the first, see O. Longham, *Price and Value in the Aristotelian Tradition*, Bergen University Press, Oslo, 1979, and R. Roover, *La Pensée économique des scolastiques*, Vrin, Paris, 1971; for the second, see K. Boulding, *A Preface to Grant Economics: The Economy of Love and Fear*, Praeger, New York, 1981, and also Pawel Dembinski, 'Economic Policy versus Social Policy: A Dilemma?', *Labour and Society*, 9. 2 (1984), 209–26.

2. The ecological problems facing the System have recently begun to attract attention in the West, and there is already a fair amount of literature on the subject. For a brief bibliography, see Vladimir Sobell, 'Central Planning and the Environment', Background Report 88/86, *Radio Free Europe Research*, 11. 28 (11 July 1986). Other relevant material can be found in 'Dossier: Pollution Europe de l'Est' ('Special feature on pollution in Eastern Europe'), published in 1986 in the July and August issues of the Swiss weekly magazine *L'Hebdo*.

    In order to grasp more fully the extent to which the physical environment sets limits to requisitioning, we need to quantify its contribution to the national product. Such an assessment has been provided for Switzerland by G. Pillet and H. T. Odum ('Energy Externality and the Economy of Switzerland', *Revue suisse d'économie politique et de statistique*, 120. 3 (1984), 409–35), who assert that 16% of the values of the resources used in Switzerland for economic purposes originates in the physical environment.

3. The following table indicates the percentage of arable land exploited by private farmers in 1982 (although it should be stressed that, legally speaking, this is not quite the same as private ownership):

| Bulgaria | 8.0% | Hungary | 12.9% |
|---|---|---|---|
| Czechoslovakia | 6.9% | Poland | 77.5% |
| GDR | 8.9% | Romania | 15.6% |
| | | USSR | 1.8% |

The above figures are taken from M.-C. Maurel, 'La Petite Agriculture en URSS et en Europe de l'Est', *Études rurales*, 99–100 (July–Dec. 1985), 157–78.

4. See A. Aslund, *Private Enterprise in Eastern Europe*, Macmillan–St. Antony's, London, 1985, and K. Rupp, *Entrepreneurs in Red: Structure and Organizational Innovation in the Centrally Planned Economy*, State University of New York Press, Albany, 1983.

5. See M. Lebkowski and J. Monkiewicz, 'Les Entreprises à participation étrangère installées dans les pays socialistes: Étude comparative', *Revue d'études comparatives Est–Ouest* (1987), No. 1, pp. 87–126.

6. The clearest example of this approach is State confiscation of produce from private farmers (so-called 'compulsory deliveries') in various Eastern European countries.

7. The same problem arises in market economies; for a wider discussion of the issue, see A. Okhun, *Equality and Efficiency: The Big Trade-Off*, The Brookings Institution, Washington DC, 1975.

8. This is similar to the issue of how the national product is to be divided between labour and capital in a market economy. Here again, there are two basic theories. According to the economic hypothesis, the division is based upon the productivity of each of the factors; however, this assumes that it depends on factors that are exogenous to the company (prices of goods, prices of factors of production). The political hypothesis states that the division is based upon the relative power of the parties concerned, and therefore need not depend on any outside factor.

The situation in CPEs resembles that of the political hypothesis since, by definition, there can be no reference to any economic variable that is external to the system. This view is shared by C. Castoriadis (*La Société bureaucratique*, 1, *Les Rapports de production en Russie*, Union générale d'éditions, Collection 10/18, Paris, 1973).

9. This is confirmed by models and discussions regarding the optimizing of production in CPEs; the central issue here is how to optimize final production, subject to limited availability of factors of production. The 'value' of each product is then only meaningful from the overall macroeconomic point of view, in which the alternative chosen is only optimal in the sense that it satisfies the System's preferences more effectively than any other alternative.

10. This is an extremely important distinction. If value were to be measured in economic terms, the System could take a corresponding number of units of value from the economy (chiefly by taxation) and use them to acquire the goods it needed. It would then be behaving exactly like the government in any market economy. However, since the System controls the means of production, it can ensure that the economy will satisfy its needs directly

without any monetary exchange. Nevertheless, the relative inadequacy of its management tools forces it to keep accounts, and these make it possible to measure the accounting value of what is requisitioned.

11. See Ch. 1.
12. See Oskar Lange, 'On the Economic Theory of Socialism', *Review of Economic Studies*, 4 (1936), 53–123. This article has been republished several times.
13. See *Capital*, 2. 2. See also the splendid analysis of Marx's theory by E. Schneider in *Einführung in die Wirtschaftstheorie*, Vol. 4, J. Mohr, Tübingen, 1970, pp. 23–44.
14. See Ch. 6.
15. M. Jensen and W. Meckling, 'Theory of the Firm: Managerial Behaviour, Agency Costs and Ownership Structure', *Journal of Financial Economics* (1976), No. 3, p. 310.
16. See also Ch. 3, pp. 66–7 ('The planning principle').
17. There is a considerable amount of literature devoted to the function of enterprises in CPEs; the most original work on the subject is undoubtedly the book by David Granick entitled *Enterprise Guidance in Eastern Europe* (Princeton University Press, 1975). See also Waldemar Kuczynski, 'The State Enterprise under Socialism', *Soviet Studies*, 30. 3 (July 1978), and Richard Portes, 'The Enterprise under Central Planning', *Review of Economic Studies*, 36 (1969), 197–212.
18. See Ch. 8 on growth.
19. The literature on the subject is too plentiful to be listed here. However, the following books deserve special mention: Wlodzimierz Brus, *The Market in a Socialist Economy*, Routledge & Kegan Paul, London and Boston, 1972; Nicholas Spulber, ed., *Organizational Alternatives in Soviet-Type Economies*, Cambridge University Press, New York, 1979; and, more recently, János Kornai's *Economics of Shortage*, North-Holland Publishing Company, Amsterdam, New York, and Oxford, 1980, which discusses the issue in terms of paternalistic treatment of enterprises by the central authority.
20. Wlodzimierz Brus (*The Market in a Socialist Economy*) has already demonstrated that decentralization is ultimately limited by the Creed and by features that are inherent in any economic tissue.
21. For a discussion of its beginnings, see Alec Nove, *The Soviet Economic System*, Allen & Unwin, London, 1978, p. 29.
22. An identical accounting base is a basic condition for the introduction of the automatic mechanisms known as norms or parameters. If, for example, a norm stipulates that 5% of net profits may be distributed to employees in the form of bonuses, its incentive effect will vary considerably according to whether the accounting unit has 100 employees or 100,000. For a more detailed discussion of this problem, see Ch. 8.
23. A now classic social, political, and economic analysis of this class is provided by Michael Voslensky in *Nomenklatura: Die herrschende Klasse in der Sowjetunion*, Molden, Munich, 1984.
24. In this connection it should be stressed that freedom to invest is more than

simply freedom to use resources belonging to the enterprise to finance investment. Even if an enterprise has the necessary resources, it may still be required to submit its investment projects for approval by the central authority, or to finance projects put forward by the latter.

25. This conceptual approach is discussed in more detail by Pawel Dembinski in *L'Endettement de la Pologne ou les limites d'un système*, Anthropos, Paris, 1984, pp. 45–65.

26. This problem is discussed from a different angle in Ch. 8.

# 5

# Money and the System:
# Which Corrupts Which?

Any discussion of the existence of money and its function within CPEs is likely to lead to confusion, since even a partial explanation presupposes a generally accepted definition of what money is. Unfortunately, there are as many definitions as there are authors on the subject, ranging from extremely relativist views[1] to the nominalist approach that is inherent in functional descriptions of money.[2]

The whole controversy turns on the basic issue of *whether the function of money is dependent upon the systemic environment in which it circulates, or whether it is independent of any system*. Each of the two schools has its own answer, but both make unproven assumptions and are therefore, in my opinion, inadequate. My own approach will be based upon observation of the kinds of relationship in which money occurs in CPEs, and of the ways in which it then functions. This approach will shed light on the 'money dilemma': the System must succeed in 'domesticating' money (by keeping its 'natural' functions separated from one another in order to ensure effective requisitioning), or else money will be free to function 'naturally' throughout the economy, making effective requisitioning impossible. *In other words, either money has been corrupted by the System, or the System is now being corrupted by money.*

In the first part of this chapter, we will examine the ways in which money functions in the various kinds of economic relationships that occur in CPEs. We will then look at how the System attempts to keep these various functions separate from one another, and how the economic tissue impedes its efforts to do so. Finally, it will be shown that the dilemma facing the System is insoluble, and will persist as long as the System resorts to requisitioning as a means of warding off the three major threats from its environment.


## ECONOMIC RELATIONSHIPS

The economic environment of the socalized sector consists of households, private enterprises (including farms), and economic agents in other countries. There are thus four possible kinds of economic relationship: the relationship between the socialized sector and agents in other countries; the relationship between the socialized sector and households; the relationship between the various agents that make up the socialized sector; and the relationship between households.[3] We will now look at all four kinds of relationship in order to see how money functions in each.


### Relationships between the socialized sector and other countries[4]

The essence of the economic relationship between the socialized sector and other countries is trade. In their trade with other countries the CPEs find themselves in a relatively weak position, since they badly need what other countries have to offer but—apart from natural resources—they themselves have nothing to offer that cannot also be found elsewhere. Thus, while CPEs cannot manage without external trade, other countries have no need to trade with CPEs. Agents in other countries can therefore insist that their own currencies are used in all trading between the two blocs. This is one reason why Eastern European currencies are not used in trade with market economies, either as a unit of account or as a means of payment. This is now a serious handicap to the CPEs, since it means that there is a permanent dividing line between foreign transactions (expressed in convertible currency) and domestic ones (expressed in inconvertible domestic currency), making it impossible to calculate gains from trade with any accuracy.[5]

The importance of which unit of account is to be used in transactions becomes immediately apparent in the preparatory phase, in which the prospective partners each make a subjective valuation of the goods. On the basis of their respective valuations, they may reach a compromise reflected in the terms of trade. However, in order for the partners to be able to agree on terms of trade, they must first agree on a single standard of value. As we have seen, only market-economy currencies can perform this function, which puts CPEs at a disadvantage since they must deal with an unfamiliar standard. The effects of this disadvantage vary according to whether imports or exports are involved.

When the socialized sector imports goods, it takes advantage of whatever competition there is between sellers on foreign markets. If, on the other hand, the seller is in a monopoly position, the importer's valuation will be limited to assessing the opportunity cost of each possible transaction in terms of the extent to which it satisfies the System's needs.

In the case of exports, the use of foreign currency as a standard of value prevents the System from making a proper comparison between the other country's valuation of the exported goods and its own production costs and preferences. Thus foreign currency does not really function as a standard of value from the point of view of the exporter, who must often use the foreign importer's valuation as a basis for setting prices.

The only value of foreign currency to CPE agents is that it is the most effective means of getting foreign exporters to part with the goods the System so badly needs. It is thus the normal means of payment in trade between the System and other countries. However, counter-trade practices have made it occasionally possible for money to be dispensed with as a means of payment, though not as a standard of value.

If the socialized sector's ultimate goal in trading with other countries is to be able to import goods, it will use foreign currency to introduce a time lapse between acquiring the currency through exports and using it to obtain imports. The means of payment thus serves as a store of wealth at the same time.

Despite the various functions foreign currency performs in trade between CPEs and other countries, it is not used as a unit of account. This is because, for accounting purposes, it remains external to the CPE, whose agents never come into direct contact with it, either literally or as a unit of account. For accounting purposes, the value of imports and exports is translated into domestic currency with the help of one or more coefficients of conversion.[6] The resulting values expressed in domestic currency merely reflect in accounting terms the real values expressed in foreign currency, and are themselves economically meaningless.

By now it will be clear that in trade between the socialized sector and other countries, the functions of domestic currency are extremely limited. It is not a standard of value, nor a means of payment, nor a store of wealth. However, it is *the sole unit of account* in the accounting method used by the System.

## Relationships between the socialized sector and households

The nature of the macroeconomic relationship between the socialized sector and households was briefly touched on in the previous chapter. Households supply the labour on which the socialized sector depends, and in exchange they receive consumer goods under terms of trade that are dictated by the System. Let us see how money functions in this unequal relationship.

The socialized sector is the sole arbiter of wage levels and prices of consumer goods, which are not subject to negotiation of any kind; valuations by households are therefore irrelevant. Thus, despite the fact that the terms of trade dictated by the socialized sector are expressed in monetary terms, money does not function as a standard of value, but merely as a *unit of account*.

The fact that the socialized sector does not allow money to function as a standard of value in its transactions with households means that instead of quantities and prices (or wages) being interdependent—as is usual in market economies[7]—quantities are dependent upon prices. Since prices are dictated by the System, households (being unable to negotiate) can only respond by adjusting the quantity of labour they supply and the quantity of goods they buy.[8]

Hence money is a unit of account but not a standard of value. Does it also function as a means of payment? As the unequal relationship between the socialized sector and households precludes the possibility of fair exchange, money cannot function as a means of exchange. However, payment can still take place despite the fact that the value of what is transferred is dictated unilaterally. Since money provides equivalence in accounting terms, it functions as a *means of payment* whenever a household acquires anything from the socialized sector or receives wages for its labour.

Furthermore, between the point at which wages are paid and the point at which households spend them on goods, money functions as a *store of wealth*. However, it does so rather imperfectly; households can choose whether or not to buy the goods the socialized sector has seen fit to make available, but they cannot use their own valuation to influence prices.

Closer analysis reveals that both the socialized sector and households are restricted in their room for manœuvre by the underlying *conditions of equilibrium*. On the one hand, households obviously cannot spend more than the sum total of wages and other benefits they receive from the socialized sector, unless they eat into their savings. On the other hand, the socialized sector is restricted from the point of view of its accounts: it cannot pay out more in wages than it receives from households in payment for the goods it releases onto the market. In theory, the System can adjust both price and wage levels so that the required proportion of national product can still be requisitioned; in practice, however, this is no easy task (see Chapter 6).

Since money does not function as a standard of value, it does not ensure that the supply of goods and services is adjusted to consumer demand, nor does it encourage labour productivity; it therefore cannot help the System to maintain a balance between its payments to households and its receipts.

To sum up, money performs several different functions in relationships between the socialized sector and households: as a unit of account, as a means of payment, and as a store of wealth. This is a quite different set of functions from those that occur in relationships between the socialized sector and other countries.

To complete the picture, we now need to see how money functions in relationships (*a*) within the socialized sector, and (*b*) between households.

## Relationships between enterprises in the socialized sector

In the previous chapter we saw why the System releases enterprises from the duty to balance their accounts. Since enterprises are not out to balance receipts and expenditure, they understandably have little reason to make their own valuations when trading with one another. Accordingly, money does not function as a standard of value in transactions between enterprises. Most prices of intermediate and investment goods are thus dictated by the producer; in CPEs, in contrast to the usual situation in a market economy, the purchaser only rarely has a say in how prices are determined. Chronic shortages throughout the economy, including the socialized sector, tip the scales even further in the seller's favour.

Ultimately, then, the customer's money will not be a sufficient incentive for producers to produce in accordance with the customer's wishes. This bears out our analysis of pseudo-economic agents in the previous chapter. Enterprises survive only by the grace of the System, which makes sure it can always requisition what it needs by organizing the movement of goods within the socialized sector and manipulating financial flows in accordance with the established accounting system; under this system, each transfer has a clearly defined monetary value which must be paid immediately. Enterprises are under a legal obligation to effect immediate payment, and are expressly prohibited from supplying goods on credit, swapping goods directly, and so forth. Money is thus the sole *means of payment* within the socialized sector.

Does money also function as a store of wealth in transactions between enterprises? It should by now be clear that the idea of a store of wealth is not relevant to such transactions. The only way money can function as a store of wealth is in its capacity as a means of payment; however, since economic agents will always have sufficient means of payment to cover their operating needs, they do not really need to build up a store of wealth, and indeed they are not allowed to. Thus, in transactions between enterprises in the socialized sector, money only possesses two out of its four market-economy functions: it is a means of payment and a unit of account, but it is not a standard of value or a store of wealth.

## *Relationships between households*

Identifying the ways in which money functions in transactions between households presents no problem at all. Since the System has no direct control over this particular sphere of circulation, money can function 'naturally' in much the same way as in a market economy: it serves as a unit of account, a standard of value, a means of exchange, and a store of wealth. In some of these functions, domestic currencies may find themselves competing with foreign currency, gold, etc.; however, a discussion of the causes and effects of such competition is beyond the scope of this study.[9]

If we analyse the functions of money in each of the four kinds of relationship that occur in CPEs, it is possible—at least in theory—to identify four separate spheres of circulation:

1. the external sphere, comprising relationships between enterprises and other countries;
2. the socialized sphere, comprising relationships between enterprises;
3. the consumer sphere, comprising relationships between enterprises and households; and
4. the private sphere, comprising relationships between households.

For convenience, the various functions of money in each of the four spheres are set out in Table 2. Using this table together with the conclusions drawn from the preceding analysis, we can investigate what basic conditions must be satisfied in order for money to perform each of its four classic functions. This will

enable us to ascertain to what extent the various functions are
independent of one another.

TABLE 2. *The functions of money in the four spheres of circulation*

|  | Unit of account | Means of payment | Store of wealth | Standard of value |
|---|---|---|---|---|
| External sphere | yes | no | no | no |
| Socialized sphere | yes | yes | no | no |
| Consumer sphere | yes | yes | yes | no |
| Private sphere | yes | yes | yes | yes |

1.  provided that it is an abstract unit derived from an account-
    ing method used by at least one of the partners in an
    economic transaction, money can function as a *unit of
    account*.
2.  in order to function as a *means of payment*, it must be
    acknowledged as such by both partners.
3.  in order to function as a *store of wealth*, it must function as a
    means of payment and, in addition, its holder must be able to
    decide exactly when he will use it.
4.  in order to function as a *standard of value*, it must be used by
    both partners to express their valuations concerning the
    transaction.

This summary shows that not all four functions are essentially
independent of one another. For example, if it is to function as a
standard of value, money must also serve (at least potentially) as a
store of wealth and a means of payment; on the other hand, either
or both of the partners may decline to use it as a unit of account.
Similarly, money can function as a means of payment without
functioning as either a store of wealth or a standard of value.

Our analysis shows that, in the four spheres in which it
circulates, the same money is supposed to function in four quite
different ways. How, then, does the System contrive to keep these
different functions separate and still run the domestic economy as
a single unit? An attempt will be made to answer this question in
the next two sections of this chapter. In the first, we will look at the

methods the System uses to try and keep the four spheres apart, while in the second we will examine the forces that act in the opposite direction, constantly breaking down the barriers the System has set up.

## The classic distinction between active and passive money

For three decades, from 1925 to 1956, an awkward silence reigned over the role of money in CPEs. Since the Creed had claimed that there would be no need for money in post-revolutionary society, its continued existence was an extremely inconvenient problem and one which the System's self-justifying ability could not dodge for ever. The System's inability to get rid of money seemed to suggest that the revolution had been a failure. Alternatively, the mere existence of money did not necessarily have to mean that capitalism had survived—but in that case the System needed to show that there was something essentially different about 'socialist money'.

In a controversial article written in 1963,* Wlodzimierz Brus put forward a theory regarding the role of money in CPEs, in which he made a distinction between *passive money* and *active money*. His analysis was based on the premiss that CPEs are divided into two distinct economic sectors: the consumer sector and the socialized sector. In the former, wrote Brus, money was *active* in the sense that real flows could only be generated by monetary flows (consumers needed money in order to acquire goods). This active socialist money was rather similar to the kind of money that formed the backbone of market economies. In CPEs, however, active money was not allowed to permeate the socialized sector; here there was only a watered-down variety, described by Brus as *passive money*. Unlike active money, passive money did not generate real flows but merely reflected them in accounting terms.

This distinction between passive and active money rapidly became a commonplace in both Eastern European and Western literature on the CPEs. Though outwardly attractive, the theory actually raised more problems than it solved, but nevertheless it was soon so widely accepted that the theoretical problems surrounding the role of money in CPEs were considered to have been solved. However, the reforms introduced in various Eastern European countries reveal how seriously the System— in common with Western Sovietologists—has underestimated its monetary problems. The director of the Institute of Economics in Poland, Józef Pajestka, has commented on the subject in the following unambiguous terms:

When it comes to the budget, finances and the monetary system, economic theory [in the CPEs] is extremely weak. It is incapable of grasping reality, and is thus unable to make appropriate diagnoses. For example, budget deficits are supposed to be 'covered' by the Polish National Bank (among others). Yet there is no way of knowing what this actually means, for in the absence of interest rates and repayment conditions it is impossible to talk of a loan. Instead, money is being issued on a completely unconditional basis; calling this a loan is quite simply a misnomer. This is a problem that theoreticians have failed even to recognise, let alone solve.[†]

Such a frank admission of helplessness strongly suggests that the theory of passive and active money—the basis of monetary theory in the CPEs—is faulty. Its main drawback is its ambiguity. Are active and passive money to be seen as the only possible kinds of money, or rather as the theoretical extremes of *a huge continuum of different kinds of money*, in which the passive and active principles may be combined in an infinite number of different ways?

The great variety of economic relationships both within the socialized sector and between the socialized sector and its environment suggests that, if the theory means anything at all, it can only refer to the extremes of a continuum. However, in that case its value in explaining the role of money is considerably reduced, and it may simply become an endless source of confusion.

* 'Pieniadz w gospodarce socjalistycznej' (Money in a socialist economy), *Ekonomista* (1963), No. 5, pp. 906–21.
† 'Reforma nie jest jeszcze procesem nieodwracalnym' ('Reform is not yet an irreversible process'), *Życie Gospodarcze*, 20 Jan. 1985.

---

## HOW THE SYSTEM CONTROLS MONEY

A situation in which the same money performs different functions in four separate spheres of the economy is really most bizarre. It is therefore intriguing to know how the System goes about controlling the economic tissue so as to prevent money from functioning in the same way throughout the economy.

### *Economic and institutional barriers*

The socialized sector is at the core of every CPE, and it is the sector over which the System and its self-organizing ability have the greatest degree of control. Since the socialized sector plays a part in three out of four spheres of circulation, we will take it as the starting-point for our analysis.

The fact that the socialized sector is involved in three different spheres of circulation raises questions regarding their economic equilibrium. Is it enough for the socialized sector to maintain overall macroeconomic equilibrium, or does the enforced separation between the various spheres require equilibrium to be maintained in each sphere separately?

1. *Equilibrium in the external sphere.* Here the socialized sector needs to avoid importing $(M)$ more than it exports $(X)$, in domestic currency:

$$X = M$$

2. *Equilibrium in the consumer sphere.* Here total wages plus social security benefits, etc. $(W)$ must equal total purchases by households from the socialized sector $(C)$:

$$C = W$$

3. Finally, *equilibrium in the socialized sphere.* Here the volume of goods and services requisitioned $(R)$ needs to equal financial accumulation $(A)$:

$$R = A$$

If the above three equations could be combined into a single macroeconomic equation, the result would be identical to the situation found in market economies:

$$X + C + R = M + W + A$$

i.e. total expenditure in the economy must be equal to its receipts, which is a truism.

In a market economy, this means that disequilibrium in any of the spheres can be compensated for by disequilibrium bearing the opposite sign in another sphere. What we then need to know is whether the System allows for such compensation, or whether the separation between the three spheres is so strict that equilibrium must be achieved in all three at once.

For accounting purposes, there is no reason whatsoever why compensation should not be allowed, since the domestic currency is the sole unit of account in all four spheres. It is therefore perfectly possible—for accounting purposes—to combine the three equations into a single macroeconomic equation; but whether this is economically meaningful is another matter altogether.

The System's self-organizing ability seriously restricts the freedom of economic agents to choose their economic partners, and agents therefore tend to become specialists in particular kinds of economic relationships. It is thus impossible for households to choose whether to purchase investment goods or consumer goods, or whether to purchase domestic or foreign goods. Similar restrictions are applicable to enterprises, which are not free to choose whether to sell (or buy) at home or abroad, or whether to sell to consumers or to other enterprises. Such specialization means that disequilibrium in any of the spheres cannot be compensated for.

If, for example, shops are left with unsold stock because not all wages are spent and, at the same time, imports exceed exports, there is no guarantee whatsoever that the surplus wages will be used to finance the trade deficit. This is because the two spheres concerned are separated from one another and money functions differently in each. It is therefore economically misleading to suggest that a surplus in one area of economic activity cancels out a deficit in another, since different accounting methods are involved in each case.

In the relationship between the socialized sector and households, money behaves just like negative ions moving from the anode to the cathode during electrolysis. Households are supplied with money when wages and other benefits are paid out by the socialized sector, this procedure being equivalent to the function of the anode. This money is then reabsorbed when the socialized sector sells the goods and services it produces to the people, much as the cathode absorbs the negative ions (units of money) that have gathered around it. Under this arrangement, each unit of wages moves from the anode to the cathode only once in the course of each period. This process demonstrates the peculiar nature of equilibrium in the consumer sphere, and how impossible it is for any disequilibrium in this sphere to be transferred and compensated for elsewhere.

Thus, of the three spheres in which the socialized sector is involved, two are so impermeable that we may safely conclude the same will be true of the third. Financial surpluses, whether from trade with other countries or with households, cannot be used to compensate for a deficit in financial accumulation in relation to the value of goods and services requisitioned. In fact, the System has only one way of compensating for disequilibrium in individual spheres, namely physical compensation, which is something only the System can put into effect. This only goes to show how meaningless macroeconomic equilibrium expressed in monetary or financial terms can be when used to analyse the economic situation in CPEs.

We have seen that the separation between the various spheres of circulation is economically significant; now it is time to look at how such separation is actually achieved.

## The role of banking

The System's banking structure plays a part in keeping the three spheres of circulation separate.

In the *consumer sphere*, as well as in the *private sphere* (which is closely related to it), money functions as a means of payment and actually changes hands during each transaction. The socialized sector uses the notes and coins that circulate within these spheres solely in order to pay wages, and recovers them by selling goods. When households have money, they can choose between hoarding it, saving it (by depositing it in a savings account), or spending it in one of two ways (either by trading with another household or by giving it back to the socialized sector in return for goods). In all four cases it is impossible to keep track of where exactly the money goes. This is because Eastern European households make little use of banking facilities such as cheques, current accounts, or giro transfers. Similarly, consumer credit is far less developed than in market economies, and is exceeded by the savings that households deposit in bank accounts. If we assume that there is no creation of money via consumer credit, financial equilibrium in the consumer sphere thus depends upon the payments that the socialized sector makes to households being equal to the purchases that households make from the socialized sector. In this way the System makes it impossible for households to act as entrepreneurs or investors, as a result of which financial intermediaries—and thus financial markets—are wholly superfluous. Under such circumstances, interest rates cannot be used as allocating mechanisms or as instruments of monetary policy.

In the *socialized sphere*, the bank has a quite different role, since it is fully involved in every transaction. Regulations prohibit enterprises from holding cash (except in order to pay wages). All payments within the socialized sector are therefore effected by means of book-keeping entries. This means that the function of the bank in the socialized sector is fundamentally different from its function in market economies. In relations between enterprises, the bank acts as a treasurer rather than a financial intermediary.

Since enterprises cannot hold cash, money does not physically circulate among them (as it does, for instance, in the consumer and private spheres). Banknotes are replaced by book money, in the form of book-keeping entries. Since the socialized sphere is formally and institutionally separate from the other spheres of circulation, such book money cannot gradually be changed into banknotes, or vice versa.

The bank supplies enterprises with the notes and coins they need to pay wages. It likewise seizes the cash paid by households in exchange for goods and services, and converts the sums in question into book money, which it then credits to the enterprises concerned. The bank is thus the sole link between the two spheres. This regulation of money circulation is an essential feature of the way in which the spheres of circulation are kept separate.

In the socialized sphere, the bank performs the functions of treasurer, funding agency, and accountant on behalf of every enterprise. In order to help the banking sector perform such complex duties, the System has traditionally opted for a unitary banking structure with numerous specialized branches. In the literature this arrangement is often referred to as the *monobank*.[10] The central feature of the monobank is the national bank, which has various agencies specializing in such areas as investment, agriculture, or external trade. In many countries these agencies are officially designated as separate bodies, but in practice their position in relation to the national bank is similar to that of a branch in relation to the parent bank in a market economy.

The fact that banks are closely involved in all activities in the socialized sector provides the System with a highly powerful instrument of financial policy.[11] By manipulating banking and financial regulations, the System can regulate enterprises' accounts and transactions in such a way that expenditure always corresponds to the supply of goods and that liquidity is always under control and in keeping with production levels. Theoretically, this mechanism protects any CPE against widespread excess liquidity, which could otherwise hamper its functioning.

The banking structure also helps to maintain the separation between the external sphere and the remainder of the economy, since it separates the two currencies that are involved in foreign trade: domestic currency, which is the unit of account, and foreign currency, which functions as a means of payment, a standard of value, and a store of wealth. The external sphere and the socialized sphere are kept separate by the State monopoly on foreign currency transactions, and by the use of multiple coefficients of conversion, which represent an attempt to accommodate inconvertibility.

The State monopoly on foreign currency transactions means that economic agents and households are prohibited from holding foreign currency without the express permission of the financial authorities. Payments by foreign purchasers are instead made directly to the specialized agencies of the monobank, and the exporter is credited the equivalent amount entirely in domestic currency. In the case of imports, the bank pays the foreign supplier on behalf of the importer, who is debited in domestic currency.[12]

The resulting separation of spheres is even more effective if the bank uses several different coefficients of conversion, since this actually severs the accounting links between the two spheres. The result is that domestic financial policy has no effect whatsoever upon the external equilibrium of the socialized sector, since the latter is expressed in foreign, not domestic, currency. This leaves the System in a particularly weak position if it wishes to use financial variables to influence its own balance of trade.

In the preceding pages we have seen how the banking structure helps the System to keep the various functions of money separate. However, the System has other mechanisms that serve the same purpose—namely, the State budget and public finance in general.

## The State budget and related instruments

Goods, services, and factors of production do not usually remain within one sphere of circulation. Though produced in the socialized sphere, only some of them are used there; the rest are consumed by households or exported. Similarly, labour is 'produced' in the consumer sphere but used in the socialized sphere. For accounting purposes, wages paid in the consumer sphere will be recorded by the enterprise as production costs, whereas the value of goods sold to households will be recorded as receipts. However, consistency in accounting terms between the differing expressions of a given flow according to which sphere it is in will be distorted if a tax or a subsidy is introduced.

Formal separation of the various spheres of circulation is pointless if they remain linked for accounting purposes. By its very nature, the System needs to be able to requisition everything it needs and at the same time keep its accounts consistent, neither of which it can do unless the spheres of circulation are separate in every sense. To achieve this, the System can resort to a number of budgetary instruments: *taxes, subsidies, and grants.*

These instruments are used to adjust financial flows at the macroeconomic level so as to ensure that loss-making production is compensated for by production that yields a surplus, without the real activity of the economy being affected. This is achieved by highly differentiated use of taxes on the one hand, and subsidies or grants on the other. By appropriate use of credit, the System can likewise ensure that each enterprise balances its accounts, irrespective of how it performs economically.[13]

Formally speaking, the organization of public finance in CPEs and in market economies is much the same: subsidies and grants are obtained from the main budget and the various para-budgets (targeted funds), which are financed from tax revenues and bank credit. However, at the macroeconomic level differences in organization begin to appear.

Owing to the constant intervention of public finance in micro-economic accounting, the same good may have several different prices at the same time, according to how it is used. The best-known example—though by no means the only one—is food subsidies. The opposite happens with spirits, whose production costs only account for 10% of their price, the rest being tax.[14] Public finance also regularly intervenes at points where goods move from one sphere to another: for instance, where prices in foreign currency are converted into domestic currency (by means of multiple coefficients of conversion, taxes, or budget grants) or again where goods move from the socialized sphere to the consumer sphere (two-tier pricing[15]).

The purpose behind such intervention is always the same: it helps to sever the link between prices and costs, so that the System can requisition what it needs without running into accounting problems. In fact, this is the only explanation for the extreme complexity and fluidity of fiscal and financial policy that is so characteristic of CPEs, which must ultimately balance their accounts at the macroeconomic level. Fiscal policy is thus a vital instrument that ultimately enables the System to balance its accounts after having ignored accounting principles to begin with.

Whereas it is quite possible to conceive of a market economy that has no financial policy (a situation some would even recommend), the System cannot possibly survive without one. *It needs a financial policy in order to separate the spheres of circulation, so that it can continue to requisition without running into accounting problems.*

Seen in this light, the overhaul of financial and fiscal policy that regularly occurs in the CPE countries is not the full-blown economic reform it is often claimed to be, but a purely technical procedure designed to ensure that financial flows can be more readily expressed in accounting terms.

## *Money as an instrument of control*

In the chapter on planning, we saw how the immense variety of goods is an obstacle to centralized management and at the same time provides enterprises with a certain amount of room for manœuvre. There comes a point where it is no longer practical to break down goods into physical units, and the enterprise's official supervisors must resort to aggregates expressed in monetary terms. The financial flows recorded in each enterprise's accounts then become an essential instrument for effecting controls and adjustments at the microeconomic level. The System imposes financial limits on each enterprise, based on relatively broad categories of expenditure: payroll, supplies (for instance fuel), foreign currency to pay for imports, etc. Similarly, profits are divided between the various categories of requirements such as budget, premiums, reserves, etc. The monobank makes sure that production units scrupulously comply with such arrangements, which are constantly changing and are not infrequently backdated. The bank is thereby responding to economic rather than accounting needs; this concern to keep control over enterprises' monetary resources and how they are used arises from the System's need to balance its accounts at the macroeconomic level without altering prices and without endangering the requisitioning process.

By supervising expenditure, the monobank is able to control the economic activity of the enterprise at all times. Such use of money as an instrument of control is vital if the System is to maintain its grip on economic activity. As the enterprise's finances and accounts are constantly supervised by the monobank, the enterprise is in a situation that would be paradoxical in a market economy: it has theoretically unlimited liquidity, but is not free to use it exactly as it wishes, since almost every transaction must be approved in advance by the monobank.

The breakdown of the company's accounts by category and the compartmentalization of the enterprise's liquid resources sheds a new light on the way money functions as a means of payment in the socialized sphere. The kinds of payment that a sum of money can be used to make vary according to the category of holder, and they are specified in advance. The relationship between money and goods thus varies from enterprise to enterprise. The fact that money is heterogeneous when used as a means of payment in the socialized sphere, notwithstanding its apparent homogeneity when used as a unit of account, suggests that it is the System which corrupts money rather than the other way around.

## The need for heterogeneous money

The System is able to allow each enterprise its own way of using money as a means of payment only because it does not require enterprises to balance their accounts. If enterprises were suddenly to become fully fledged economic agents, they would be forced to use money as a homogeneous means of payment, whether the System liked it or not.

Heterogeneity of means of payment in the socialized sphere is essential if requisitioning is to be effective. It allows centralized management of the economy to be more flexible by enabling accounts to be kept consistent. The monobank's control over the way money is used throughout the socialized sphere prevents excess liquidity in one sector of the economy from boosting demand in another. By maintaining heterogeneity in means of payment (with the help of the monobank), the System can break up supply and demand into separate, watertight compartments, so that disequilibrium in one compartment will not affect the situation in any of the others. The System can thus keep things under control, and requisition whatever it needs.

What kind of monetary policy will allow the System to keep its accounts consistent without breaking down the walls between the compartments? There are two alternative, and quite different, instruments: *creation of money (with parallel elimination of an equivalent amount), and financial and fiscal policy.*

*By varying the amount of money available* in a given area of the economy, the System can easily restore equilibrium in any compartment where money has become scarce. However, such creation of money must be balanced by the elimination or sterilization of excess liquidity in the particular compartment where it is threatening equilibrium. Were it impossible to sterilize liquidity, the creation of money might increase the volume of units of account to an unacceptable level and turn them into homogeneous means of payment, which would not be in the interests of the System. Excessive creation of money is thus a risky business, since it may obscure and disturb the functioning of the economy and make it more difficult to perceive what is happening in accounting terms.

However, as long as the System can effectively sterilize excess liquidity, the money supply can continue to follow requisitioning requirements and changes in economic potential. In that case, the money supply becomes a totally endogenous variable, which shows some similarity between the System's monetary policy and the theories of the Banking School.[16] However, this kind of monetary policy may begin to threaten the System's requisitioning powers if at any time the monobank's control slackens and excess liquidity is allowed to leak from one compartment to another.

The use of *financial and fiscal policy* does not entail such dangers, since no money is created; instead, money is merely transferred, whereby excess liquidity in one compartment of the economy is used to compensate for scarcity in another. In some ways, then, the use of financial and fiscal policy may appear more logical and less hazardous for the System than the use of credit to create money. However, no policy is effective unless it can be implemented fairly rapidly; in this respect the use of credit is more flexible, since tax rates and subsidy levels cannot be altered in the short term (although in the medium term they fluctuate far more in CPEs than in market economies). In other words, this kind of intervention keeps the total volume of money in circulation constant, and in that respect is similar to monetarist theories such as those of the Currency School in England in the early nineteenth century.[17]

The System is faced with a dilemma when deciding which of the above instruments of monetary policy to choose. If it chooses financial policy, it is indicating that its chief concern is to ensure consistency between flows of homogeneous units of account which only incidentally function as heterogeneous means of payment. In contrast, if it chooses to vary the money supply and create money, the role of heterogeneous means of payment in restoring partial and sectoral equilibrium is emphasized at the expense of consistency in macro-flows of homogeneous units of account.

The money dilemma facing the System stems from the System's attempts to keep the various functions of money separate and raise barriers that will prevent money from functioning 'naturally', i.e. uniformly, throughout the economy. The System must keep money under control; if it does not, the prospect of gain may well encourage enterprises to use the ensuing freedom in such a way as to interfere with requisitioning.

What kind of resistance does the System encounter and what, if anything, can it do about it? There appears to be a clash within CPEs between the System's attempts to control money and prevent it from functioning as a homogeneous means of payment, and the tissue's use of its inevitable room for manœuvre to resist— not to say corrupt—the System. In the event, the tissue ensures that money is more homogeneous than the System would like.

## Attempts at economic reform: A challenge to monetary policy*

Ever since the 1960s, in order to make up for its deteriorating economic performance, the System has been toying with the idea of economic reform. The main principles behind all such reform are as follows:

1. wages must be more specifically linked to productivity; and
2. the degree of freedom and the amount of resources made available to each enterprise must depend upon its financial performance.

Even hesitant attempts to apply these principles may well lead to the appearance of four new monetary phenomena which no monetary policy can afford to ignore:

1. the volume of income ultimately available to the people will no longer be subject to macroeconomic control;
2. the more freedom the enterprise has, the fewer compartments in which its money reserves remain 'trapped', and thus the greater the range of choice provided by each unit of money;
3. the enterprise will become more responsive to prices (although this does not necessarily mean that its behaviour will become financially more efficient); and
4. the more freedom the enterprise has, the greater its inclination to save, in other words, to use money as a store of wealth.

Although at the moment these four factors are still fairly insignificant, they do to some extent interfere with the circulation of money in CPEs. Since reforms tend to break down the barriers that have traditionally separated the spheres of circulation, the System may find itself facing new kinds of monetary problems.

In a situation where the circulation of money has become homogeneous, the three main challenges facing the System are:

1. how to determine the optimum quantity of money;

2. how to allocate money efficiently; and
3. how to do both of the above and still survive.

* See Pawel Dembinski, 'Quantity versus Allocation of Money: Monetary Problem of the Centrally Planned Economies Reconsidered', *Kyklos*, 41. 2 (1988); D. M. Nuti, *Financial Innovation under Market Socialism*, EUI Working Papers, No. 87/285, Florence, 1987; and X. Richet, 'L'État, la décentralisation et la monétisation: Les Réformes du système monétaire en Hongrie', *Économie et Humanisme*, 294 (Mar.–Apr. 1987).

## HOW MONEY CORRUPTS THE SYSTEM

We have now seen what means the System uses to tighten its hold on money. Below, we will see how the way in which the tissue uses money is likely to corrupt the System, by circumventing the barriers thrown up by the System as it tries to prevent money from functioning homogeneously throughout the economy.

## *Fungibility*

The domestic currencies of all the Eastern European CPEs are the sole legal tender, that is, they must be used in exchange for any transfer of goods or services from one economic agent to another. The fact that direct swaps between enterprises are prohibited by law reinforces this role of the domestic currency and emphasizes its *fungibility*.

Currency is said to be fungible if none of its units can be differentiated from the others, that is, if every one of its units has the same economic characteristics. However, we have seen how the System, in order to keep control of economic activity, prevents money from circulating freely within the socialized sphere, something which would appear to be incompatible with fungibility. In order to explain this paradox, we need to assume that the System restricts the fungibility of money to its capacity as a unit of account, and turns it into a rationing coupon where its capacity as a means of payment is concerned.

As Mary Douglas has shown,[18] rationing coupons only circulate within an institutional framework. The fundamental difference between money and rationing coupons lies in their transferability:

in the case of rationing coupons, this is limited to those who supply and who use the good in question, whereas in the case of money it is unlimited. Another important difference is one of range, that is, the degree to which holders of either rationing coupons or money exercise control over the goods available within the economy. Rationing coupons are proof of purchasing rights backed up by the availability of the good, whereas in the case of money the relation to goods is less apparent—the number and prices of available goods are highly unstable, as are preferences and needs. The degree to which money provides control over goods is thus variable; it increases as confidence in money increases.

Rationing coupons would ensure the System far more effective control over economic activity than money can. Yet there are two quite specific reasons why the System does not substitute rationing coupons for money as a means of payment within the socialized sphere. First of all, rationing coupons would require the issuer to anticipate all economic activity with perfect accuracy. Secondly, accounts cannot be kept on the basis of rationing coupons.

1. The System is free to requisition whatever the economy produces and to allocate it as it sees fit. However, this power is limited inasmuch as the System is unable to determine production in advance, and can only respond after the event. The System is therefore not in a position to issue the right number of each kind of rationing coupon. A major disadvantage of rationing coupons is that uses cannot be adjusted afterwards to fit in with what is available. Money administered by the monobank is much more flexible from this point of view, since accounts can subsequently be balanced in the light of actual circumstances—either by varying prices and taking appropriate fiscal measures, or by altering the rules governing the use of money or even sterilizing certain kinds of liquidity.

2. Money, being a unit of account and therefore fungible by definition, makes it possible to keep both macroeconomic and microeconomic accounts in respect of all transfers of goods between production units, something that rationing coupons cannot do. As we have already seen, accounts are vital if requisitioning is to be carried out consistently. What is more, rationing coupons are only a workable solution if the entire economy can be

perceived in terms of quantitative variables; however, such is the diversity of products that the System, in its capacity as planner and manager, is obliged to amalgamate them. This it can only do if money is fungible.

Nevertheless, despite the advantage of fungibility, it does expose the System to a certain number of risks. The System cannot be sure of limiting fungibility to the unit of account function. In fact, there are *three danger points* at which, despite all the System's efforts, the tissue may imperceptibly turn the fungible unit of account into a fungible means of payment and thereby interfere with requisitioning:

1. Though kept under close surveillance, the holder of money still has some freedom of choice. Such microeconomic freedom can multiply very rapidly indeed, and thus reduce both the degree of control exerted by the System and the exent to which it can keep track of economic activity in accounting terms. This is a serious dysfunction which limits the effectiveness of requisitioning.

2. Since the System keeps prices fixed, the total value of production is determined by the quantity of each good produced, *regardless of quality*. This specific link between quantity and accounting value enables enterprises to produce goods whose accounting value exceeds their utility. This phenomenon, often wrongly referred to as inflation, is the second kind of dysfunction connected with the fungibility of money.

3. The third kind of dysfunction occurs when unchecked flows of money or goods move from one sphere to another, a phenomenon that may be described as leakage.

## The explosive effects of freedom

The kinds of dysfunction just described are due to the fact that, despite the vice-like grip of the monobank, money provides more freedom when used as a means of payment than rationing coupons. In a modern economy, allocation entirely in kind is simply not feasible, owing to the insurmountable problems of administering several million material balances in real time, and of guaranteeing that all the goods within a given material balance are identical. The

System is thus forced to rely on money. By enabling enterprises to make a choice among the range of goods covered by a single material balance, money functions as a homogeneous means of payment as well as a uniform unit of account.

This freedom of choice is reflected in the fact that enterprises do not actually produce what the System wants. Whether the System likes it or not, it is the enterprise that decides what range of articles will be produced within a given category, on the basis of production parameters specific to each individual good (risk and effort involved, available inputs, etc.). The enterprise then makes its choice from a number of goods that are interchangeable as regards production (for example, screws of differing diameters). Sadly, they are not usually so interchangeable in use, which may cause production problems further down the line; the more the various types of production are interconnected, the greater the risk that this will happen.

Arrangements in which money functions as a homogeneous means of payment interfere with the workings of the System, since they increase uncertainty regarding the product range and thus the risk that production will not be able to satisfy needs.[19] At the same time, requisitioning will be less effective.

Microeconomic freedom multiplies throughout the production process, the eventual outcome of which thus becomes almost impossible to predict. The same applies to requisitioning.

## Insidious 'inflation'

In the Promised Society, says the Creed, the social utility of each good should be similar to the value of the labour that is socially necessary for its production. Accordingly, the System simply declares that value in use is identical to labour value, the 'real' relationship being held to be irrelevant. In CPE theory, a good derives its value from the fact that it has been produced, not from its ability to satisfy a need; for accounting purposes, therefore, the good acquires value before any needs have become apparent. Hence the rigidity of CPE price structures, and the System's refusal to take valuations by individual economic agents or enterprises into account. However, this attitude to value makes it possible to produce goods that have accounting value but no value in use. The macroeconomic consequences of this will vary according to the sphere of circulation concerned.

*In the external sphere*, the discrepancy between accounting value and value in use will only be visible on the export side. For internal purposes, accounting value (the cost expressed in domestic currency) and value in use (the price paid by the purchaser in foreign currency) are brought into line either by means of a subsidy, or by applying an *ad hoc* coefficient of conversion to the foreign currency earnings. Such procedures are, of course, mere window-dressing.

*In the socialized sphere*, there are two quite distinct alternative possibilities: goods that have no value in use either remain unsold, or else they are bought and used regardless.

If the money-induced freedom of enterprises to refine their product range results in products that nobody wants, they will remain unsold. The surplus stock is financed one way or another, so that there is excess liquidity in relation to total available and usable goods. In a market economy, such excess liquidity is absorbed as the prices of useful goods rise, and the result may well be inflation. Despite the fact that prices in CPEs respond only very weakly to such excess liquidity, there are authors who describe this as 'inflation'.[20] The only conceivable justification for applying this term to CPEs is that the situation described fulfils the basic initial conditions for inflation in a market economy—but even so the term is inappropriate, as we will see below.

In practice, only a small proportion of goods actually remains unsold; most goods whose accounting value is unrelated to their value in use do nevertheless find a buyer. This is because the buyer is not offered a choice, and at the same time the enterprise must produce and can afford to ignore costs. The macroeconomic consequences are harder to determine, since they cannot be readily identified for accounting purposes. Shoddy goods are used in the production of other goods, which also turn out shoddy, *and so on until the entire economy has been 'infected'*; yet, owing to the rigid price structure, this is not reflected in accounting value. The insidious nature of such 'infection' makes it all the more damaging; though widespread, it has so far resisted all attempts to pin it down. This phenomenon, which is quite alien to market economies, has not yet been analysed in sufficient depth to justify giving it such a misleadingly familiar name as 'inflation'.

*In the consumer sphere*, the effects of the rigid price structure are similar to those found in the socialized sphere: either consumer goods are so unattractive that they remain on the shelves and consumers are left with cash on their hands, or else consumers buy the goods regardless and put up with the consequences (inadequate diet and ill-health, poor-quality vehicles that waste fuel and pollute the environment, inferior products that need extra work to make them fit for their intended use, and so on). Under such circumstances living standards can hardly improve, and indeed they may even get worse. If even the shoddiest goods are sold because the consumer has no alternative, there will be no disequilibrium in macroeconomic terms; but behind this pleasant façade the economic situation and the standard of living will be steadily deteriorating.

If goods remain unsold, or again if demand for certain goods exceeds supply, households will be left with a certain amount of unspent cash. In the literature dealing with Eastern Europe the standard term for such surplus cash is 'inflationary overhang'. There are those who maintain that such cash remains idle and is bound to end up in savings accounts, and that involuntary savings are thus a major factor in Eastern European economies; this, they then claim, is evidence of 'inflation' or 'tension in the consumer sphere'.[21]

However, it is just as conceivable that consumers will respond to a surplus of cash by *getting rid of it as soon as they possibly can*. This they will do by purchasing anything which is likely to be a more satisfactory store of wealth than money. The result is that consumer demand becomes extremely volatile, and the consumer goods market is ransacked sector by sector for anything which will do as an alternative to cash. In this way the entire supply of goods is soon exhausted, and shortages become endemic in the consumer sphere.[22]

If there is a surfeit of cash and public confidence is low, money will circulate more rapidly among households. The job of administering the surplus cash and allocating consumer goods is then taken over by black-marketeers and speculators. The volume of business transacted in this unofficial sector will depend on the amount of cash available and the speed at which it circulates (which is liable to increase dramatically within the private sector whenever confidence is low).

Given the use the System makes of the fungibility of money and the rigid price structure, the economy as perceived in accounting terms no longer reflects the economy as it really is. As a result, the System has no real idea of what is going on. Moreover, since the quality of what is requisitioned is also in doubt, requisitioning is bound to be less effective.

## Leakage

A good deal of the goods produced by the economy (e.g. food, building materials, office equipment, fuel, and certain industrial inputs) are used by both households and enterprises. In its attempts to make sure that such goods are correctly allocated, the System is hampered by the behaviour of individuals with access to both spheres at once, who take advantage of this privileged position to transfer goods or money from one to the other. Were such leakage to occur on a large scale, the monetary equilibrium of both spheres would be affected.

There are two conceivable kinds of leakage: consumer goods may be leaked to the socialized sector, or vice versa. The former is often legal, since—unless it is trying to defraud the State—the enterprises concerned will notify the monobank. The purchases usually involved are office supplies (paper), fuel, and food; this reduces the volume of goods available to households and may therefore increase the amount of unspent cash.

The other kind of leakage, which is completely illegal, involves the transfer of goods from the socialized sector to households—in other words, theft. Anything that households need and that is unavailable in the consumer sphere is likely to be stolen and sold on the black market. There is thus a flourishing illicit trade in building materials, fuel, spare parts, and goods originally intended for export. Usually the resulting shortages do not appear in production accounts; instead, the quality of everything produced simply gets worse. All of this adds to the insidious inflation described earlier. On reaching the private sphere, the loot is swapped among households and helps to increase living standards and speed up the circulation of money. Though the national income is redistributed and the speed at which money circulates within the private sphere is increased, the amount of cash available to households remains unchanged.

To sum up, such leakage should probably be seen, not as a third kind of dysfunction that is quite separate from the other two, but rather as a phenomenon that serves to exacerbate the other kinds of dysfunction. It helps to sever the link between value in use and accounting value (price), and transfers disequilibrium from the consumer sphere to the socialized sphere. And, of course, it also makes requisitioning less effective.

We have now examined the various aspects of the monetary links between the System and the tissue. We have seen how the System endeavours to keep the various spheres of circulation separate from one another, and how the tissue makes use of the freedom provided by the fungibility of money to frustrate the System's aims. There are thus two opposing forces at work within CPEs, in a never-ending struggle: the System, fighting to keep money under control; and the tissue, using the same money to thwart the System and interfere with requisitioning. In other words, while the System tries to corrupt money, the tissue is using money to corrupt the System.

Our analysis of the money dilemma shows that the System's control over the tissue is not sufficient to ensure that the various spheres of circulation will remain separate. Apparently, once money is used as a universal unit of account, there is no power on earth that can prevent it becoming—at least to some extent—a universal means of payment. The unit of account and means of payment functions cannot be kept entirely separate, and the System is forced to adopt a unit of account, but opposes its becoming a universal means of payment.

This chapter has shown that the System is not in a position to guarantee effective requisitioning. In addition to the necessary structures and mechanisms, effective requisitioning also necessitates compliance on the part of the tissue. Unfortunately, money allows the tissue to sabotage the System's efforts at every turn.

The planning dilemma facing the System is an artificial one, since we have seen that it can easily remain credible in terms of the Creed without impairing its requisitioning powers, in particular by resorting to the trickery of retrospective planning. The System also has the power to overcome any obstacles to requisitioning that enterprises may put in its way, since—at least in theory—it can turn them into submissive pseudo-economic agents. However, even this is not enough to ensure effective requisitioning, which ultimately depends on the behaviour of the tissue. The use of money is one of the main factors that enables the tissue to set limits to requisitioning; here, in fact, the tissue controls the System rather than the other way round.

All of this seriously affects the extent to which the System can fulfil its mission in a hostile environment. If neither the quality nor the quantity of what is requisitioned are sufficient for the System to cope with the pressures from its environment, the System's very survival is at stake. This sheds a new light on the nature of the economic problems facing the System. The traditional signs of economic disequilibrium—inflation, poor technology, and external deficit—take on a new, specific meaning in the context of CPEs, since their adverse influence upon the effectiveness and/or volume of requisitioning indirectly jeopardizes the survival of the System. The fact that the System's unilaterally asserted right of allocation is unable to protect it against the pressures from its environment means that its economic problems are bound to become critical. The significance of 'economic' problems in CPEs can thus only be fully understood in the context of the workings of the System. Currently, however, economic theory is not capable of such an analysis. This book will therefore conclude by suggesting a conceptual framework in which, for once, the economic problems facing the CPEs are not misrepresented.

## Notes

1. Such as those expressed by Thomas Crump, who believes that anything a society refers to as 'money' must be considered as such; he calls this approach 'cultural tautology' (*The Phenomenon of Money*, Routledge & Kegan Paul, London, 1981).
2. See e.g. T. Mayer, J. Duesenberry, and R. Aliber, *Money, Banking and the Economy* (2nd edn.: W. W. Norton & Co., New York and London, 1986,

p. 5): '. . . economists define money by its functions. Anything that functions as a medium of exchange or a standard of value or, according to many economists, as an extremely liquid store of wealth is considered money.'

3. A fifth kind are the relationships between households and agents in other countries, but these are insignificant from the point of view of the System.

4. For the purpose of this analysis, the term 'other countries' essentially means market economies.

5. This issue is discussed in greater detail in Ch. 8. See also Pawel Dembinski, 'L'inconvertibilité est-elle un obstacle aux échanges entre les économies planifiées de l'Europe de l'Est et les économies de marché?' *Revue d'études comparatives Est–Ouest*, Dec. 1985, pp. 109–30.

6. I use this term 'coefficient of conversion' in preference to the standard expression 'exchange rate', since it stresses the fact that the process involved is merely an accounting procedure rather than the literal exchange of one currency for another.

7. Such interdependence is essential to the functioning of market economies; it is usually stated in the form 'prices are dependent upon quantities, but at the same time quantities are dependent upon prices'.

8. See Ch. 6, which discusses the relationship between the System and its social environment.

9. The *Wall Street Journal* of 9 Feb. 1987 contains an article describing how in Poland the dollar has become established as the sole standard of value and means of payment in asset transactions between households.

10. G. Garvy (*Money, Banking and Credit in Eastern Europe*, Federal Reserve Bank of New York, 1966, excerpted in Alec Nove and D. M. Nuti, eds., *Socialist Economics*, Penguin Education, Harmondsworth, 1972) appears to have been the first to use this term.

11. It is my opinion that the term 'monetary policy' cannot properly be applied to CPEs. I prefer the term '*financial* policy', which avoids the risk of confusion with the situation in market economies.

12. The effects of this arrangement on the terms of trade are discussed in Ch. 8.

13. It will be clear that fiscal policy serves quite different purposes in CPEs and in market economies. In CPEs, fiscal policy enables the System to requisition whatever it needs and still keep its accounts consistent. In market economies, the crucial issue is how the government uses financial policy to influence its revenue. The functions of public spending will then include nudging economic agents in the desired direction and protecting certain sectors of the economy that would otherwise face extinction.

14. See I. Krasnikov, 'La Marchandise numéro un', *Une opposition socialiste en Union soviétique aujourd'hui*, Maspero, Collection 'Samizdat $xx^e$ siècle', Paris, 1976.

15. See Ch. 4.

16. See M. Burchardt, 'Die Banking-Currency-Controverse: Beitrag X', *Kredit und Kapital* (1985), No. 5, pp. 457–78, and also S. Gedeon, 'The Post-Keynesian Theory of Money: A Summary and an Eastern European Example', *Journal of Post-Keynesian Economics*, 8. 2 (1985), 208–21.

17. R. Portes, 'Central Planning and Monetarism: Fellow Travelers', *Marxism, Central Planning and Soviet Economy*, MIT Press, Cambridge, Mass., 1983, pp. 149–65.
18. M. Douglas, 'Primitive Rationing: A Study in Controlled Exchange', R. Firth, ed., *Themes in Economic Anthropology*, Tavistock, London, 1967, pp. 119–45.
19. The policy of enforced substitution, described in detail by János Kornai in *Economics of Shortage*, North-Holland Publishing Company, Amsterdam, New York, and Oxford, 1980, can only eliminate shortages at the production stage; further down the line, however, it is only likely to make things worse.
20. There are many examples of this: R. Portes, 'Central Planning and Monetarism'; P. Jansen, *Die Inflationsprobleme in der Zentralverwaltungswirtschaft*, G. Fischer, Stuttgart, 1982; F. Seurot, *Inflation et emploi dans les économies socialistes*, PUF, Collection 'Libre échange', Paris, 1983; P. Wiles, *Economic Institutions Compared*, Blackwell, Oxford, 1979, p. 372.

   For a detailed discussion of how the various authors use the term 'inflation' with reference to CPEs, see D. M. Nuti, 'Hidden and Repressed Inflation in Soviet-Type Economies: Definitions, Measurements and Stabilisation', *Contributions to Political Economy*, 5 (1986), 37–82.
21. See, in particular, F. Seurot, *Inflation et emploi dans les Économies socialistes*.
22. See Ch. 6.

# III

# External Dilemmas

We have now seen the internal, or organizational, dilemmas that face the System as it attempts to fulfil the mission assigned to it by the Creed. If the System somehow succeeds in overcoming these obstacles and securing access to enough good-quality resources to be sure of withstanding the pressures from its environment, then it will also succeed in avoiding external dilemmas. If not, however, the unsolved internal dilemmas will become an increasingly pressing problem.

At this stage in our study, therefore, it is important to know whether the economic performance currently achieved by the System in Eastern Europe is sufficient for it to ignore its internal dilemmas. Such information is essential for an understanding of the full economic relevance of the analyses contained in Parts I and II.

In other words, *the economic problems that face the System in its struggle for survival will be analysed as indicators of the gravity of the systemic problems discussed in Part II*. Economists are likely to find this approach paradoxical, since it implicitly treats economic problems as dependent and thus places serious limits on the relevance of standard economic analysis.

Economic theory first emerged in societies in which economics was independent of politics. There is therefore reason to suppose that it is only relevant to societies in which this is still the case. The premisses on which economic theory is based only hold true in market economies; by definition, therefore, economic theory is biased (despite claims to the contrary) and is not applicable to other economic systems. Three of the basic premisses are:

1. the existence of *Homo oeconomicus* (whether or not subject to restrictions on his behaviour);
2. the existence of market forces, without any overriding controls from above; and

3. the existence of money as an instrument used by *Homo oeconomicus* to take advantage of the freedom provided by market forces.

Even cursory examination of the Eastern European economies gives an intuitive idea of how they work. Deeper analysis, of the kind contained in this book, makes it quite clear why the basic premisses of economic theory simply do not apply in CPEs. As we have seen, this difference is so fundamental that it would be quite wrong to treat CPEs as though they were merely a peculiar kind of market economy.

Any research programme that attempts to analyse CPEs on the basis of classic economic theory is therefore bound to be biased and unscientific. The approach taken here is quite different: an attempt has been made to devise a specific conceptual framework for CPEs, while retaining as much of classic economic theory as possible. Parts I and II of this book have shown how the workings of the System influence its economic behaviour. Part III will conclude by looking at the actual or potential influence of economic problems on the workings of the System.

Part III is divided into three chapters, which deal in turn with the three major economic problems that the System encounters in coping with its environment. While these environmental constraints all hinge on availability of resources—an eminently economic issue—they also fundamentally affect the workings of the System. Thus the three external dilemmas (the social dilemma, the military dilemma, and the dilemma of growth) each have an economic dimension and a 'systemic' dimension, which—as the following analysis will show—are inextricably linked.

# 6

# The Social Dilemma: Rationing versus Consumer Sovereignty

Within its national frontiers the System has a monopoly on power which it uses to satisfy its requisitioning requirements. However, it cannot requisition everything in sight, for two very good reasons:

1. Despite its monopoly on power, the System can never be sure it will not be overthrown by popular revolt. As recent history has repeatedly shown, economic hardship is high on the list of factors likely to trigger off a rebellion, so the System must avoid requisitioning too much.

2. There are two ways the System can keep its balance on this particular tightrope. One way is to requisition whatever it needs, and use rationing to allocate whatever is left—a policy the people will only put up with for so long. The other is to allow consumers to decide what they will consume, in the hope that they will no longer be driven to revolt and that, in return, they will increase their productivity—thus increasing the volume of resources available for requisitioning by the System.[1]

If the System decides to use the rationing approach, it will certainly increase its short-term chances of requisitioning what it needs, but in the long term it is likely to trigger off a rebellion, which will then have to be put down by force. The alternative approach requires the System to requisition less in the short term in the hope of being able to requisition more in the long term. Thus the first alternative ensures immediate survival but puts the future at risk, whereas the second alternative involves taking risks in the present in the hope that the future will be better than ever.

At the root of this 'social dilemma' lies a twofold economic problem. On the one hand, the System must decide on what basis national income is to be distributed between consumption and accumulation; and on the other, it must decide how to maintain financial equilibrium in the consumer sphere.


## MACROECONOMIC RATIONING

### *The prerogatives of the central authority*

In both market economies and CPEs, national income is ultimately distributed between what society consumes and what it accumulates (i.e. gross investment, when seen from the expenditure point of view). However, each system has its own particular way of doing this.

*In market economies*, the distribution of national income is based on free, independent decisions by the individual. As an owner of labour or capital, he receives a remuneration (wages or return on capital) which he allocates to either consumption or savings (after paying tax to the State). When deciding how to use his income, the individual must strike a balance between two forces which are pushing him in opposite directions. On the one hand, in order to attract a large proportion of income into savings, financial inter-mediaries offer the highest possible return on deposits, which are then made available to investors. At the same time, producers of consumer goods try to induce the individual to spend his money rather than save it, by offering him products whose prices and quality are particularly attractive.

In both of these sectors, supply and demand are brought into equilibrium through adjustments in price levels. Thus, if the proportion of income allocated to consumption exceeds what producers of consumer goods can supply, the prices of such goods will rise. Similarly, if the supply of savings is less than investors' demand for loans, the return on deposits will increase. In other words, in market economies there is automatic equilibrium between the way incomes are allocated and the way production is distributed.

*In CPEs*, neither households nor socialized-sector enterprises are allowed or able to decide how their income will be distributed between consumption and savings/investment. Such decisions may only be made by the System, which uses this power to make sure it can requisition what it needs. This method of distributing the national product may be termed 'macroeconomic rationing' of consumer goods, since the total volume of goods produced to satisfy consumers' needs is limited in advance, the rest being earmarked for other uses (see Table 3).

TABLE 3. *The distribution of physical production between accumulation and consumption* (%)

|  | 1960 | 1965 | 1970 | 1975 | 1980 | 1985 |
|---|---|---|---|---|---|---|
| *Bulgaria* | | | | | | |
| Consumption | 72.5 | 71.7 | 69.2 | 67.2 | 74.8 | 75.7 |
| Accumulation | 27.5 | 28.3 | 30.8 | 32.8 | 25.2 | 24.3 |
| *Czechoslovakia* | | | | | | |
| Consumption | 82.4 | 90.9 | 73.1 | 71.4 | 74.0 | 82.9 |
| Accumulation | 17.6 | 9.1 | 26.9 | 28.6 | 26.0 | 17.1 |
| *GDR* | | | | | | |
| Consumption | 80.6 | 78.8 | 74.4 | 76.6 | 77.3 | 82.9 |
| Accumulation | 18.2 | 21.2 | 25.6 | 23.4 | 22.7 | 17.1 |
| *Hungary* | | | | | | |
| Consumption | — | — | 73.2 | 69.8 | 78.5 | 90.1 |
| Accumulation | — | — | 26.8 | 30.2 | 21.5 | 9.9 |
| *Poland* | | | | | | |
| Consumption | 76.0 | 74.1 | 74.9 | 65.8 | 81.0 | 74.0 |
| Accumulation | 24.0 | 25.9 | 25.1 | 34.1 | 19.0 | 26.0 |
| *USSR* | | | | | | |
| Consumption | 73.2 | 73.6 | 70.5 | 73.4 | 76.1 | 73.5 |
| Accumulation | 26.8 | 26.4 | 29.5 | 26.6 | 23.9 | 26.5 |

*Sources: Comecon Data 1983*, Vienna Institute for Comparative Economic Studies, 1984, pp. 10–20; *Economic Survey of Europe in 1986/87*, Economic Commission for Europe, UN, New York, 1987, p. 167. No information was available for Romania.

Nevertheless, despite these extensive powers, the System is subject to a number of constraints. To begin with, it has a historical mission to fulfil: the building of the Promised Society necessitates immediate availability of resources. Therefore, if the

System could have its way, it would most probably requisition the entire national income and allocate all of it to accumulation.

Secondly, the way national income is distributed affects the System's short-term chances of survival, which ultimately depend upon the tissue. If not enough priority is given to consumption, the resulting social discontent may be enough to topple the current regime; indeed, this has already happened several times in Eastern Europe.[2] Although in theory the System's Messianic vocation requires it to treat consumption as a cost that should be minimized or even eliminated altogether, in practice there are limits to what the System can do in this regard.

Finally, the System's need for accumulation not only now but in the future leaves it in something of a bind. Even though it has made itself the sole owner of the means of production and moreover has the power to force people to work, the volume of resources available for accumulation will ultimately depend on how *well* people work. This is a matter of motivation, which will in turn depend on the proportion of national income allocated to consumption.

In short, consumption is the price the System must pay if it is to remain faithful to its mission, prevent social discontent from reaching an unacceptable level, and ensure sufficient resources for future accumulation. This suggests that we should take a closer look at the variables that influence the terms of trade between the tissue and the System.


## The macroeconomic terms of trade

The way in which national income is distributed is considerably different in CPEs and in market economies. In the latter, it is distributed by means of a financial flow which is ultimately traded for either capital goods or consumer goods. The point at which physical supplies of each category of goods match demand is determined by price levels.

In CPEs prices are fixed, which means that any macroeconomic distribution of national income in terms of value will be economically meaningless unless there is a corresponding distribution in physical terms. In this context, the terms of trade between the tissue and the System acquire a special meaning.

The chapter dealing with the dilemma of methods (Chapter 4) approaches this problem in the only possible way, namely, from the point of view of the labour theory of value, which is the basis for CPE price structure. Since labour remains the inalienable property of the individual, the terms of trade between the tissue and the System equal the ratio between the respective accounting values of national income and of consumption.[3] If, for instance, national income is valued at 10 units and consumption at 6 units, then labour gives up 10 units and only gets 6 units back. The System, however, sees things quite differently: it gives up 6 units and only gets 4 units back (in the form of requisitioning). The result is that both the System and consumers feel cheated, since they both think they are giving up more than they are getting back.[4]

Having seen the macroeconomic significance of the terms of trade, we must complete the picture by examining their microeconomic effects—in other words, we must look at the terms of trade that govern the relationship between the System and the individual.

## The microeconomic terms of trade

The individual supplies productive effort and in return receives a wage or, more broadly, a remuneration in the form of a certain number of units of money.[5] This wage is not in accordance with the microeconomic terms of trade, for it is not based either on the value of the labour supplied by the individual, or on the value of the goods the individual can buy with his wage, or on the individual's share of social consumption. This is because the method the System uses to determine wages does not take account of labour productivity,[6] nor does it have any direct effect upon the prices of goods. In other words, the System can quantify the value of the labour supplied by the individual only on the basis of its quantitative component (time). This means that individual terms of trade cannot be ascertained directly, since in CPEs the value of individual effort is unmeasurable.

In the absence of a satisfactory single method of measuring the microeconomic terms of trade, it is necessary to adopt a piecemeal approach. First of all, a distinction must be made between the nominal and real dimensions of the microeconomic terms of trade. The factors that influence the microeconomic terms of trade will be seen to differ according to which dimension is being considered.

1. In the *nominal dimension*, the terms of trade are entirely determined by the System, which (with the help of the trade unions) is responsible for determining the wage grid. In this nominal ratio, the individual thus has no control over the denominator—nor indeed over the numerator, since the accounting method used by CPEs is based on fixed prices for consumer goods, irrespective of their quality and of demand.

2. In the *real dimension*, on the other hand, the situation is rather different. Although the System determines the quantity and range of consumer goods, it cannot determine how they are distributed among individuals. Ultimately, the 'basket' consumed by each individual will depend not only on his money wage, but above all on his access to the consumer goods available on the 'market'. This means that the System can only determine the denominator by resorting to microeconomic rationing of all consumer goods; moreover, this is reckoning without such redistribution of goods as takes place via the black market. Failing this, the denominator (which varies from individual to individual) cannot be controlled directly by the System. The individual has even greater control over the numerator, since he determines the quality of his labour and the effort that he puts into it.[7]

There is no institutional interface between the two dimensions, so both sides are free to take unilateral advantage of the situation, with the System using the nominal dimension and the individual the real dimension. The likely result is a ding-dong battle in which the individual uses the real dimension to adjust the terms of trade in his favour and the System uses the nominal dimension to get its own back. In this context, popular revolt is to be seen as the ultimate weapon that the people can use against the macro-economic terms of trade (i.e. the physical allocation of what is produced, as determined by the System) so as to alter the microeconomic terms of trade.

Every individual involved in the production process or the political and economic management of a country thereby either has access to a certain number of goods or possesses a certain degree of decision-making power. Thus any worker in a CPE country who is unhappy with the nominal terms of trade dictated by the System can adjust the real terms of trade to his own advantage—either by reducing the quality of the labour he supplies (which will not, however, improve his standard of living), or by using goods, factors of production, or decision-making powers for his own private purposes. The possibilities are endless, and both economic literature and popular anecdotes are constantly revealing new methods used by individuals to bend the terms of trade in their favour. These methods (all of which interfere to a greater or lesser extent with requisitioning) include corruption of officials, misuse of working-time in the form of absenteeism or private work carried out during official working hours, and outright theft of goods that are then sold or swapped for other goods the particular individual happens to need.

Clearly, then, the wide range of methods the individual can use to adjust the real terms of trade means that in practice the System's control over the macroeconomic terms of trade is considerably less than would appear at first sight. Any individual who feels he has been unfairly treated by the System can use the real dimension to rectify the situation. However, if such behaviour becomes widespread, the result is likely to be a general deterioration in moral or ethical standards which may in the long term confront society with serious problems. In the short term, such behaviour will rapidly damage the economic tissue by arousing individual passions to a level where macroeconomic rationality no longer has any effect. As a result, the tissue is likely to be pervaded by irrationality and chaos.[8]

The struggle between the tissue and the System over terms of trade is reflected in the variables that govern financial equilibrium in the consumer sphere. These will be discussed below.

## FINANCIAL EQUILIBRIUM IN THE CONSUMER SPHERE

Our analysis of the money dilemma stressed not only the importance but also the precarious nature of financial equilibrium in the consumer sphere. We now need to examine how that equilibrium is affected by the struggle between the tissue and the System over terms of trade.

## The components of financial equilibrium

Financial equilibrium in the consumer sphere depends upon two kinds of flow—the income paid to the people by the socialized sector, and the payments made to the socialized sector by the people—being equal. If payments exceed income, the people are eating into their reserves, while if income exceeds payments those reserves will increase. In both cases there is financial disequilibrium.

The socialized sector pays income to the people either for economic reasons (wages) or for reasons of social policy (pensions and miscellaneous social security benefits). Essentially, households spend that income by purchasing goods produced by the socialized sector; any remaining income can be used to obtain goods from the private sector or unofficial sources. Only a small percentage of income ends up in savings accounts, for two reasons: income is low in relation to needs, and the inhabitants of CPE countries show a marked preference for liquidity. The motives behind this preference are most probably the same in CPEs as Keynes found them to be in market economies, namely the transactions motive, the precautionary motive, and the speculative motive.[9] However, the possession of money for speculative purposes has a totally different significance in CPEs and in market economies. In market economies, says Keynes, it depends on movements in financial markets; in CPEs, on the other hand, it depends on the supply of goods and expectations concerning it. In other words, the portion of income that is not immediately spent consists of two quite distinct components, which are known (in Keynesian terminology) as savings and liquidity held for precautionary and speculative motives.

In order for there to be financial equilibrium in the consumer sphere (i.e. in order for the flow of income paid by the socialized sector to be equal to the flow of payments it receives from the consumer sphere), one prior and one retrospective condition must be met.

The prior condition is quite simply that the total value of the supply of consumer goods from the socialized sector must not be less than the total income the socialized sector pays to the people. If $W$ is the total income paid by the socialized sector and $O$ is the total value of products allocated for consumption, the prior condition can be written thus:

$$W = O$$

The retrospective condition is that the socialized sector must recover value equal to the income it has paid to the people, either through the sale of goods, or through deposits in official savings banks. If $P$ is the value of purchases by the people from the socialized sector over a given period and $S$ is the savings the people entrust to the socialized sector, the retrospective condition can be written thus:

$$W = P + S$$

We can then describe the prior conditions as being 'necessary' and the retrospective condition as being 'sufficient' for there to be financial equilibrium in the consumer sphere. Before examining the various kinds of possible disequilibrium, however, we need to see why the System is at such pains to maintain equilibrium in the consumer sphere.

Whether or not it is achieved, financial equilibrium does not affect the macroeconomic terms of trade between the System and society, since the financial situation in the consumer sphere does not influence the way in which national income is distributed. Accordingly, even if the supply of goods does not match the amount of cash held by households, CPEs do not provide any automatic mechanism whereby it can be adjusted. The individual will only take action in the real dimension against such macroeconomic disequilibrium at the point where he notices that his own microeconomic terms of trade have worsened. In other words, temporary financial disequilibrium does not mean instant retaliation by the workers.

However, the System strives to maintain financial equilibrium in the consumer sphere precisely because it cannot afford to risk prolonged macroeconomic disequilibrium triggering off microeconomic responses such as a reduction in the quality of labour, misuse of State goods for private purposes, or even social discontent that may threaten the System's very survival.

## The ambiguous nature of financial disequilibrium

A breakdown of the various kinds of financial disequilibrium will enable us to identify the economic circumstances in which the financial situation is serious enough to make the people resort to violence in order to adjust the terms of trade—in other words, serious enough to threaten the System's survival. Our analysis will be divided into two stages, enabling us to introduce three different criteria in succession. Two of these will appear in the first part of the analysis, the third will be introduced later on. The first two criteria are as follows:

1. The first criterion, derived from the prior condition for financial equilibrium described above, concerns the relationship between the value of products that the socialized sector allocates to consumption ($O$) and the income that the socialized sector pays to consumers ($W$). There are three possible situations:

the supply of goods equals total income: $O = W$;
the supply of goods exceeds total income: $O > W$;
the supply of goods is less than total income: $O < W$.

2. The second criterion, derived from the retrospective condition for financial equilibrium, concerns the relationship between purchases by households from the socialized sector ($P$) and their income ($W$). Once again, there are three possible situations:[10]

income equals purchases: $W = P$;
income exceeds purchases, which implies hoarding: $W > P$;
income is less than purchases, which implies 'dis-hoarding':
   $W < P$.

By combining the two criteria, we can conceive of nine possible instances of financial disequilibrium in the consumer sphere, as shown in Table 4.

TABLE 4. *The nine possible instances of financial disequilibrium in the consumer sphere*

| Retrospective equilibrium | Prior equilibrium | | |
|---|---|---|---|
| | $O > W$ | $O = W$ | $O < W$ |
| $W > P$ | 1 | 2 | 3 |
| | $O > P$ | $O > P$ | $O \geqslant P$ |
| $W = P$ | 4 | 5 | 6 |
| | $O > P$ | $O = P$ | absurd |
| $W < P$ | 7 | 8 | 9 |
| | $O \geqslant P$ | absurd | absurd |

The nine situations can immediately be divided into three categories:

*situations 6, 8, and 9*: here purchases by consumers from the socialized sector would have to exceed the supply of goods, which is absurd;

*situation 5*: this situation is ideal in all respects, since consumers spend all of the income they receive from the socialized sector and purchase all of the goods supplied;

*situations 1–4 and 7*: these situations may appear similar, but in actual fact there are important differences between them. Why exactly do households not spend all their income? And do they save the difference, or do they hoard it for precautionary or speculative motives?

We will now introduce the third criterion, in which the degree of popular satisfaction with the supply of consumer goods—an indicator of the level of social discontent—is specifically taken into account. Although purchases can obviously never exceed supply, the first two criteria tell us nothing about the relationship between consumer demand ($D$) and supply by the socialized sector ($O$). We therefore need to extend our classification to consider what happens when purchases equal, exceed, or are less than consumer demand. For simplicity's sake, we will assume that demand only concerns everyday needs. The introduction of this third criterion will make our classification more thorough, but at the same time more complex.

If purchases equal demand ($P = D$), any difference between households' income and expenditure can only be the result of a decision to save.

Things are different if purchases are less than demand, even though demand has not been satisfied ($P < D$). This means that the range of goods supplied by the socialized sector does not meet the people's needs, and that the people are then forced to increase their precautionary and speculative reserves in order, for example, to obtain what they need from other sources.

Applying this to situations 1, 2, and 3 above:

(a) the difference between $P$ and $O$ indicates wastage of productive effort;

(b) the difference between $P$ and $D$ indicates dissatisfaction (discontent with the terms of trade) on the part of the people. The workers will then unilaterally readjust the real terms of trade and, should this fail to have the desired effect, the result may be social unrest;

(c) the difference between $P$ and $W$ indicates an increase in speculative and precautionary reserves, which is an indicator of the degree of financial disequilibrium.

This gives the System at least three reasons to avoid situations 1, 2, and 3.

In situation 4 financial equilibrium is guaranteed, so the System only has to worry about (a) and (b).

In situation 7, it may be that there is no waste of productive effort, provided that $P$ happens to equal $O$; however, the System still has to cope with problems (b) and (c).

Our introduction of the third criterion thus shows that, whereas previously it was impossible to differentiate between five of the nine situations, the System now has good reason to prefer situation 4 to situation 7, which in turn is an improvement on situations 1, 2, and 3.

We have still not examined the situation in which purchases exceed demand ($P > D$), in other words, exceed households' everyday needs. If this were the case, the surplus of income in relation to expenditure observed in situations 1, 2, and 3 would represent voluntary savings.

The motives for accumulating stocks of goods in excess of everyday needs are precaution and speculation, phenomena which appear whenever the people foresee a deterioration in supply or a rise in prices. In situation 7, such motives may even be strong enough to induce households to eat into the monetary reserves they have previously built up.

Our classification clearly indicates that financial disequilibrium is not necessarily an indicator of social discontent. However, there is definitely social discontent in situations where needs remain unsatisfied ($P < D$). The most complex, and potentially most dangerous, of such situations are those in which part of the supply remains unsold even though people have surplus financial resources (which they convert into precautionary and speculative reserves), and at the same time their needs exceed their purchases ($D > P$, $W > P$, and $O > P$).

We then have to ask ourselves how, quite apart from the issue of financial equilibrium, purchases by the people in CPE countries can be less than both income and demand at a time when, in overall terms, there is surplus supply.

Such disequilibrium is paradoxical in purely macroeconomic terms, since—if $D > P$—situations 1, 2, and 4 satisfy the necessary condition for financial equilibrium ($O = W$). The explanation for this paradox is microeconomic: faced with a range of goods that fails to satisfy their preferences and requirements, households will hold on to their money rather than buy something that is shoddy or useless. In allowing households this freedom of choice, the System rather restricts its own freedom of choice as to the allocation of goods for accumulation or consumption. As soon as households reject what is on offer and decide to hold onto their money for the time being, social discontent and financial disequilibrium become inevitable and the System is potentially at risk.

The same total value of goods supplied may represent any one of an infinite number of different ranges of goods which will each satisfy households' needs to a different extent. Unsold products mean wastage, and so it is to the System's advantage to supply households with a range of goods that meets their needs, since in this way it can ensure that it requisitions the greatest possible volume of goods. This will also considerably improve each individual's terms of trade without altering the macroeconomic terms of trade, it will reduce wastage to a minimum, and it will ensure financial equilibrium, which will in turn reduce the danger of social unrest. In other words, the closer the supply of consumer goods comes to satisfying demand, the better for the System.

Unfortunately, since the System has encouraged enterprises not to worry about balancing their accounts, there is no way that the supply of consumer goods from the socialized sector can be regularly adjusted to take account of demand. The absence of consumer sovereignty in CPEs means that there is very little the System can do to protect itself against social unrest. All it can do is make occasional and often spectacular gestures that temporarily avert the danger of revolt by reducing requisitioning; however, such gestures only treat the symptoms, not the underlying causes.

As evidence of this, social discontent will be found to occur not only in the cases described in our classification above, but as soon as demand exceeds financial resources (income flows plus liquidity reserves), irrespective of supply levels and even when there is financial equilibrium.

In the next section we will see what the System can do to try and make sure that the people's income is simultaneously equal to their purchases, to supply, and to demand—in other words, how it endeavours, by macroeconomic rationing, to keep social discontent under control without allowing consumer sovereignty to develop.


## MULTIDIMENSIONAL EQUILIBRIUM IN THE CONSUMER SPHERE

In this section we will examine why the System is unable to respond to disequilibrium in the consumer sphere by adjusting supply, and will then go on to examine how it attempts to restore equilibrium $(W = P = O = D)$ by influencing both the level of income paid to households and the level of purchases or, alternatively, demand. (See Table 5.)


### *Consumer freedom or consumer sovereignty?*

Though an instrument of the Creed, the System nowadays specifically recognizes the right of households and individuals to make certain economic choices, so long as these do not encroach upon the System's exclusive power to make decisions on macroeconomic and general matters. Thus, for example, households are

TABLE 5. *Indicators of equilibrium in the consumer sphere in Eastern Europe* (average annual percentage growth rates 1981–1985)

| | Bulgaria | Czecho-slovakia | GDR | Hungary | Poland | Romania | USSR |
|---|---|---|---|---|---|---|---|
| 1. Wages | 4.2 | 3.1 | 3.2 | 8.5 | 31.0 | 6.0 | 4.0 |
| 2. Retail prices | 0.9 | 2.0 | 0.1 | 6.7 | 31.5 | 5.0 | 0.4 |
| 3. Industrial production of consumer goods | 4.3 | 2.7 | 4.1 | 2.0 | 0.4 | 4.0 | 3.7 |
| 4. Agricultural production | 1.2 | 1.9 | 1.7 | 2.2 | −0.5 | 2.0 | 1.1 |
| 5. Real wages (1 minus 2) | 3.3 | 1.1 | 3.1 | 1.8 | −0.5 | 1.0 | 3.6 |
| 6. Real industrial production of consumer goods (3 minus 2) | 4.4 | 0.7 | 4.0 | −4.7 | −31.1 | −1.0 | 3.3 |
| 7. Real agricultural production (4 minus 2) | 0.3 | −0.1 | 1.6 | −4.5 | −31.0 | −3.0 | 0.7 |
| 8. Real supply to consumers ((average of 6 and 7) minus 5) | −0.95 | −0.8 | −0.3 | −6.4 | −30.5 | −4.5 | −1.6 |
| 9. Increase in savings deposits from 1980 to 1985 | 51.3 | 40.0 | 25.0 | 68.0 | 238.0 | — | 40.0 |

*Note:* Obviously the above figures are only *indicators*, particularly in the case of item 8 where an attempt has been made to combine monetary data (wages) and real data (supplies to the consumer sphere). This indicator is based upon a number of hypotheses which are not discussed here.

*Source:* Items 1–4 and 9 are taken from *Economic Survey of Europe in 1986/87*, Economic Commission for Europe, UN, New York, 1987; the remaining items are calculated on the basis of these.

free to choose between the various alternative occupations offered by the System.

However, in order to avoid excessive disequilibrium on the labour market, the System dictates how many places will be available at training colleges. Access to training is thus subject to fixed quotas, to which demand must simply adapt. A similar situation prevails on the labour market: the supply of labour by individuals must adapt to demand. Freedom to choose one's occupation is thus not the same as unlimited power to choose where one will work—a hairdresser cannot force an electronics firm to employ him, but is free to choose between various alternative hairdressing jobs.

The same thing happens on the consumer goods market, where money functions as a means of payment and as a store of wealth.[11] As such, it enables those with sufficient cash to choose between various alternative transactions. Let us see what factors determine the range of possible choices.

The answer is, basically, supply. In CPEs, the socialized sector supplies consumers with a given range of goods which is determined almost entirely by exogenous factors. Money, functioning as a means of payment, then enables this range of goods to be distributed among individual consumers. If the range of goods does not meet households' needs, they will use their freedom by refusing to buy certain goods and hoarding their means of payment instead. In market economies, this freedom implies consumer sovereignty—but is the same true of CPEs?

In market economies, every producer is essentially out to make money. Since he must remain solvent, he resorts to all kinds of tricks to induce solvent consumers to exchange their money holdings for his products. He either adapts his supply to fit in with demand, or uses advertising or market manipulation to adapt demand more closely to his supply. Ultimately, his economic survival depends on his ability to make consumers part with their cash. The basis of this automatic mechanism whereby supply follows demand is consumer sovereignty.

The System, on the other hand, is geared to the satisfaction of social needs, if necessary at the expense of individual ones. According to the Creed, economic power is vested in society as a whole, which uses its own means of production to satisfy its demand to the best of its ability. Producers must follow the System's instructions, which by definition are a reflection of the balance that society has struck between its needs and its economic capabilities. This indirectly satisfies social demand, which is patently unrelated to demand as expressed by consumers.

If the System required producers to respond to consumer demand, there is no doubt that the chances of achieving equilibrium in the consumer sphere would increase—but the System would pay a price.

Sooner or later, the System would lose the power to decide how national income is distributed, and thus the power to requisition what it needs. Under the pressure of demand, the producer would alter not only his product range, but even his entire product line, thereby altering his own demand for supplies. Consumer demand would thus also indirectly affect producers of both capital goods and intermediate goods, and eventually the entire economy — which the System would then no longer control.

In order for the producer to respond to consumer demand, he would have to become dependent upon the income he derived from consumers. This would involve enterprises becoming fully fledged economic agents, exactly like their market-economy counterparts. The dilemma of methods[12] would then be resolved, since requisitioning would no longer be possible — but that would mean the end of the System.

The adjustments involved in establishing consumer sovereignty would be fatal to the System; although the risk of social discontent would be eliminated, the System would no longer be able to build the Promised Society or withstand the pressures from its international environment. Therefore, so long as the System can successfully use macroeconomic rationing to keep social discontent within acceptable limits, it will put up with the social dilemma rather than risk letting consumer sovereignty destroy it from within.

The System has a number of instruments that it can use to influence financial equilibrium in the consumer sphere so that its macroeconomic rationing will be less noticeable at the individual level. However, even the most sophisticated instruments can never entirely eliminate the risk of social unrest or of individuals making unilateral adjustments to the microeconomic terms of trade.

## Adjustment of incomes

Since it cannot do anything about the supply of goods, the System must endeavour to bring about what equilibrium it can in the consumer sphere by influencing financial flows, namely, the total volume of income and the total volume (or, more precisely, the value) of purchases.

The System has three kinds of instrument that it can use to determine, or at least influence, the total volume of income made available to the people by the socialized sector:

1. income policy;

2.  sterilization of a certain proportion of income; and
3.  forced savings and fiscal policy.

For convenience, we will assume that both the supply of consumer goods and consumer demand are determined by exogenous factors. Equilibrium between supply and demand is perfectly compatible with financial disequilibrium, for if $O$ equals $D$, that by no means implies that $W$ equals $P$, let alone that $O$ equals $W$. In order for there to be real equilibrium in the consumer sphere, $W$ must equal $O$ and also, as far as possible, $P$. The System uses the three instruments listed above in an attempt to achieve such equilibrium.

*Income policy*[13] involves drawing up wage grids and rules for the allocation of social welfare benefits and, at the same time, determining the total volume of income to be distributed to the people.

Financial equilibrium depends not so much on how income and wages are distributed as on their total volume, which must equal the value of goods and services supplied. If the total volume of income and wages is determined in advance, any later adjustments can only be achieved by altering the way in which income and wages are distributed.

The System can determine the way in which national income is distributed in physical terms, without determining its total volume. The risk is then that total income will exceed the value of what is supplied. Such excess liquidity tends to generate new needs and thereby increases the risk of social unrest.

Even if an increase in total wages does not alter the way in which national income is distributed in physical terms, it will affect each individual's nominal terms of trade, so that—at least to begin with—he will think he is richer. Dazzled by this peculiar monetary illusion, he will resolve to convert this nominal improvement in the terms of trade into a real one, by increasing his demand. If he actually succeeds in acquiring the goods he wants, well and good; however, if everybody does the same, the pressure of demand will increase dramatically and the entire consumer sector will be thrown out of balance. In order to prevent this without having to determine the total volume of income, the System can attempt to influence households' *disposable* income as opposed to their gross income. It can do this with the help of two different instruments.

*Sterilizing a certain proportion of income.* This instrument is used to counteract the negative effects of a lenient wages and income policy. Sterilization is quite different from confiscation. An example of sterilization is increasing the deposits on returnable bottles, which macroeconomically speaking will reduce the volume of money in circulation. Another method is to issue a wide variety of coins (or postage stamps), which will tempt people to collect them rather than spend them (or stick them on letters). The effects of such measures are of course relatively minor, but they do have the advantage of being inconspicuous, since the macroeconomic rationality behind them often goes completely unnoticed.

The practice of paying for goods in advance is another example of how income can be sterilized. The individual whose nominal terms of trade have improved can find an outlet for his increased demand if he purchases goods that will only become available later. Since he is required to pay immediately and in full, the money paid is sterilized (i.e. removed from circulation) for the time it takes for the good he has purchased to become available. This last method is similar to the third kind of instrument the System uses to influence disposable income, namely, fiscal policy.

*Fiscal policy and targeted savings.* In Eastern Europe relatively little use so far has been made of fiscal policy as a means of influencing households' behaviour. There are various reasons for this, which have to do with the Creed, the way the System works, and various historical factors. Since the System can distribute national income as it sees fit, without consultation, there is no need to use fiscal policy as an instrument for allocating resources between consumption and accumulation. However, there are some advantages to fiscal policy. To begin with, it allows incomes to be equalized without necessarily being redistributed and, secondly, it allows the System to influence financial equilibrium in the consumer sphere. However, its importance should not be exaggerated, since it only affects very high incomes, which are mostly not generated by the socialized sector. Besides classic fiscal measures, the CPEs occasionally introduce temporary taxes for specific purposes, such as an automatic 1 per cent levy on all wages to enable a hospital to be built or a historical monument to be restored.

The targeted savings method consists of introducing compulsory savings books for specific purposes, such as housing or cars. While such measures are often motivated by considerations of social policy, they also sterilize a proportion of income by turning it into long-term savings. This method has two advantages: it leaves the System in control of the volume of income it pays to the people, so that the monetary illusion can be maintained, but it does not require the volume of consumer goods to be increased.

Together, these three instruments enable the System to adjust total disposable income so that it always remains very close to the value of goods supplied. However, even these instruments have their limits. Extreme social pressure leaves the government with no choice but to relinquish its control over wages and incomes, and the resulting financial disequilibrium in the consumer sphere is too serious and persistent for the above-mentioned instruments to have any effect.

Given the problems involved in trying to balance the supply of goods and the level of disposable income, the System may decide to concentrate instead on influencing the total value of purchases.

## Influencing the value of purchases

If disposable income is rising and the System cannot alter the physical composition of the supply of consumer goods, the obvious temptation is to try and influence the value of purchases. There are two instruments available for this purpose:

1. alteration of prices; and
2. currency reform, if alteration of prices proves insufficient.

By *altering prices* of consumer goods, the System is able to alter the value of purchases without affecting their supply. This is a way of leaving the distribution of national income unchanged while absorbing excess liquidity, and thus improves financial equilibrium in the consumer sphere.

However, prices are usually altered *upwards*, which adversely affects the terms of trade as perceived by individuals: the real value of their nominal income falls while access to goods remains unchanged. Being abrupt, alteration of prices is likely to spark off social unrest and the System may eventually be forced to back-pedal. Therefore, although this measure is financially very effect-ive, the System does not resort to it often. On the other hand, when price rises *are* used, they are large enough to absorb a considerable period of disequilibrium in one go. In the periods between rises, price levels remain very stable, a fact that the System's self-justification uses to demonstrate the superiority of central planning.

By altering prices, the System is thus able to reduce liquidity in the consumer sphere and also reduce inflationary overhang. However, since excess liquidity is never fairly distributed among consumers, price rises will increase the discrepancies between individual terms of trade. In fact, in this respect price rises are no different from the excess liquidity they are supposed to eliminate. When the supply of sought-after goods is exhausted by specu-lators, who take a generous commission before reselling the goods on the open market,[14] the System prosecutes the speculators as though they were the main cause of the disequilibrium. However, price rises are no fairer or more efficient, since they lead to redistribution in much the same way as speculation does—only this time it is the System that benefits most.

If there is too much excess liquidity—or it is too unfairly distributed—for it to be safely absorbed by a price rise, the system can resort to *currency reform*. This drastic measure can be used to confiscate varying proportions of cash holdings from specific categories of consumers, by applying a series of rates of conversion whereby the old currency is not converted into the new one at a uniform rate. However, since it is so drastic, currency reform is also a last resort; no country can afford to keep using it to restore financial equilibrium in the consumer sphere, as it can with price rises.

If consumers suspect that a currency reform is in the offing, they will most likely respond by getting rid of their cash, and the speed at which money circulates among households will increase. Households will then avoid using domestic currency as a store of wealth, preferring some more appropriate medium such as foreign currency or gold, while at the same time the domestic currency will continue to function as a means of payment—a classic example of Gresham's Law.

Now that we have seen how the System can influence supply, income, and purchases, let us look at what it can do about demand.

## Influencing demand

Here the System can use one of two diametrically opposed methods: either it can increase confidence in order to dissuade people from hoarding, or else it can introduce microeconomic rationing in addition to the macroeconomic rationing it is already regularly using.

*In order to increase confidence*, the System must prove to consumers that their expectations about deteriorating supply are wrong. Though ideal as far as the System is concerned, this method is not always practicable. It necessitates a sufficient supply of consumer goods to convince the people that everyone's nominal terms of trade are going to stop getting worse. Only then will people stop hoarding, so that the System can gain some breathing-space. Therefore—at least to begin with—the System must create the impression of prosperity, which means increasing the supply of sought-after goods, which in turn depends upon there being sufficient stocks. Ultimately a balance must be struck between consumers' expectations of shortage (leading to increased demand) and the amount of resources that the System can put into convincing them that these expectations are unfounded.

Experience indicates that this is likely to be rather a touch-and-go affair, since available resources will often be exhausted before consumers' expectations begin to change. The System's efforts may then actually be counter-productive, since consumers' expectations of shortage will merely be confirmed and the merry-go-round of hoarding and speculation will become even more hectic. A wave of pessimism can thus be extremely damaging to the consumer sphere, creating a vicious circle in which successive shortages lead to a net increase in demand, making the original disequilibrium even worse.

Since the System cannot rely on reasoning to get what it wants, it must resort to microeconomic *rationing*. This extremely un-popular method must be used whenever people are led by pessimistic expectations to steer clear of money and start hoarding, so that supplies become exhausted, speculation flourishes, and chaos reigns. However, microeconomic rationing destroys confidence and only ostensibly brings supply and demand into equilibrium, since the brunt of the adjustment is borne by the unofficial sector. Like currency reform, rationing is a last resort, but if disequilibrium builds up to danger level there may be no alternative.

In order to keep the risk of popular revolt within acceptable limits and ensure that unilateral adjustments of the individual terms of trade do not interfere too greatly with requisitioning, the System must make sure that the standard of living rises, if only slowly; if it does not, the discrepancy between aspirations and reality may drive the people to acts of desperation. In fact, unless the System is prepared to reduce requisitioning so as to release resources for consumption, there is only one solution—constant growth. This is the price the System must pay if it is to ensure that the social dilemma remains a purely economic problem rather than a systemic one.[15]

In the next chapter we will see that growth is essential not only in view of the relationship between the System and the people, but also in order to ensure the System's military survival—without which the System's economic problems must inevitably lead to its downfall.

## Notes

1. See Ch. 8.
2. See, *inter alia*, J. Osers, 'Die osteuropäischen Krisenerscheinungen und ihr sozioökonomischer Hintergrund', *Osteuropa Wirtschaft* (1982), No. 4.
3. See Ch. 4.
4. In an article entitled, 'Régulation de la part salariale et crise en système socialiste' (W. Andreff and M. Lavigne, eds., *La Réalité socialiste: Crise, adaptation, progrès*, Economica, Paris, 1985, pp. 143–67), D. Redor not only successfully describes the macroeconomic terms of trade, but also shows that from the point of view of households the terms of trade are worsening in every Eastern European country.
5. For simplicity's sake, we will ignore what is known as 'social (or collective) consumption', even though the resources it uses also limit the extent of requisitioning. Social consumption will be assumed to remain constant.
6. This statement needs to be qualified somewhat in the light of recent reforms. In Hungary, for example, a higher proportion of wages than in other Eastern European countries is made up of bonuses linked to certain types of financial results achieved by enterprises. Even so, the statement remains essentially valid.

7. This problem of the quality of the labour supply has been scarcely touched upon in Western economic theory. A fascinating exception is H. Leibenstein's *Beyond Economic Man: A New Foundation for Microeconomics*, Harvard University Press, Cambridge, Mass., 1976; see also Ch. 8.

8. This is J. Drewnowski's explanation for the crisis that has been afflicting Polish society for most of the past decade: see 'The Anatomy of Economic Failure in Soviet-Type Systems', J. Drewnowski, ed., *Crisis in the Eastern European Economy*, Croom Helm, London, 1982.

9. John Maynard Keynes, *The General Theory of Employment, Interest and Money*, Macmillan, London, 1967, pp. 170 ff. Though simple and clear, Keynesian terminology has not found favour with most writers on the subject of financial equilibrium in CPEs; instead, they prefer to talk of 'voluntary savings' (depositing in savings banks) and 'involuntary savings' (which may be either hoarded or deposited in an account); see e.g. F. Seurot, *Inflation et emploi dans les pays socialistes*, PUF, Collection 'Libre échange', Paris, 1983. However, this distinction is no more appropriate than Keynes's classification of liquidity holdings; since only deposited savings are measurable, it is impossible to break savings down into voluntary and involuntary savings, and hoarding can only be measured in residual terms. I therefore prefer the Keynesian terminology, which is not only clearer but also universal. The term 'savings' is therefore used here to mean all savings bank deposits, irrespective of underlying motives.

10. Unspent sums are described here as being hoarded, whether the underlying motives are savings or the building up of cash reserves for precautionary or speculatory purposes. For simplicity's sake, we will assume here that savings (as defined above) are exogenous, and therefore need not be specifically taken into account.

11. See Ch. 4.

12. See Ch. 4.

13. See J. Adam, *Wage Control and Inflation in Soviet Bloc Countries*, Macmillan, London, 1979. This book contains a detailed analysis of the various instruments that the System can use in order to restore equilibrium in the consumer sphere.

14. D. O. Stahl II and M. Alexeev, 'The Influence of Black Markets on a Queue-Rationed Centrally Planned Economy', *Journal of Economic Theory*, 35 (Apr. 1985), 234–51.

15. See Ch. 8.

# 7

# The Military Dilemma:
# Brain versus Brawn

In addition to social pressures, the System is subject to two further types of constraint: those relating to its international relations, and those arising out of its trade with market economies. According to the System's self-justification, the Bolshevik revolution was the prelude to world revolution. This gave the 'motherland of socialism' international responsibilities.[1] This dimension of the role assumed by the USSR, and later by the entire Eastern bloc, requires the System to behave as an international power. As the bastion of 'real socialism', it must not only hold its own in a politically hostile international environment, but must also make new converts by showing the world how to abolish capitalism and build the Promised Society.

The System's role in international relations requires a considerable volume of material resources, which are theoretically obtained by requisitioning (with all its economic implications). In this chapter we will look at the pressures that this brings to bear upon the CPEs and the ways in which the System can attempt to reduce such pressures. A central element in our analysis will be the *arms race*, in which the Eastern bloc has been involved for forty years.[2]

In the first section we will compare the economic implications of the arms race in CPEs and in market economies. The second section will attempt to analyse the economic conditions that will enable the System to take part in the arms race without risking social discontent. Finally, the third section will identify the systemic obstacles that the Eastern European countries need to eliminate if they are to alleviate the economic problems caused by their involvement in the arms race.

## THE NATURE OF THE ARMS RACE

The arms race can mean any one of several different things, according to one's point of view.[3] From the point of view of the human race, it means above all an ever more explicit and, apparently, uncontrollable threat to life on earth. From the point of view of the military, it is a way of both practising one's profession and fulfilling one's responsibilities towards one's country and/or the prevailing ideology. From the point of view of politicians, it is an instrument of policy, a 'stepping-stone to peace'.

The two super-powers more or less openly agree that the ideological differences that separate them are profound ones, and that their political goals are bound to lead them into conflict. They each acknowledge that their role in international relations requires them both to seek military parity or superiority. In general, the influence of economic factors on the arms race is considerably underestimated. It is therefore worth examining the various forms the arms race can take and the economic effects each of them has on market economies and CPEs respectively.

The arms race is a contest, in which relative performance matters more to the competitors than absolute performance. Accordingly, each side is constantly trying to outdo the other, a process which in theory can escalate *ad infinitum* but in practice is limited by the competitors' economic capabilities. For convenience, we will take two extreme cases with very different economic implications: the quantitative arms race, and the qualitative arms race.

If both competitors possess the same technological skills, in other words if their weapons are very similar in quality, then the arms race will be entirely *quantitative*. The competitor with the greatest quantity of each weapon will then come out on top, as happened during the Second World War, first with Hitler, and later with the Allies. Such a quantitative race is currently going on in the field of conventional arms (numbers of troops, tanks, and aircraft, artillery firepower, naval strength, and numbers of standard nuclear warheads).[4]

The arms race can take a quite different form, on the other

hand, if the competitors do not share the same technology and are both trying their best to develop new weapons. The resulting *qualitative* arms race does not involve trying to acquire more weapons than one's opponent, but developing new weapons capable of knocking out those held by the other side. Often, though by no means always, it begins with offensive weapons and moves on to defensive weapons. A recent example of the qualitative arms race is the period between 1945 and the late 1950s, in which the A-bomb (and subsequently the H-bomb) unquestionably gave the United States superiority over the USSR. Unlike the quantitative arms race, the qualitative arms race is not susceptible to statistical analysis, since by definition each competitor is producing different weapons which cannot be compared without the necessary technological and military expertise.

The above examples show that the form taken by the arms race is determined by the state of technology. If both competitors share the same technology, they will compete in terms of quantity, but if each has its own technology the race will be either entirely or chiefly qualitative. However, in today's world technology is neither entirely shared nor entirely separate. There are two kinds of technology: advanced technology (which each competitor keeps hidden by declaring it top secret) and conventional technology (which, if not actually freely available, is certainly negotiable and can thus be shared by both sides). Research is constantly adding to the amount of advanced technology, but at the same time formerly advanced technology is constantly being released for public use.

The arms race, which has now been going on for over four decades, is currently based on both advanced and conventional technology, and accordingly is both qualitative and quantitative. We therefore need to see which of the two components prevails on each side. Apart from one or two extreme instances, such as the A-bomb and the Strategic Defense Initiative, no technological breakthrough by either of the competitors has ever succeeded in knocking out the other side's weaponry altogether. Therefore, in the event of such a breakthrough, the other competitor can do one of two things:

1. increase the quantity of its weapons to make up for their inferior quality; or

2. try to speed up improvements in the quality of its weapons.

Indeed, there is no reason why it should not try to do both at once. However, in both cases there are a number of economic and systemic conditions that must be met. In other words, the form taken by the arms race depends upon each competitor's economic capabilities, which in turn depend upon the prevailing economic system.

## THE ECONOMIC IMPACT OF THE ARMS RACE

Let us begin by looking at the current state of things. One way we can do this is by measuring quantities of arms; the other involves investigating both competitors' technological and systemic capabilities and examining the respective economic impact of the arms race in each of the scenarios described earlier.

Whereas economic theory can perfectly well be used to analyse the relationship between the rate of growth in GNP and the rate of growth in military expenditure in a country such as the United States, it is of no help whatsoever with regard to the Soviet Union.[5] Our knowledge of how CPEs operate is as yet too imperfect to allow an objective assessment of statistics or estimates relating to Soviet arms expenditure. Since economic theory cannot help us, we must attempt to analyse the problem in terms of systems analysis. By placing the subject in its true context, this approach sheds an entirely new light on it. (See Table 6.)

## *The role of expenditure*

In the United States economy, as in any market economy, production of goods and services depends upon demand by economic agents. As long as there are idle factors of production in the economy, any increase in demand will lead to an increase in production, while prices remain constant. Once demand exceeds the productive capability of the economy, in the sense that its factors of production are fully employed, supply responds by a general rise in prices, customarily referred to as inflation. Since the early 1970s the Western economies have been under-using their

TABLE 6. *Various estimates of the share of defence expenditure in Soviet gross national product*

|  | O* | S 79 | S 80–1 | S 82–3 | LEE CP | LEE P70 | ROS | DIA | CIA |
|---|---|---|---|---|---|---|---|---|---|
| 1970 | 4.7 | 10.0 | 12.0 | — | 11.7 | 12.9 | 14.0 | 13.0 | 13.0 |
| 1971 | 4.0 | 9.7 | 9.7 | — | — | 13.6 | — | 13.0 | 12.0 |
| 1972 | 4.0 | 9.6 | 9.6 | 11.4 | — | 13.7 | — | 13.0 | 13.0 |
| 1973 | 4.0 | 9.0 | 9.0 | 10.8 | — | 14.5 | — | 13.0 | 12.0 |
| 1974 | 4.0 | 8.7 | 8.7 | 10.4 | — | 14.8 | — | 13.0 | 13.0 |
| 1975 | 4.0 | 8.6 | 10.3 | 10.3 | 14.5 | 15.5 | 15.3 | 14.0 | 13.0 |
| 1976 | 3.0 | 8.3 | 9.9 | 9.9 | — | — | — | 14.0 | 13.0 |
| 1977 | 3.0 | 8.0 | 9.6 | 9.5 | — | — | 16.5 | 14.0 | 13.0 |
| 1978 | 3.0 | — | 9.4 | 9.2 | — | — | — | 15.0 | 13.0 |
| 1979 | 3.0 | — | — | 9.0 | — | — | — | 15.0 | 13.0 |
| 1980 | 3.0 | — | — | 8.8 | — | 19.4 | — | 15.0 | 14.0 |
| 1981 | 3.0 | — | — | 8.7 | — | — | — | 15.0 | 13.0–14.0 |
| 1982 | 2.0 | — | — | — | — | — | — | — | 13.0–14.0 |
| 1983 | 2.0 | — | — | — | — | — | — | — | — |

\* The following abbreviations are used for the headings in this table:

O ('Official'): official statistics on arms expenditure compared with Western estimates of GNP (Soviet macroeconomic statistics only refer to net national product).

S (SIPRI): from the *World Armaments and Disarmament Yearbook* (Taylor & Francis, London and Philadelphia).

LEE CP ('Current prices'): from W. T. Lee, *The Estimation of Soviet Defense Expenditures, 1955–1975: An Unconventional Approach*, Praeger, New York, 1977, p. 97.

LEE P 70 ('1970 prices'): from *CIA Estimates of Soviet Defense Spending*, Hearings before the Subcommittee on Oversight of the Permanent Select Committee on Intelligence, House of Representatives, Washington DC, 1980, p. 22, table 3.

ROS: S. Rosenfielde, *False Science: Underestimating the Soviet Arms Build-up*, Transaction Books, New Brunswick, NJ, and London, 1983, p. 201.

DIA (Defense Intelligence Agency) and CIA (Central Intelligence Agency): from *Allocation of Resources in the Soviet Union and China: 1983*, Hearings before the Subcommittee on International Trade, Finance and Security Economics of the Joint Economic Committee, Congress of the United States, Washington DC, 1984; DIA, p. 21; CIA, pp. 214 and 231.

*Source:* This table is taken from A. S. Becker, *Sitting on Bayonets: The Soviet Defense Burden and the Slowdown in Soviet Defense Spending* (RAND/UCLA, Center for the Study of Soviet International Behavior, University of California, 1986, p. 13), in which the various methods used are described in detail.

factors of production, as shown by their unemployment rates, which have fluctuated between 5 and 12 per cent of the working population.

Within the market-economy system all government expenditure (including military spending) helps to increase demand for goods and services and thus remunerate factors of production left idle owing to insufficient demand. If under conditions of under-employment, which are normal in market economies, the government orders a billion dollars' worth of ships for the navy, part of this sum will be paid to shipyard workers in the form of wages, part will be passed on to subcontractors, and the rest will be profit for the shipyards. The subcontractors will divide up the sums they receive from the shipyards in the same way. In the United States, military orders currently provide employment for some 2 million people, or 2 per cent of the working population.[6]

In market economies, government spending functions as a tool of economic policy; it can be used to expand overall demand so as to increase the total volume of remunerated productive effort and combat underemployment, thereby improving living standards and ensuring that more effective use is made of the means of production. As Keynes made clear over fifty years ago, government spending is not merely a macroeconomic cost, for it triggers off a multiplier effect that benefits the whole economy.

The above remarks apply to all expenditure, however allocated. Yet a new warship will not have the same impact on general welfare as, say, a new road. If we accept that, in peacetime, new armaments as such make no contribution to welfare, it will be clear that the effects of government spending upon welfare will depend on how it is allocated. If the result of discontinuing arms expenditure were simply a reduction in total government expend-iture by the equivalent amount, the effect upon welfare would be nil. On the other hand, if the same amount could otherwise have been allocated for other purposes, or if other expenditure has had to be cut in order to finance military spending, the negative impact upon welfare is evidently considerable. Our analysis will be based on the former hypothesis, namely, that additional armaments are financed by increased public spending.

The effects of military expenditure upon market economies are threefold:

1. the volume of factors of production used is increased;
2. total production by the economy is increased; and

3. the level of welfare is unaffected.

In CPEs, the effects are very different. The System's mission and its use of its requisitioning powers are such that the means of production are always fully employed. As the supreme administrator, the System has a historical duty to ensure that the work of building the Promised Society continues to progress, and it must therefore always requisition as much as it can. To make this task easier, the System releases enterprises from the duty to respond to demand.[7] There is accordingly no such thing in Eastern Europe as factors of production lying idle for lack of outlets, as is so often the case in market economies.

Given the hostility that prevails in international relations, arms are essential to the System's physical survival. The System therefore exerts maximum pressure on the tissue to produce arms which it can then requisition. Accordingly, defence manufacture has top priority throughout Eastern Europe, the necessary factors of production being obtained from other areas of the economy.[8] Any additional military expenditure inevitably involves transferring factors of production away from civilian allocations, so that civilian manufacture decreases. In short, more weaponry means less welfare.

The effects of military expenditure upon CPEs are thus as follows:

1. factors of production are transferred from other areas of the economy, without any increase in their total volume;
2. total production by the economy remains unchanged; and
3. the level of welfare deteriorates, since fewer socially useful goods can be produced.

However, in order to obtain a complete picture of the economic impact of military spending upon each of the two systems, we need to look at its long-term effects.

## The long-term impact of military spending

A large part of modern arms expenditure goes into research and development, either directly via the State budget, or else indirectly via firms that obtain military orders. In the United States in 1983, approximately 46 per cent of total R & D costs were financed from the federal budget, and 75 per cent of this sum went into military research. At the same time, industries that were the main suppliers of the US armed forces put up to 15 per cent of their receipts back into research.[9] Thus military spending directly or indirectly finances a major part of all US research and development. Although no such data are available for the Soviet Union,[10] it is a fairly safe bet that a major proportion of Eastern European research is directly related to the armed forces.

In the medium or long term, in either system, military R & D spending produces civilian spin-offs. There is thus a link between the amount of military research and the future level of welfare. In market economies military and civilian research are in a symbiotic relationship, and the consumer soon benefits from technology developed for military purposes. Thus, in a matter of years, Western lifestyles have been revolutionized by new developments in aviation, (tele)communications, computers, and materials science; many of these discoveries were first made for military purposes and were often directly financed by the armed forces. In this way, market economies allow the consumer to take advantage of developments in the military sector without too much of a time-lag, and military financing of R & D leads to increased welfare in the medium term (or, exceptionally, the long term). This effect is in direct proportion to the share of R & D in total military spending.

In order to obey the Creed, if not simply in order to survive, the System must requisition as much as it can. Accordingly, in CPEs factors of production are never idle. To some extent they are absorbed by military research, the short-term opportunity cost to the System of such research being equivalent to the volume of arms that could otherwise have been produced. However, if research bears fruit in military terms, the long-term diagnosis is different. In CPEs, the balance between present and future needs is subject to very specific rules, since the System is well aware that its means are limited and therefore dislikes taking economic risks, of which financing research—even military research—is one. Moreover, the civilian spin-offs are insignificant and only occur with a considerable time-lag, far greater than in market economies. The System's obsession with security causes it to cloak all military research in the utmost secrecy, which completely isolates it from the civilian sector. Hence technological progress achieved under the impetus of the arms race does not necessarily herald an improvement in consumers' living standards; the contribution of military technology to future welfare is minimal.

The economic burden of the arms race is thus considerably greater in CPEs than in market economies, since not only do armaments divert resources from other uses, but they fail to produce spin-offs in the form of future welfare. Having reached this conclusion, we are now in a position to look at the current state of the arms race and analyse the military dilemma facing the System.

## The current state of the arms race

All statistical sources are agreed that the Eastern European armed forces are numerically superior in almost every type of conventional weaponry as well as in most kinds of standard nuclear weapons. In the light of the foregoing, this can be interpreted in one of two ways:

1. the numerical superiority enjoyed by Eastern Europe gives it an unassailable lead in the arms race; or
2. its numerical superiority is offset by the inferior quality of its weaponry, making it difficult to tell who is really in the lead.

Various technological and military data suggest an essential difference in the way the two sides approach the arms race: *in the case of the NATO countries it would appear to be mainly qualitative, as opposed to mainly quantitative in the case of the Warsaw Pact.* In that case, numerical superiority should not be seen as an absolute advantage, but as the System's way of making up for its technological inferiority—since the System cannot develop such good weapons as the West, it makes sure it has more of those it can develop.

This interpretation is confirmed by the persistent efforts of the Eastern European countries to get hold of advanced Western technology and use it for military purposes.[11] By placing legislative

and other restrictions on 'sensitive' exports, the West in turn
attempts to stop such leakage and so maintain its technological
advantage.[12]

The economic effects and the economic burden of arms spending are set out in Table 7, according to type of economic system
and type of military effort. The four economic variables considered here are:

1. volume of factors of production used (FP);
2. total production by the economy (TP);
3. present welfare (PW);
4. future welfare (FW).

TABLE 7. *Economic effects of arms race scenarios*

|  | Quantitative arms race | | | | Qualitative arms race | | | |
|---|---|---|---|---|---|---|---|---|
|  | FP | TP | PW | FW | FP | TP | PW | FW |
| Market economies | + | + | 0 | 0 | + | + | 0 | + + |
| CPEs | 0 | 0 | − 0 | − | 0 | 0 | − | − + |

Table 7 shows that there are four possible scenarios, each with
very different advantages and disadvantages for each of the
competitors. In order to grasp this properly, the table needs to be
read in two different ways: firstly from the economic perspective,
and secondly from the political and strategic perspective.

The *economic perspective*, which involves reading the table
horizontally, indicates which approach to the arms race will
minimize the economic burden of the military effort, irrespective
of what the other side does. Seen from this point of view, it is
clearly in each side's interest to go for qualitative effort; however,
the result must be, at the very least, parity with the other side. The
economic advantages must therefore be weighed up against the
political and strategic advantages, which ultimately determine
whether the System can survive.

The *political and strategic perspective* indicates which approach
to the arms race will maximize the chances of gaining—or

consolidating—the military advantage. Here the table will be read differently by each of the competitors. In order to gain a relative advantage, each side must pursue two objectives at once—that is, it must minimize its own economic burden, and maximize the economic problems that its choice of approach causes the other side. It will be seen that the market economies will gain the maximum strategic advantage if they go for qualitative effort and at the same time are technologically far enough ahead of the CPEs to force the latter to step up their quantitative effort. The CPEs, for their part, will maximize their relative advantage if they succeed in turning the tables in this scenario.

Accordingly, the current state of the arms race is to the advantage of the NATO economies and is particularly burdensome to the Warsaw Pact economies, which are forced to respond to the West's mainly qualitative approach by putting all their effort into increased quantity. As our analysis clearly shows, it is in the economic and strategic interest of the market economies to keep the arms race the way it is, by holding on to their technological advantage at all costs; whereas the CPEs need to close the current technology gap, or at the very least prevent it from getting wider. Unless the System manages to reverse current trends, it may well find that its requisitioning powers can no longer provide sufficient resources to compensate for the West's technological advantage.

Given present economic constraints on the CPEs, arms control agreements are key instruments in changing the nature of the arms race. This is because such agreements place ceilings on the *quantitative* development of certain categories of weapons, whereas there is no conceivable agreement that can control *qualitative* development, since it is totally unpredictable. Arms control agreements thus give an undoubted economic advantage to whichever side has adopted a mainly quantitative approach, since they release resources which can then be devoted to improving quality. However, in the long run this can turn out to be more of a disadvantage than an advantage.

If, for example, all conventional weapons are subject to strict numerical controls and the West continues to widen the technology gap despite greater efforts by the System to catch up, the Eastern European countries will simply fall further and further behind, since they will be prohibited from having more weapons and will never be capable of developing such good weapons as the West. Hence their ambiguous attitude towards arms control proposals. If they cannot achieve superiority in terms of quality, they had better make sure they achieve it in terms of quantity. The chances of reaching an agreement to limit all conventional weapons would therefore seem slight, since such an agreement can only work to the System's disadvantage. Yet, since their requisitioning powers are limited, the Eastern European countries must continue to seek controls on conventional weapons—which are a heavier burden on their economies—so as to concentrate more of their resources on areas with a higher qualitative component.

Rather different reasoning lay behind Gorbachev's proposal in 1985 that the United States abandon its Strategic Defense Initiative. A decision to call a halt to 'Star Wars' research would have reduced the United States' advantage in terms of quality, and would accordingly have given the Eastern European countries a real chance to narrow the technology gap and at the same time reduce their quantitative effort, which their economies were finding harder and harder to sustain.

The only real obstacle to mobilizing the necessary resources to sustain such an effort is that the System must maintain a level of consumption that will allow it to requisition what it needs without the people rising in revolt. If there is already serious social discontent, the slightest additional burden may well bring the situation to boiling-point. In other words, the closer the System is to an internal revolt, the smaller its chances of surviving militarily. The age-old question 'guns or butter?' is as relevant today as it ever was.

The essence of the military dilemma is as follows. The System is systemically speaking capable of adopting a quantitative approach to the arms race, but this swallows up increasingly scarce economic resources. Yet the System does not appear capable of increasing the qualitative component of its military effort, which would reduce the economic burden of the social and military constraints on the System. We must therefore see what prevents the System from doing something so clearly to its political and economic advantage.

WHY THE SYSTEM CANNOT ACHIEVE QUALITY

## Failure to innovate: An endemic disease of the System

'Innovation' is a convenient term with which to sum up current trends in the world economy. However, the term covers such a variety of phenomena that no attempt will be made to define it here; suffice it to say that, from the purely economic point of view, there are two main kinds of innovation, namely *product innovation* (relating to uses) and *process innovation* (relating to production techniques and technology).

As we saw in Chapter 1, the Creed ignores innovation altogether, for the following reasons:

1. Demand has no economic function, since the party is already essentially aware of social needs. Accordingly, new needs cannot arise without the party knowing about them and guiding production so as to satisfy them in the best possible way. This assumption enables the Creed to assert that CPEs are superior to market economies because they are not exposed to the uncertainties of fashion and they avoid waste. Capitalism, says the Creed, is wrong because it remains subject to the fluctuations and whims of demand.

2. The Creed also indicates that forces of production reached their final stage of development with late nineteenth-century capitalism. Innovation in production processes is therefore bound to be insignificant, since production techniques have already developed to their fullest extent and can no longer seriously be altered.

Not surprisingly, since it grew out of the Creed, the System is poorly equipped to deal with the problems currently posed by innovation. In our discussion of the System's internal dilemmas (see Part II), it was stressed that the System heartily dislikes anything that is unknown or unforeseen—the very essence of innovation. From the point of view of the System, allowing for the unforeseen means giving the tissue a measure of freedom which may be used to the System's disadvantage.

Technical coefficients derived from the table of inputs and outputs indicate the current state of production processes and are used by the System to organize the distribution and circulation of goods within the economy. Any innovation in production processes will not only alter such coefficients without warning, but will alter their components: for example, production of the same good will involve different inputs. Furthermore, in market economies process innovations are only adopted if they improve company results, otherwise they are discarded; but how is the System to tell whether a given production process is better than another?

Various criteria come to mind: how the process affects production costs in accounting terms, or the use of scarce materials, or foreign currency flows, etc. Such a variety of criteria only makes the choice more confusing and increases the risk of error. Indeed, such information as is available confirms that the System is inconsistent in its approach to this problem, and that it bases its decisions to introduce new production processes on highly random and unstable criteria. As a result, whenever the System introduces a process innovation, it is taking an economic risk that it cannot quantify in advance—hence its extreme aversion to innovation and its preference for imitation instead.

Product innovation is similarly stifled, since CPE enterprises have only the barest interest in responding to users' needs, whether the users concerned are consumers or other enterprises.

The relevant literature mentions two separate sources of innovation,[13] namely *demand pull* and *scientific push*. Scientific push presupposes viewing progress 'as the result of an organized, rationalized system capable of foreseeing and planning change', whereas demand pull is based on a 'system of social organization in which decision-making is decentralized, and which accepts a high degree of competition between agents'.[14] Clearly, only scientific push is compatible with the way the System works, while demand pull is completely foreign to it. To what extent, then, does the System succeed in using scientific push to encourage innovation and so lighten the economic burden of the arms race?

## The costs and implications of scientific push

From the very beginning the System has always seen scientific research as an essential aspect of its activities. Statistics confirm that the number of research workers, research establishments, etc. is far higher in the Eastern European countries than in the West.[15] Thus the conditions for innovation by means of scientific push are satisfied.

Were our analysis to stop here, we might conclude that the System possesses an unending source of technological progress. However, we should not be too hasty in jumping to such a conclusion, since it presupposes that the results of scientific research are automatically translated into technological progress; yet, as Caron has shown, this process is neither automatic nor immediate in either economic system. In order to be translated into technology, research must be not only operational but also useful, which is to say profitable. In market economies, the risk taken by the entrepreneur or investor provides the necessary link. The final verdict lies with the user, whose decision whether or not to purchase will determine whether the entrepreneur's choice has been economically wise. In market economies, then, the results of scientific research are selected and later translated into technological progress according to criteria based on the solvency of the companies that have taken the risk of innovating. Ultimately, the sanction of demand is essential if scientific push is to make a real contribution to increased economic efficiency.

As we saw in Part II, the System has chosen to run the economy on the basis of requisitioning rather than efficiency. This has led it to release enterprises from the duty to balance their accounts, thereby eliminating a simple, accurate criterion which could otherwise have guided it in its choice of technology. As things stand, then, the System is incapable of coping with the economic risk inherent in all innovation; accordingly, whenever an innovation is adopted, the risk is borne by the economy as a whole. Let us assume, for example, that an industry has introduced new technology and that the necessary investment has been made, but that the effects upon production are disappointing. The enterprise concerned will cover the costs of production without suffering any further adverse effects, other than perhaps the dismissal of its director. Macroeconomically, on the other hand, the invested resources will have been inefficiently used, i.e. wasted—but there will be no evidence of this in the accounts.[16]

In other words, there is no mechanism to guide the System in the process of trial and error that necessarily precedes the selection of the most efficient technology from among the possibilities thrown up by scientific research. The absence of such a mechanism means that, even if scientific push comes up with an abundance of new technical solutions, the System will be incapable of determining which of those solutions will reduce its production costs. Consequently, whenever the System (whether of its own accord or, for instance, because of the arms race) opts for product innovation, it cannot compare costs for want of a mechanism with which to assess economic efficiency.[17]

What makes this especially serious is a particular feature that distinguishes the military sector from the rest of the economy, namely, the fact that the ultimate recipient of the goods—the military hierarchy—is in a position to insist that producers satisfy its requirements in all respects. In this way, *the military sector can determine the quality of the equipment supplied to it, but the System completely loses control over the resources swallowed up by military production.* Let us take a closer look at what this implies.

## External valuation

The accounting method[18] used by the System is the only way it has of assessing the value of what is produced. However, agents in other countries disregard valuations made on the basis of this accounting method and subject the goods produced by CPEs to their own valuations, in the form of prices in foreign currency. Within the System, the same is true of the people, who make their own valuations of the products available, either by readjusting the real dimension of the microeconomic terms of trade, or—if that is not enough—by means of social unrest. As regards valuations, the military sector is in a similar position; however, the difference is that in this case the System authorizes the military sector to make its own valuations in order to maximize the System's chances of military survival.

The military sector assesses the supplies it receives not in terms of their cost (which is irrelevant), but in terms of their intrinsic ability to help the System keep up in the arms race. Goods may therefore be rejected if they fail to meet the prescribed quality standards. Nevertheless, the power of the military sector over arms manufacturers is not as great as the power of customers over companies in market economies, since such companies will eventually go bankrupt if customers decide not to buy their goods. In the absence of such an automatic mechanism, the System has no hesitation in punishing or rewarding particular managers or employees in order to make them supply the military sector with goods that will ensure the System's military survival. Furthermore, in order to remove any obstacles that might prevent arms manufacturers from fulfilling what is ultimately no more than a moral duty to meet the requirements of the military sector, the System puts its requisitioning powers almost entirely at their disposal. Thus the armament sector works under artificial conditions of abundance that the System creates around it by quite simply seizing the necessary factors of production and intermediate goods from other sectors of the economy.

Accordingly, the military sector is a bottomless pit into which resources vanish almost literally without trace, since there is no way of measuring their value. The accounting method used by the System is incapable of quantifying the value of the resources swallowed up in this way, since the supplies are highly varied, come from innumerable different sources, and tend to be in kind. Outside observers are naturally in even less of a position to judge, which is why Western estimates of the proportion of economic resources devoted by Eastern European countries to military expenditure vary considerably.[19]

Nevertheless, despite the System's efforts, its ability to make the tissue produce weapons of higher quality than the rest of what is produced by the economy remains limited. Even the most extensive powers cannot increase the range of technological opportunities or guarantee that scientific push will achieve a level of productivity that will enable the CPEs to turn their military effort into one based on quality rather than quantity.

Thus the System, given the current state of the arms race and its own peculiar characteristics, is faced with the following alternatives:

1. it can risk devoting a large part of the available resources to product innovation, the results of which are by definition unpredictable; or
2. it can follow the technological path already marked out by the West, improving its own products where it can, and using quantity to make up for any inferiority in terms of quality.

The System is well aware of its own intrinsic shortcomings and has traditionally opted for the second alternative. It therefore puts enormous effort and considerable resources into acquiring technical documentation and other information on the technological and scientific research carried out by the other side. Such informational input is essential for improving not only the quality of Soviet armaments, but also—and this is often forgotten—the allocation of economic resources.

Imitation is one of the classic features of the System, and is particularly evident in the economic field,[20] of which armaments are only the most visible element. Popovski quotes the director of a Soviet institute of industrial economics as saying that if the USSR were somehow to succeed in catching up with the United States, it would then have to wait for the United States to draw ahead again, since it would have no idea which way to go next.[21]

To sum up, having allowed the armed forces to value goods in terms of their usefulness, the System is forced to satisfy military demand without, however, being able to control or determine in advance the quantity of resources that will be absorbed. In view of this, as well as the fact that its requisitioning powers are limited by consumption requirements, the System understandably prefers to satisfy military demand by refining products already developed by other countries rather than by risking innovation, which would mean taking unforeseeable economic risks. Hence the System has a natural tendency to seek to perfect its armaments by means of imitation rather than by innovation in the true sense of the term.[22] However, it should be stressed that this is a general tendency rather than a hard-and-fast rule—for there are exceptions, particularly in the field of space research (see also Table 8).

TABLE 8. *The state of high technology in the United States and the USSR*

| | United States ahead | Parity | USSR ahead |
|---|---|---|---|
| Aerodynamics | | X | |
| Computers and software | ←X | | |
| Conventional warheads | | X | |
| Electro-optical sensors | X→ | | |
| Guidance and navigation | X→ | | |
| Lasers | | X | |
| Life sciences | X | | |
| Materials | X | | |
| Microelectronic manufacturing | X→ | | |
| Nuclear warheads | | X | |
| Optics | X→ | | |
| Power sources | | X | |
| Production/manufacturing | X | | |
| Propulsion | X | | |
| Radar | X→ | | |
| Robotics and machine intelligence | X | | |
| Signal processing | X | | |
| Signature reduction (stealth) | X | | |
| Submarine detection | X | | |
| Telecommunications | X | | |

*Note:* The arrows indicate trends.

*Source:* US Congress, House of Representatives, Committee on Armed Services, Hearings on H.R. 5167, Department of Defense Authorization of Appropriations for Fiscal Year 1985, Part 4, Research, Development, Test, and Evaluation: Title II (US Government Printing Office, Washington DC, 1984), p. 63.

## Ensuring quality: The 'dual economy' or 'quality through imports'?

Given its reluctance to innovate, then, the System's answer to the military constraint is to increase the quantity of what it already has. But how can it prevent insidious inflation and unilateral adjustment of individual terms of trade from interfering with military production?[23]

Two hypotheses are often used to 'prove' that military supplies will always be of perfect quality. According to the first hypothesis, the socialized sector is subdivided into two subsectors, one civilian and one military. The military subsector operates according to completely different rules, similar to those that govern market economies, and military production is therefore automatically shielded from the negative influences mentioned above. CPEs are thus really dual economies. According to the second hypothesis, imported production facilities and intermediate goods play an essential part in ensuring that military supplies are of infinitely higher quality than the rest of what is produced domestically. However, neither hypothesis stands up to closer analysis.

The 'dual-economy' hypothesis immediately raises questions regarding the functioning of the military subsector. The System is based on social ownership of the means of production and requisitioning, so how can there possibly be room for a miniature market economy in its midst? Any arrangement based on market forces would be totally unworkable, if only because military production takes place under conditions of artificial abundance in which costs play no part. The System need only offer employees in that sector sufficiently attractive terms of trade and subject them to military discipline to ensure that they will work satisfactorily and refrain from adjusting their terms of trade unilaterally.

However, neither artificial abundance nor improvements in individual terms of trade can protect military production from insidious inflation. Even if the military sector operates differently from the rest of the economy, it has to use intermediate products that the rest of the economy has made. This means that even the armaments sector is infected by the endemic shoddiness that prevails in all CPEs. The only way round this would be to create a parallel economy purely for military needs. Although there are those who allege that this actually happened during the Stalin era, such is the complexity of today's economies and so limited is the volume of available resources that this hypothesis can now be rejected.[24]

The 'quality through imports' hypothesis also needs to be

qualified. While there is no doubt that—like all military supplies—imports for the military sector have priority, there is
equally no doubt that only some of the inputs and production
capacity used by the military sector are imported. This is partly
because the West places limits on what can be supplied, but also
because the Eastern European countries only have limited
amounts of foreign currency.

In other words, neither importation nor a so-called 'military
subsector' are enough to ensure weapons of perfect quality.
Certainly, the combined effect of the relatively high rate of imports
and the special treatment of certain industries does raise the
quality of military supplies well above that of normal production;
but this does not essentially alter the dilemma facing the System as
it tries to find an economic strategy that will enable it to sustain its
military effort.

Military survival and the need for greater international
influence are among the System's main concerns, and in theory
there is nothing to stop it putting all its economic resources into
strengthening its military power. In practice, however, it is
prevented from doing so by a number of economic constraints.
The System's room for manœuvre in this area is limited, for it can
only keep on requisitioning so long as the people are relatively
satisfied; if, on the other hand, social discontent reaches such a
level that the survival of the System is at risk, requisitioning must
be cut back until things settle down again. Since the social
constraint and the military constraint are economically interdependent, the System must constantly make concessions in order
to keep either of them from getting out of control—which, given
the limited capabilities of the economy, is no easy task. So long as
the System can requisition enough goods and services of sufficient
quality to maintain an internationally credible level of military
power and still avoid social discontent, there is no problem. But as
soon as the opportunity cost of using resources to ward off one
immediate threat is an increased threat from another quarter, the
System is in serious trouble.

It is hard to say where the System currently stands with regard
to the above dilemma, since there are no means of telling how
serious are the current threats to the System. However, the
System's eagerness to gain a respite in the arms race suggests that

it is starting to run out of the economic resources it needs to damp down social discontent. Certain Kremlinologists have detected friction between military and civilian pressure groups within the System,[25] which could well be a sign that shortage of resources has started to get out of hand. Suppose the economy no longer produces enough to insulate the System against both the social and the military threats to its survival. If so, the System is faced with the eminently economic problem of how to use limited resources as efficiently as possible, and the Creed's assertion that class consciousness will automatically allocate resources in the best interests of the System—without any need for objectivizable economic criteria—may be starting to ring rather hollow. Could shortages be forcing the System to adopt efficiency as a basis for its economic policy? Indeed, does it have any choice in the matter?

The following chapter examines the dilemma that faces the System when resources run short: either it must accumulate foreign debt, or else it must rely on economic growth. As we shall see, neither alternative is without its dangers.

## Notes

1. There is plenty of literature on this subject, and new analyses are constantly appearing. Of these, A. Ulam's remarkable book entitled *Expansion and Coexistence: The History of Soviet Foreign Policy 1917–1973*, 2nd edn. Praeger, New York and Washington, 1974, has stood the test of time. For an analysis of the current situation, see Hélène Carrère d'Encausse, *Ni paix ni guerre*, Flammarion, Paris, 1986.

2. See A. Ulam, 'Forty Years of Troubled Coexistence', *Foreign Affairs*, 64. 1 (Autumn 1985).

3. For a 'game theory' interpretation of the arms race, see the *Economist*, 9 Nov. 1985, pp. 89–94.

4. Highly detailed reports on the armed forces and weaponry maintained by the major powers are published annually by the Stockholm International Peace Research Institute (SIPRI) and the London-based International Institute for Strategic Studies (IISS). Also worth mentioning is the US Government publication *World Military Expenditure and Arms Transfers, 1985*, US Arms Control and Disarmament Agency, Government Printing Office, Washington DC, 1985.

5. The problem of estimating Soviet military expenditure has been a matter of considerable interest to Western experts, who all have their own ideas on the subject, each based on a different viewpoint and therefore different methods. To begin with there is the CIA (*Soviet Defense Spending*, Feb. 1985), which attempts to discover what the Soviet army would cost if the United States had to pay for it. Then there are studies such as those by S. Rosenfielde

(*False Science: Underestimating the Soviet Arms Build-up*, Transaction Books, New Brunswick, NJ and London, 1983, and 'The Underestimation of Soviet Weapons Prices: Learning Curve Bias', *Osteuropa Wirtschaft* (1986), No. 1, pp. 54–64), who attempts to assess the 'true value' of the Soviet arms effort in roubles. Mention should also be made of the approach adopted by G. Duchêne ('Place de l'effort de défense dans les comptes nationaux de l'URSS', W. Andreff and M. Lavigne, eds., *La Réalité socialiste: Crise, adaptation, progrès*, Economica, Paris, 1985), who attempts, using macro-economic statistics, to determine the economic impact of the arms race on the entire Soviet economy. Finally, see C. G. Jacobsen, ed., *The Soviet Defence Enigma*, Oxford University Press, 1987.

6. See *World Armaments and Disarmament: SIPRI Yearbook 1985*, London, 1985, and *The Military Balance, 1985–1986*, IISS, London, 1985.
7. See Ch. 4.
8. See A. S. Becker, *Guns, Butter and Tools: Tradeoffs in the Soviet Resource Allocation*, The Rand Corporation, Santa Monica, Calif., Oct. 1982 (P-6816).
9. Bureau of Census, *Statistical Abstract of the United States 1984*, Washington, DC, 1983, pp. 343 f.
10. According to Pentagon estimates (see the 6th edition of *Soviet Military Power*), half of all Soviet spending on research and development goes to the military sector; see 'Build-up of Soviet Arms "beyond Legitimate Needs" ', *Financial Times*, 3 Mar. 1987.
11. See 'Un document secret soviétique: Les Bons Comptes de l'espionnage scientifique et technique' (Top-secret papers reveal how Soviet spies obtain science and technology on the cheap), a two-part feature in *Le Monde*, 30 Mar. and 2 Apr. 1985.
12. See D. Buchan, *Western Security and Economic Strategy towards the East*, IISS, London, 1985; see also T. E. Gustafson, *Selling the Russians the Rope? Soviet Technology and US Export Controls*, Rand Corporation, Santa Monica, Calif., Oct. 1981 (R-2649-ARPA).
13. See F. Caron, *Le Résistible Déclin des sociétés industrielles*, Perrin, Paris, 1985.
14. Ibid., pp. 124 f.
15. For an analysis of the role of science under the System, see M. Popovski, *La Science manipulée*, Mazarine, Paris, 1979.
16. See S. Gomulka, 'L'Incompatibilité entre le socialisme et l'innovation rapide', *Revue d'études comparatives Est–Ouest* (1984), No. 3, pp. 91–104; other writings on the subject by the same author can be found in *Growth, Innovation and Reform in Eastern Europe*, Wheatsheaf, Brighton, 1986.
17. The writings on this subject by R. Amman and J. Cooper are based on extremely solid technical and technological documentation; see *Innovation in Soviet Industry*, Yale University Press, New Haven, Conn., 1983. The political aspects and the causes of this problem have been discussed by a number of authors, such as A. Kozminski and K. Oboj, 'Collaboration de la recherche scientifique et de l'industrie à l'innovation technique', *Revue d'études comparatives Est–Ouest* (1984), No. 2, pp. 87–97.

18. See Ch. 4.
19. According to NATO estimates, the military sector absorbs 13–16% of Soviet gross domestic product: 40% of machine tool production, 35% of metallurgical production, 20% of fuel production, and more than 4% of the workforce; see 'L'Armée rouge plus gourmande qu'on ne le dit' (Red Army greedier than previously thought), *Le Figaro*, 16 Jan. 1987. See also US Congress, Joint Economic Committee, *East European Economies: Slow Growth in the 1980s*, compendium of papers, Government Printing Office, Washington, DC, 1985, 1. 447–97.
20. See L. Pasinetti, *Structural Change and Economic Growth*, Cambridge University Press, Cambridge and London, 1981.
21. M. Popovski, *La Science manipulée*, pp. 90–1.
22. In a fascinating study ('Le Lend-lease américain pour l'Union soviétique', *Revue d'études comparatives Est–Ouest* (1984), No. 3, pp. 21–90), H. Dunajewski shows the extent to which imitation has determined the subsequent development of the Soviet industrial base, including the armament sector.
23. See Chs. 5 and 6.
24. For a detailed discussion of the dual-economy hypothesis from a historical point of view, see S. Bialer, *The Soviet Paradox: External Expansion, Internal Decline*, A. Knopf, New York, 1986, pp. 286 ff.
25. See D. Herspring, 'Soviet Military Politics', *Problems of Communism*, Mar.–Apr. 1986, pp. 93–7, in which the author analyses six recent works on this subject.

# 8

# The Dilemma of Growth: Intensive Growth versus Growth on Credit

The social dilemma and the military dilemma both have the same systemic and economic roots, namely, the System's apparent inability to allocate resources—which by definition are finite—among a number of goals that are mutually exclusive but equally important to the System's survival. In the short term, neither the systemic nor the economic situation can be altered in such a way as to reduce the various threats to the System. But what about the medium and long term?

Systemic alternatives have already been discussed in Part II of this book. We have seen that any economic reform capable of increasing the efficiency of the CPEs must eventually undermine the System, and it seems unlikely that the Communist parties would willingly permit the destruction of an instrument which has served them so well, and without which they cannot possibly maintain their grip on Eastern Europe.

Thus the only solution the System can afford to consider in order to improve its chances of survival is a purely economic one: increased production. The only way it can achieve this is through growth, which as things stand must either be intensive or else be achieved by running up a foreign debt. In this chapter we will be looking at both alternatives, which are the only choices the System has.

First of all, we will examine the System's objectives with regard to economic growth and how it can set about trying to achieve it. Next, we will discuss the System's efforts to obtain the necessary resources through international trade. We will see that only the accumulation of foreign debt will enable the System to obtain the resources it needs in the short term without putting its own survival directly in jeopardy.

The first section of this chapter will examine to what extent the System is actually capable of achieving growth, while the second will discuss the System's attempts to carry on international trade on the basis of 'autarkic logic'. Finally, the third section will show that since international trade is based on 'comparative logic', CPEs are not capable of carrying on such trade in any meaningful sense, and that the only option they have left is to accumulate foreign debt—which is a threat to their future.

## OPPORTUNITIES FOR GROWTH

### Methods of growth

Ever since the late 1950s, there has been a tendency for growth rates in Eastern Europe to fall steadily, despite the System's extremely ambitious growth targets (which are indicative of the strong pressure on the productive sector to fulfil the System's requirements). This suggests that growth rates may never be sufficient to achieve the System's targets or sustain requisitioning. The question of what factors the System can mobilize in order to achieve growth is thus of crucial importance. Accordingly, we need to identify which of the possible methods of growth is compatible with the physical and systemic conditions currently prevailing in the CPE countries.

In discussing market economies, neo-classical economic theory essentially uses the term 'growth' to mean an increase in production, which in market economies can only come from an increase in the volume of factors of production. This means that technological progress is treated as an exogenous variable. The function of production thus remains unchanged, only the volume of factors increases. In CPEs, on the other hand, the range of alternative methods of growth is in theory wider, since it includes not only growth in the sense in which the term is used in economic theory (referred to in CPEs as *extensive* growth), but also what is known as *intensive* growth.[1]

Intensive growth is the result of more efficient technical and/or organizational management of the economy; it thus entails a change in the function of production, and leads to increased production without any increase in the volume of factors used. With reference to market economies, economic theory disregards this type of growth, for it simply takes it for granted that any potential for such growth will be exploited as a matter of course. Any producer wishing to survive in a competitive environment will indeed automatically choose the most efficient of the available technical alternatives; in other words, in market economies the profit motive leads to technological and/or organizational efficiency. In market economies, microeconomic agents are chiefly concerned with choosing the most efficient methods of production and/or organization; it is here that the much-vaunted spirit of enterprise comes into its own.

By depriving enterprises of their function as economic agents and abolishing competition, the System has shifted the problem of choosing efficient methods from the microeconomic to the macro-economic sphere. Accordingly, it is the System's job to make the tissue adopt a method of growth that will make the best use of both the available factors of production and existing technical and organizational knowledge.

We therefore need to see whether any factors of production are currently lying idle, for this would enable the CPEs to choose between extensive and intensive growth.

Westerners, used as they are to chronic unemployment, are apt to be mystified by the employment situation in the CPEs—for, instead of there being a surplus of labour (i.e. surplus demand for jobs), there is always *surplus demand for labour*. Statistics published by the United Nations Economic Commission for Europe[2] show that the employment rate in Eastern European countries is some 8–10 per cent higher than in Western European countries; in the case of women the difference is as much as 20 per cent. Such differences existed even before the crisis in the 1970s, that is, at a time when the market economies were enjoying full employment. Currently, with Western unemployment running at approximately 10 per cent of the active population (as opposed to zero unemployment in Eastern Europe), the figures are about 17 per cent for men and 30 per cent for women. This means that the CPEs only have minimal reserves of man-hours, which are certainly not enough to sustain extensive growth for any length of time. In other words, if the CPEs are ever to achieve lasting growth again, it will have to be intensive.

The term 'intensive growth' is somewhat ambiguous, since it specifies the technical source of the increase in the value of the national product, but fails to specify its content. The same increase in national income may thus be due either to an increase in the quantity produced—quality remaining constant—or to an increase in quality coupled with a smaller increase in quantity. This distinction is ignored by economic theory, in which price is the only means of measuring the value of domestic production, it being implicitly assumed that any increase in quality will automatically cause the price of the good concerned to rise. Yet this distinction between quantitative and qualitative methods of growth is essential if opportunities for growth in CPEs are to be analysed properly.

Our analysis of the social and military constraints on the System has demonstrated that their impact depends to a large extent on the physical composition of domestic production. The better the quality of consumer goods, the greater the System's chances of keeping the people satisfied with the same volume of goods. The same is true of requisition: the better the quality of arms produced, the fewer will be needed to achieve military parity. Hence, in order to survive, *the System needs not only to induce the tissue to achieve intensive growth, but also to make sure that such growth is essentially qualitative.*

How can the System do both at once?

## Mobilizing labour[3]

The fact that there is still surplus demand for labour in the Eastern European countries, despite the exhaustion of labour reserves, can be explained by the method of growth traditionally adopted there.[4] So long as growth could be maintained by an increase in the rate of employment, surplus demand for labour was not a major macroeconomic problem and for a long time was simply seen as a necessary evil associated with extensive growth. So long as the CPEs could count on large labour reserves (rural overpopulation and women), the very real side effects of surplus demand for labour went unnoticed. However, labour reserves were finally exhausted in the early 1970s, and the situation changed dramatically. Since then the System has given high priority to combating the side effects of surplus demand for labour, which have become all too evident and are now rightly seen as the main obstacle to intensive growth.[5]

The literature on CPE labour markets identifies the following phenomena as the main symptoms of dysfunction (these phenomena are in practice interlinked, but will be discussed separately for the purposes of analysis):[6]

1. *hoarding of labour* by enterprises, i.e. the tendency of production units in CPEs to be seriously overmanned. Such behaviour can be explained at the microeconomic level by the concern of enterprises to avoid the ill-effects of the prevailing labour shortage. Repeated throughout the economy, such behaviour further increases the pressure of macroeconomic demand for labour;

2. *wage drift*, which leads to expansion in total wages and raises the problem of how to provide sufficient consumer goods to match such expansion (see Chapter 6 on the social dilemma);

3. *public resentment* of the fact that differences in qualifications are not reflected in wage differentials;

4. *poor labour discipline* (high labour turnover, absenteeism, alcoholism), chiefly because the labour shortage leads to labour being remunerated on the basis of scarcity rather than productivity (which cannot be measured).

Such dysfunction precludes efficient use of labour, which is essential if extensive growth is to be exchanged for intensive growth. The present problems, which are a legacy of earlier voluntarist growth, prevent the labour market from functioning efficiently and the chances of intensive growth are thus nipped in the bud. The System is caught in a vicious circle of its own making.

In the previous chapter we saw how the System prevents CPEs from curing their ills through innovation. The same is true of the potential contribution of technological progress to intensive growth. Given that requisitioning is limited by consumption requirements, the volume of resources available in Eastern Europe for the purpose of increasing investment (essential if growth is to accelerate under present conditions) without at the same time aggravating the various constraints on the System is currently very small. In order to avoid becoming repetitive, we will limit this analysis to policies that are used to mobilize labour.

The economic impact of work carried out within an economy depends upon two factors, namely, the quantity of labour involved (the volume of labour) and its average productivity. Policies designed to mobilize labour can therefore also be divided into two categories, according to which of these two factors they affect.

The following are examples of measures designed to increase the volume of labour:

1. increasing the length of the working week or working year;
2. deferring the age of retirement;[7]
3. measures whereby people's leisure time is used for productive purposes (legislation to combat 'parasitism', forced labour, reduction of frictional unemployment).

Productivity, on the other hand, depends on two different but essentially related factors: the worker's zeal, and the material conditions in which he works. It is hard to draw a clear line between these two factors.[8] Zeal depends upon the worker's willingness to work; however, with the best will in the world, productivity cannot be increased if the necessary means (production equipment, organization, management, inputs, transport, basic infrastructure) are lacking. Thus productivity depends not only on zeal, but also on the right material conditions.

Policies designed to increase productivity by encouraging zeal can be divided into policies based on condign power, compensatory power, and conditioned power:

1. those based on *condign power* range from measures to combat absenteeism and alcoholism to dismissal or even imprisonment;
2. those based on *compensatory power* involve wages being linked to actual production;
3. those based on *conditioned power* include the glorification of work on behalf of society, and appeals to personal honour

(decorations, commendations, individual publicity) or to national pride, international solidarity, etc.

In the chapters dealing with the System's internal dilemmas we saw how the range of policies designed to stimulate productivity by improving working conditions was limited by features inherent in the System. Basically, the System has a choice between four types of employment policy, all of which—at least in theory—are capable of inducing intensive, qualitative growth:

1. policies that increase the available amount of labour;
2. policies that use penalties to encourage productivity;
3. policies that use rewards to encourage productivity; and
4. policies that use persuasion to encourage productivity.

We will now examine the systemic and economic feasibility of each of these policies.

## Growth-inducing policies and their limitations

The foregoing discussion suggests that employment policies need to be assessed according to both economic and systemic criteria. The economic criteria concern the System's need to achieve lasting growth that is both intensive and qualitative in nature, while the systemic criteria are used to examine whether such policies interfere with the functioning of the System, which they can do in any of the following ways:

1. they can upset financial equilibrium in the consumer sphere (see the chapters devoted to the money dilemma and the social dilemma);
2. they can alter individual terms of trade (see the same chapters); or
3. they can affect the labour market by reducing or, alternatively, aggravating the chronic problem of excess demand.

Table 9 classifies the various policies according to their economic and systemic feasibility. We can see from the table that only Type 3 and Type 4 policies do not interfere with the functioning of the System and are likely to induce the kind of economic growth that the System needs in order to cope with the social and military constraints. Type 1 and Type 2 are merely makeshift solutions.

TABLE 9. *Feasibility of types of growth-inducing policy*

| Criteria | Policies | | | |
|---|---|---|---|---|
| | Type 1 Increasing the amount of labour | Type 2 Encouraging zeal by penalties | Type 3 Encouraging zeal by rewards | Type 4 Encouraging zeal by persuasion |
| Content of growth | quantitative | quantitative | qualitative | qualitative |
| Duration of growth | short-term | short-term | long-term | long-term |
| Method of growth | extensive | extensive | intensive | intensive |
| Effect on wage pyramid | nil | nil | considerable | nil |
| Effect on financial equilibrium | nil | nil | considerable | nil |
| Effect on individual terms of trade | considerable | considerable | considerable | nil |
| Effect on labour market | congestion | nil | decongestion | nil |

There is no doubt that the optimal type of policy is Type 4, which is based on persuasion. Not only does it lead to qualitative growth without any need for additional manpower, but it has the further benefit of not interfering with the normal functioning of the System, since it does not affect either equilibrium in the consumer sphere, or the microeconomic terms of trade, or the labour market. However, it does have one major drawback as far as the System is concerned, which is that it does not depend for its implementation on the System, but on the people's willingness to let themselves be persuaded by propaganda. If neither propaganda nor education succeed in persuading the people, Type 4 policies are bound to fail, optimal or not.

As regards economic efficiency, Type 3 policies are comparable to Type 4, but their implementation, which does depend on the System, may well cause the System serious, irreversible damage. The economic efficiency of such policies depends upon the System's adaptability, which—as we saw in the chapters dealing with the System's internal dilemmas—is limited. Let us take a look at the main limitations.

In order for Type 3 policies to have any chance of success, the System must satisfy the following four basic conditions:

1. The productivity indicator used to determine wages must be based on productive effort alone. This is the necessary and sufficient condition for ensuring that productivity and wages keep in step.

In market economies, productivity (and therefore effort) is measured by the value of what is produced. In CPEs, where prices have a different function, measurements of productivity based solely on value are likely to be misleading. It is standard practice for enterprises to improve their productivity indicators simply by manipulating prices and/or costs, something which is perfectly possible under the accounting method. Such increases in productivity do not reflect any real increase in effort, and do not, therefore, justify an increase in wages. In order for wages to be based on actual rather than apparent effort, the System must change its accounting method.[9]

2. The additional effort the worker must make in order to increase productivity must be in keeping with both the resulting increase in productivity and the resulting increase in wages.

As mentioned above, labour productivity depends both on the worker's zeal and on the material conditions in which he works. If the necessary material conditions for increased productivity are not satisfied, all the zeal in the world—even well-paid zeal—will not help. Unfortunately, Type 3 policies have no direct effect upon material conditions.[10]

Moreover, from the point of view of the domestic economy, economic agents are so interdependent that there is no way of measuring each agent's exact contribution to increased productivity. Very often, circumstances external to the agent determine what proportion of his effort can actually be translated into increased productivity. The same phenomenon occurs within enterprises, in which individual wages are based upon overall productivity. The larger the number of workers employed by the production unit where wages are determined, the smaller the reward the individual worker receives for a marginal increase in production. Hence individual motivation can be stifled if the workforce is too large.

3. In addition, the desire for a higher nominal wage must be sufficient to increase the worker's zeal, which brings us back to the

problem of the relationship between the nominal and real dimensions of the microeconomic terms of trade.

Even if the System can adapt and succeed in meeting the first two conditions, it may well fail to meet the third, since it can never be certain that the lure of a higher nominal wage will be sufficient to increase productivity. The greater the discrepancy between the nominal and real dimensions of the individual terms of trade, the less attractive a higher nominal wage will be. How great the discrepancy is will depend not upon the prices of consumer goods, but upon their availability.

If, for example, consumer durables are in chronically short supply, an increase in nominal wages will be less motivating than if such goods are readily available. If the supply of goods fails to satisfy demand, the stability of the consumer sphere is threatened and motivation collapses. Since the volume of wages is no longer determined by the planner but by apparent productivity, the likelihood of Type 3 policies leading to such disequilibrium is considerable. The only way the System can prevent this is by creating an automatic link between the consumer and the available range of goods—in other words, by allowing consumer sovereignty to develop.[11]

4. Finally, before attempting to encourage productivity by increasing wages, the System must be certain that individuals will not use existing mechanisms to improve their situation other than by increasing physical productivity.

If Type 3 policies lead to a deterioration rather than an improvement in individual terms of trade (for example, if consumer goods are in short supply), the individual will take steps to recover what he believes is his rightful share by adjusting the real terms of trade, over which he has virtually complete control. The possibilities are endless: corruption, theft, speculation, fraud, doing private work during official working hours, etc. If such behaviour becomes typical, the entire tissue will be corrupted and the System's economic policies will be sabotaged at every turn—in short, the System will lose control of the economy.

As the above analysis shows, none of the alternatives available to the System is at all promising. The problem is the System's refusal to question its own basic principles. If it is to achieve the economic performance it seeks, the System has no choice but to dismantle its own survival mechanism;[12] yet this would strike at the very roots of the System and immediately threaten its existence. In other words, the System's attempts to achieve intensive, qualitative growth are a much more immediate threat to its survival than its efforts to cope with its social and international environment.

Let us now see whether there is any other way for the System to obtain the resources it so badly needs in order to handle the social and military constraints.

## THE TEMPTATIONS OF TRADE

### *Comparative logic versus autarkic logic*[13]

The economic organization of the System is particularly suited to *autarky* (economic self-sufficiency) since, at least in theory, the System is not subject to disruption from outside sources. However, should the System urgently need an injection of resources from abroad, autarky ceases to be an asset and instead becomes a very serious liability.

Whenever, in order to sustain its military effort or reduce social unrest, the System has to import high technology or food from the market economies, it does so not on the basis of their market value, but simply on the basis of their ability to satisfy its immediate needs. Such behaviour cannot be accounted for by traditional economic theory; it is the result of *autarkic logic* based on meta-economic considerations.

Autarkic logic has no place in economic theory, which acknowledges only one kind of rational basis for international trade, namely *comparative logic*. External trade is then seen as a means of minimizing costs rather than as a means of obtaining essential goods. Thus comparative logic does not consider what needs are directly satisfied by the imported good, but merely the resulting 'gains', or saving of resources. According to this classic theory, international trade brings the following advantages:

1. the range of importable goods is extended to include all goods whose international price is less than the cost of producing them domestically;
2. comparative trade increases the chances of economic growth by producing a net transfer of resources, and would thus enable the System to increase the volume of resources available for consumption and/or requisitioning.
3. the composition of trade flows can be determined simply by comparing costs and prices. Comparative logic would thus enable the System to satisfy—at a price—its pressing need for goods that the domestic economy either fails to produce in sufficient quantity or fails to produce at all.

However, comparative logic can only work properly if a certain number of systemic conditions—usually taken for granted in the pure theory of international trade—are satisfied. In order to tell whether comparative trade can provide the System with the resources it so badly needs, we therefore need to see whether the System satisfies these systemic conditions. If it does not, we must then investigate the effects of a policy based on comparative logic in an economy that is systemically incapable of implementing such a policy properly.


## The conditions for comparative trade

According to traditional theories of international trade, trade flows between countries can be explained in terms of the relative costs at which the countries produce the goods concerned. Trade is carried on by arbitrageurs who take advantage of the difference between the trading partners' domestic prices.[14]

Models of international trade assume a single rationality behind the behaviour of all agents in all trading countries, namely, maximization of receipts, with the proviso that they must never be less than costs. The domestic agent is confronted directly with foreign prices and must take them into consideration in his accounting. In other words, the same rationality conducts the behaviour of all agents in market economies, irrespective of whether they engage in domestic or international trade.

In order to prevent this rationality from interfering with requisitioning, the System turns enterprises into pseudo-economic agents by releasing them from the duty to balance their accounts. It has thus replaced microeconomic rationality (the basis for traditional theories of trade) by macroeconomic rationality (which is the prerogative of the party). According to macroeconomic rationality, only the System is capable of distinguishing between what is essential and what is superfluous to its needs. The term 'socially essential' is used to refer to a specific physical good of which only the quantity imported matters, its monetary value being of secondary importance.

In the case of trade according to comparative logic, the situation is reversed, and monetary value has priority. In market economies, microeconomic agents respond only to market value. They use exchange rates to compare production costs, expressed in domestic currency, with international prices. This means that the pure theory of international trade is only applicable in an environment in which domestic currencies are fully convertible.

Furthermore, international trade will only fulfil the promises of comparative logic if there are no significant differences in structure between domestic markets. If there is a domestic seller's market and an international buyer's market, domestic customers will quite definitely prefer to buy on the international market—even if there is a difference in price—whereas domestic producers will prefer to sell everything they produce on the home market. However, according to pure theory, such a situation cannot last long, since the balance of trade of one of the trading partners will be in constant deficit; this will result in an automatic readjustment, either by a fall in the exchange rate of the domestic currency, or by a change in the structure of the domestic market to bring it nearer to that of the international market—producers must adapt to demand or die.

To sum up, in order for trade to be fully comparative and produce the results in terms of growth that are promised by theory, both trading partners' economies must satisfy the following conditions:

1. the choice of what to trade in must be left to microeconomic agents who can only survive if they balance their accounts;

2. agents must integrate signals from world markets into their accounts, with the help of exchange rates;

3. agents must be able to make decisions and take the risks inherent in decisions to specialize in a particular direction; and

4. any disequilibrium in the balance of trade must be corrected either by a change in the structure of the domestic market or by a shift in the exchange rate of the domestic currency.

These conditions are clear evidence of the considerable systemic differences between CPEs and the classic trading partners of pure theory. This suggests that CPEs are bound to run into trouble if they attempt to reap the benefits of comparative trading without first making the necessary systemic changes. As we have seen in earlier chapters, the System does not permit independent economic agents to operate, only pseudo-economic agents; the functions of the domestic currency are different in international and domestic transactions; and, finally, the System has no natural inclination to take the requirements of international specialization into consideration when deciding how to use what it has requisitioned.

In the following section we will look at the systemic considerations that make the System base its foreign trade on autarkic rather than comparative logic. If the domestic economy cannot provide the necessary exports at a time when internal needs are increasing, the System obtains the resources it needs for short-term survival by accumulating foreign debt—thereby jeopardizing its long-term survival instead.

## THE WORKINGS OF AUTARKIC LOGIC

The reason why the System does not allow enterprises to determine the composition of trade is that it does not want its macroeconomic rationality to be verified by microeconomic rationality. Since, according to the Creed, only the System is capable of perceiving what is socially essential, the System claims the exclusive right to determine the physical composition of import flows, and insists on approving virtually all imports in advance.

In CPEs, the composition of all international trade carried on by enterprises is monitored by the System; though the exact procedures vary, it essentially does this by supervising all conversions of foreign currency into domestic currency. The System has a *monopoly on foreign currency transactions*, a legal arrangement which means that all foreign currency held by entities or individuals is the property of, and is administered by, the System. The System allocates foreign currency in accordance with its own needs; however, additional mechanisms (customs tariffs, taxation, conversion rates) are used to signal to enterprises when it will be in their microeconomic interest to request the System to finance import transactions.

The System's monopoly on foreign currency transactions allows it not only to regulate the use of foreign currency, but also to ensure a constant supply of it. All domestic exporters are required to surrender their foreign currency earnings to the bank, irrespective of the price in domestic currency paid in exchange. How can the System be sure that all foreign currency receipts are surrendered to the monobank? The answer is that it also has a *monopoly on external trade*, which means that enterprises may enter into trading relations with foreign partners only if authorized to do so by the System. This monopoly, coupled with the all-pervasive nature of the monobank, ensures that all export receipts are surrendered to the System. Even if an enterprise were to succeed in keeping part of its foreign currency receipts secret, it could not use them to import anything without the System finding out. There is thus little point in an enterprise holding foreign currency, since all such holdings are automatically sterilized by the System's monopoly on external trade.

## Inconvertibility

In addition to the monopolies just referred to, a major determining factor in trade between the System and the market economies is the inconvertibility of currencies.

If the conversion of a given currency ceases to be an exceptional, isolated transaction and instead becomes a normal, frequent one, the currency may be considered convertible.[15] Economic evidence of convertibility is provided by the existence of a specific market in which, following an infinite number of individual confrontations, buyers and sellers agree on a price for the currency (in other words, an exchange rate). If all agents outside the market come to accept the exchange rate as an established fact, the currency may be considered economically convertible; this means that each unit of the currency has a high likelihood of being converted on the market at a pre-established rate, regardless of whom the currency is held by or the purpose for which it is being used.

This economic definition of convertibility suggests that some domestic currencies will be more convertible than others, since the market for them is larger and more accessible and their exchange rate is less unpredictable. If we accept that economic convertibility is a continuum and that it diminishes in direct proportion to the number of actual conversions carried out, at what point exactly does a currency cease to be economically convertible? There are two possible indicators: one is the size of the market (in other words, the number of transactions carried out), and the other is the difference between the prices at which the currency is bought and sold (in other words, the transaction costs).

Convertibility can also be usefully defined in legal terms: if the conversion—or the attempted or proposed conversion—of a currency is not subject to legal penalties of any kind, then the currency may be considered convertible. The emphasis here is thus on the permissibility of the transaction, in contrast to the economic definition which stresses its feasibility.

On the basis of the above analysis, the following definition may be proposed: *the convertibility of a currency means the possibility of any unit of the currency—irrespective of its location and irrespective of the type of agent it is held by or destined for—actually being converted.* Here the word 'possibility' has a double meaning: firstly, the economic conditions for conversion must be satisfied, and secondly, there must be no legal obstacle to the transaction.

At this point, it will be clear that inconvertibility is directly related to the System's monopolies on foreign currency transactions and external trade. Eastern European currencies are inconvertible in both the legal and the economic senses of the term, since the two monopolies prevent the establishment of a foreign exchange market (if we disregard the black market, which is only accessible to individuals, not to enterprises).[16] As we saw in the

chapter devoted to the money dilemma, this enables microeconomic accounts to remain unaffected by foreign currency flows,
which makes trade flows even more subject to macroeconomic
rationality.

Is trade under such conditions likely to increase the volume of
resources available for requisitioning by the System? To answer
this question, we need to look at the mechanisms whereby the
balance of trade is kept in equilibrium.

## The balance of trade

Inconvertibility and the monopolies on foreign currency transactions and external trade are sufficiently powerful instruments to
have a profound effect upon trade between CPEs and market
economies. They enable the System to obey the dictates of
autarkic logic by importing whatever it considers essential; however, the economy must first generate the necessary foreign
currency to pay for such imports. In other words, autarkic logic
does not absolve the System from the duty to remain solvent.

Although autarkic logic makes it easier to import essential
goods, it seriously discourages enterprises from exporting. The
System's use of condign or compensatory power[17] to induce
enterprises to export only works in the case of homogeneous goods
for which there is a world price, i.e. raw materials or agricultural
produce. Thus autarkic logic can only ensure solvency in those
CPE countries that have sufficient quantities of such homogeneous
goods for export. The USSR is undoubtedly such a country, but
the remaining Eastern European countries are not (see Table 10).

As soon as solvency depends on exporting finished goods, the
limitations of condign power become apparent, since it cannot
guarantee either that the exports will be of sufficiently high quality
or that they will sell. Only the manufacturers are sufficiently
familiar with their particular technology and with international
demand to know how to adapt so that their goods will be bought
by customers in the market economies. Unfortunately, the nature
of the System and of autarkic logic is such that enterprises are not
encouraged to adapt to demand, whether domestic or international.

TABLE 10. *Estimated percentage of homogeneous goods in East-West trade, 1986*

|  | The six small countries of Eastern Europe | | Soviet Union | |
|---|---|---|---|---|
|  | Exports | Imports | Exports | Imports |
| 1. Raw materials | 23 | 17 | 16 | 20 |
| 2. Fuel | 19 | 4 | 66 | 1 |
| Manufactured goods including: | 56 | 76 | 13 | 76 |
| 3. semi-finished goods | 21 | 31 | 10 | 38 |
| 4. capital goods | 11 | 34 | 2 | 31 |
| 5. consumer goods | 24 | 12 | 1 | 7 |
| 6. Total share of homogeneous goods (1 + 2 + 3) | 63 | 52 | 92 | 59 |

*Source: Economic Survey of Europe 1986/1987*, Economic Commission for Europe, UN, New York, 1987.

If homogeneous exports are not sufficient to ensure a level of solvency commensurate with the import of essential goods, the System must rely on receipts from exports by the tissue. Since enterprises are unresponsive to financial considerations and since the domestic seller's market is far more attractive from their point of view than the international buyer's market, there is very little the System can do to make them export manufactured goods. Incentives such as subsidies, tax relief, and even favourable exchange rates for foreign currency earnings have all failed to induce enterprises to increase their exports, and thus to increase the volume of resources the System can import in return.

In fact, the only way the System can increase exports is to give export production top priority, in other words, to encourage it by paying wages that bear no relation to productivity and by giving export production precedence over other sectors of the economy as regards inputs. The effects of such a policy may be quite as devastating as the effects of ignoring costs in the armament sector.[18]

It is clear that trading on this basis cannot significantly increase the volume of available resources. Certain Eastern European countries have therefore succumbed to the temptations of comparative logic, with its prospects of greatly increased trade, gains from trade (a net transfer of resources into the economy), and—most important—solvency. Can such a 'free trade' policy give the System the resources it needs in order to reduce the social and military pressures that threaten its survival? Let us see.

## THE LURE OF COMPARATIVE LOGIC

### Growth on credit

Around 1970, comparative logic began to win converts in those CPE countries where the fall in growth rates and the increase in social discontent had reached crisis proportions. The lessening of the military pressures on the System in the wake of *détente* encouraged Poland and Hungary to break away from traditional autarkic policies.

Comparative logic seemed the answer to the System's prayers— an apparently effortless means of achieving quite unprecedented growth. The fact that there was a glut of capital on Western markets at negative real interest rates made comparative logic all the more attractive. All the CPEs had to do was borrow money to import the technology that the System had proved incapable of creating, and trust that the resulting upsurge in exports would be sufficient to pay back the debt. As the 1970s progressed, comparative trade became established as the quick way to growth and technological development, and comparative logic seemed to provide the answer to all the economic problems raised by the social and military constraints on the System. Not every Eastern European country was equally keen to venture along this path; the two pioneers, Poland and Hungary, were followed much more cautiously by Czechoslovakia, Bulgaria, and Romania. The USSR and the GDR, for their part, remained relatively untempted by comparative logic; in particular, the GDR—thanks to its special relationship with the Federal Republic of Germany—has always been able to view trade in a somewhat different light from its Eastern European neighbours.

The temptations of comparative logic have left the System in a paradoxical situation: while using its self-targeting ability to adopt a new approach to trade, it refuses to use its self-organizing ability to dismantle organizational arrangements based on the old approach. Thus Eastern European currencies are still not convertible, the System still has a monopoly on foreign currency transactions and external trade, and enterprises are still not required to balance their accounts. In the first flush of enthusiasm this inconsistent use of the System's self-targeting and self-organizing abilities has gone unnoticed, especially since the use of credit has simultaneously enabled the System to finance a huge inflow of investment goods. However, the change of approach does mean that, in addition to the social and military constraints with which it was already having trouble coping, the System has saddled itself with a new constraint—*the need to remain solvent.*

## Import suction and export aversion

The System's motto in adopting comparative logic was 'Import whatever is cheaper, and export whatever can be sold for more than it costs to produce.' All of a sudden, the System was relying on enterprises to determine the composition of trade by comparing costs and prices. At the same time, it was releasing more foreign currency for import purposes and issuing more import and export licences.

Formulae for the maximization of gains from trade[19] were drawn up to help enterprises make decisions regarding international trade; these formulae compared domestic prices or production costs with world prices by means of coefficients of conversion, in theory set so as to ensure that trade was macroeconomically as efficient as possible. However, in basing trade entirely upon such formulae, the System forgot that its own peculiar characteristics might prevent it from reaping the benefits of comparative logic, especially since it was still operating on unaltered economic principles.

The System's requisitioning powers rely on (*a*) the fact that its agents are not economic agents in the full sense of the term, (*b*) its ability to make money function in different ways and to create artificial abundance, and (*c*) its accounting method, which is based on a tautology. Under such circumstances, the effects of 'economic' calculus are bound to be rather surprising. To see what they are, let us look at what motivates enterprises to import and to export respectively.

*Imports.* The System's accounting method enables producers to either pass on increased costs to the customer or else obtain compensation in the form of grants. Thus, assuming that foreign currency is readily available, a producer will prefer to import (regardless of the price in foreign currency or the rate of conversion) whenever an input is unavailable on the domestic market, or simply if the quality of the foreign input is higher, or there is better after-sales service, or the supplier will keep to the agreed delivery dates. Even if the System uses its monopoly on foreign currency transactions to withhold the necessary foreign currency, the producer can still get hold of it by distorting the information it makes available to the System.

This tendency to import is enhanced by differences in structure between the world market and CPE domestic markets: the world market is a buyer's market, whereas in CPEs producers call the tune. Not surprisingly, therefore, producers will buy on the world market whenever they can, particularly since this opens the door to all kinds of personal privileges (trips abroad to visit suppliers, opportunities for bribery, etc.).

Accordingly, the adoption of comparative logic and the relaxation of foreign currency controls has resulted in import suction that the System is powerless to prevent.

*Exports.* Since the domestic market is a seller's market, producers have no trouble in selling what they produce. Prices are stable and there are practically no requirements regarding quality, after-sales service, or delivery dates. Under such circumstances, increasing production is bound to have a favourable effect on the firm's results, since demand is by definition insatiable. A producer who decides to export is faced with the problem of uncertain prices, must keep to agreed delivery dates, and may even be unable to sell his products at all if they fail to meet the buyer's quality standards. Since there are so many snags involved in exporting, producers will prefer to sell on the domestic market; despite the fact that exporting is likely to be more profitable, a seller's market is always preferable to a buyer's market. Hence comparative logic makes the tissue *highly averse to exports*. Such aversion is less apparent when the System is governed by autarkic logic, which relies more upon condign power and accepts whatever foreign currency earnings are generated by the export of homogeneous goods.

Obviously, the combined effect of import suction and export aversion is that the balance of trade, or even the balance of payments, will be constantly in deficit.

## Borrowing abroad and gains from trade

We have just seen that import suction and export aversion are both caused by features inherent in the System. The result has been serious and persistent disequilibrium in the balance of payments of the various Eastern European countries, which means that during the 1970s and 1980s there has been a *net transfer of resources from the market economies to the CPEs in the form of loans*. The CPEs have thus enjoyed temporary gains from trade, not so much because they have been converted to comparative logic as because their trading partners are prepared to lend them money (see Tables 11 and 12).

TABLE 11. *Eastern European debts in convertible currency* (year-end figures in millions of dollars)

|                | 1981 | 1982 | 1983 | 1984 | 1985 | 1986* |
|----------------|------|------|------|------|------|-------|
| Bulgaria       | 3.1  | 2.9  | 2.4  | 2.1  | 3.6  | 4.9   |
| Czechoslovakia | 4.4  | 3.8  | 3.5  | 3.1  | 3.4  | 4.5   |
| GDR†           | 15.2 | 12.8 | 12.1 | 11.2 | 13.4 | 14.5  |
| Hungary        | 8.7  | 7.9  | 8.2  | 8.8  | 11.7 | 15.0  |
| Poland         | 25.4 | 26.5 | 26.4 | 26.9 | 29.7 | 33.8  |
| Romania        | 10.1 | 9.7  | 8.9  | 8.0  | 6.6  | 5.9   |
| TOTAL          | 67.1 | 63.8 | 61.6 | 59.4 | 68.5 | 78.6  |
| USSR           | 25.4 | 25.7 | 22.9 | 22.1 | 27.7 | 36.0  |
| TOTAL          | 92.5 | 89.6 | 84.6 | 81.5 | 96.3 | 114.6 |

* Provisional figures.
† Convertible currency debts plus debts with Federal Republic of Germany.

Capital goods account for a large share of the imports achieved with the help of Western loans. However, it remains to be seen to what extent such loans have been used by the CPEs to become

TABLE 12. *Debt-service ratio\* in Eastern European countries*

|  | 1981 | 1982 | 1983 | 1984 | 1985 | 1986[†] |
|---|---|---|---|---|---|---|
| Bulgaria | 32 | 32 | 29 | 26 | 20 | 41 |
| Czechoslovakia | 20 | 19 | 21 | 18 | 17 | 20 |
| GDR[‡] | 89 | 70 | 50 | 43 | 41 | 45 |
| Hungary | 43 | 40 | 39 | 48 | 54 | 60 |
| Poland | 157 | 174 | 142 | 99 | 96 | 67 |
| Romania | 32 | 43 | 35 | 27 | 29 | 28 |
| All countries | 64 | 69 | 58 | 47 | 47 | 45 |
| USSR | 24 | 20 | 16 | 17 | 20 | 25 |
| All countries | 44 | 44 | 36 | 32 | 34 | 36 |

\* Sum total of medium-term and long-term interest and repayments (not including rescheduled debts) expressed as a percentage of one year's exports.
† Provisional figures.
‡ Not including debts with the Federal Republic of Germany.

*Source*: OECD, Financial Market Trends, No. 36, Paris, Feb. 1987.

more specialized and thus consolidate their comparative advantages in the long term.[20] At all events, such investment has certainly raised the technological standard of production, particularly in the more sensitive sectors—i.e. those supplying the armed forces[21]— and has therefore helped to *relieve the military burden*. At the same time, some of the imported capital goods have been used to produce consumer goods, which at least in the early 1970s went some way towards *reducing social pressure*. The import of capital goods has therefore greatly contributed to the physical survival of the System. However, this is a meta-economic effect and, as such, cannot be accounted for by comparative logic.

Borrowing abroad has thus given the System a much-needed shot in the arm, enabling it to increase temporarily both the volume and the quality of what it requisitions. However, borrowing has also introduced a new constraint—the need to remain solvent. Thus, far from alleviating the social and military constraints on the System, external trade may simply have given the System a new constraint to go with the two it already had. Indeed, borrowing abroad in an attempt to get rid of the constraints on the System may end up making the System's position in relation to its environment worse rather than better.

Our analysis of the various ways in which the System could achieve a lasting increase in the volume and quality of available goods shows that all of them put the survival of the System at risk. In short, the way in which the System is organized is incompatible with growth. The hoped-for benefits of international trade are cancelled out by the additional constraint of needing to remain solvent, and by the systemic inability of the CPEs to engage in comparative trade.

So what choices does the System have left? All it can do is keep juggling the three constraints, with the constant risk that it will run out of economic resources and be forced either to yield to environmental pressure or to make systemic concessions. Yet the philosophical principles on which it is based, and the organizational demands of the Creed, make it clear that such concessions can only go so far if the System is to be sure of surviving. The scope for systemic concessions (usually described as economic reforms) is thus restricted in advance, and so therefore are their chances of providing any lasting relief from constraints on resources. The effect of limited reforms designed to perfect the workings of the System is certainly not to be discounted,[22] but is clearly limited by the internal dilemmas discussed in Part II. These dilemmas make it clear that the essential workings of the System cannot be reformed without the System itself being damaged. Such reform cannot solve the economic problem at the root of the external dilemmas discussed in Part III, which is that the System is incapable of allocating scarce resources efficiently. This is because such reform does not essentially alter the workings and the philosophical basis of the System as described in Part I—it merely disguises them. This is the reason why this book, though devoted to the workings of the System (the factor that frustrates all attempts at reform), barely makes any direct reference to reform as such; indirectly, however, reform is the subject of the entire book.

Are economic reforms a way of bringing the Promised Society nearer, or are they merely evidence that the System is becoming increasingly bogged down in an apparently endless transitional period? Given the increasing pressure of environmental constraints on the System, one cannot help thinking that its main concern must now be sheer survival rather than the attainment of the Promised Society. Do the economic problems arising out of the System's relationship with its environment mean that the Creed's days in Eastern Europe are numbered, and that the System is about to make way for a market economy run by an authoritarian one-party regime? Will Hungary emerge as a kind of East Korea? This is one possible scenario, but it is certainly not the most likely one, since it would require the System to commit suicide—an improbable event. However, should the party leadership ever find itself with its back against the wall, it may conceivably prefer to jettison the Creed and salvage what material achievements it can, rather than go down with the sinking ship.[23]

## Notes

1. One of the first economists to build models for both types of growth in a socialist economy was Michal Kalecki: see *Introduction to the Theory of Growth in a Socialist Economy*, Basil Blackwell, Oxford, 1970.
2. ECE, *Labour Supply and Migrations in Europe: Demography 1950–1975 and Perspectives*, UN, New York, 1980, pp. 18 ff.
3. This section is based on an article by the author and M. Bacchetta entitled 'Le Défi de l'emploi en économie centralement planifiée' (The employment challenge in centrally planned economies), *Revue d'études comparatives Est–Ouest* (1986), No. 4, pp. 75–95.
4. The literature is unanimous on this point. See e.g. M.-A. Crosnier, 'L'URSS: Le Systeme salarial en question', *Problèmes économiques et sociaux*, La Documentation française, 22 Mar. 1985; T. Globokar and M. Kahn, 'Travail à l'Est: Des réalités contrastées', *Courrier des pays de l'Est*, May 1985, pp. 3–23; and E. Teague, 'Labour Discipline and Legislation in the USSR, 1979–1985', *Radio Liberty Research Bulletin*, 16 Oct. 1985.
5. For an analysis of this phenomenon from a historical perspective, see Wlodzimierz Brus, *Histoire économique de l'Europe de l'Est (1945–1985)*, La Découverte, Paris, 1985, and Z. Fallenbuchl, 'Communist Pattern of Industrialization', *Soviet Studies*, 21. 4 (1970), 459–84.
6. The side effects of surplus demand for labour are discussed in great detail by authors such as J. Adam (*Employment Policies in the Soviet Union and Eastern Europe*, Macmillan, London, 1982), F. Seurot (*Inflation et emploi dans les pays socialistes*, PUF, Paris, 1983), and János Kornai (*The Economics of Shortage*, North Holland Publishing Company, Amsterdam, New York, and Oxford, 1980).
7. See in this connection H. Yvert-Jalu, 'Les Personnes âgées en Union Soviétique', *Population*, June 1985, pp. 829–54.
8. Economic theory often uses the term 'X-efficiency' in this connection; see H. Leibenstein, *Beyond Economic Man: A New Foundation for Microeconomic Theory*, Harvard University Press, Cambridge, Mass., 1976.
9. The political consequences of such a step have been discussed in Ch. 4.
10. The underlying reasons have been discussed in Ch. 3.

11. The consequences of such a measure are discussed in detail in Ch. 6.
12. Discussed in Ch. 2.
13. This section borrows a number of arguments from earlier writings on the subject: see Pawel Dembinski, *L'Endettement de la Pologne ou les limites d'un système*, Anthropos, Paris, 1984, and 'Systems' Adaptations to East–West Trade', in B. Csikos-Nagy and D. Young, eds., *East–West Economic Cooperation in the Changing Global Environment*, Macmillan, London, 1986.
14. There are numerous handbooks of international economics, but the writings on the subject by J. Chipman are still (despite their age) the most comprehensive, since they present the classic theory of international trade in a way that takes full account of the various stages in its development (*Econometrica*, 1965 and 1966).
15. Pawel Dembinski, 'L'Inconvertibilité est-elle un obstacle aux échanges entre les économies planifiées de l'Europe de l'Est et les économies de marché?', *Revue d'études comparatives Est–Ouest* (1985), No. 4.
16. In early 1987 Poland decided to try a new approach. Enterprises with foreign currency holdings (as a result of a system of allowances designed to encourage exports) were invited to put them up for sale by auction. However, what was being auctioned was the right to hold the currency, rather than the currency itself. The initial results of the new approach were rather disheartening. The amount of foreign currency on offer was only $80,000, while demand totalled $4,000,000—well above the black-market rate.
17. See Ch. 3.
18. See Ch. 7.
19. For a summary of such measures, see W. Trzeciakowski, *Indirect Management in a Centrally Planned Economy: System Constructions in Foreign Trade*, PWN & North Holland, Oxford and Warsaw, 1978.
20. In *L'Économie internationale des pays socialistes*, Armand Colin, Paris, 1984, M. Lavigne analyses the main components and the direction of East–West trade, and shows that, despite industrialization, homogeneous goods (raw materials and agricultural produce) still make up the bulk of Eastern European exports.
21. In this connection two studies deserve special mention: G. Sokoloff, *Economy of Détente: The Soviet Union and Western Capital*, Berg Publishers, 1987, and E. Zaleski and H. Wienert, *Technology Transfer between East and West*, OECD, Paris, 1980.
22. A comprehensive and frank analysis of the Hungarian 'reforms' has been published by János Kornai ('The Hungarian Reform Process: Visions, Hopes and Reality', *Journal of Economic Literature*, 24 (Dec. 1986), 1687–737). See also J. Winiecki, 'Pourquoi les réformes économiques échouent-elles dans les systèmes du type soviétique?', *Revue d'études comparatives Est–Ouest* (1987), No. 3, pp. 47–72.
23. S. Bialer (*The Soviet Paradox: External Expansion, Internal Decline*), A. Knopf, New York, 1986 and M. Voslensky (*Nomenklatura: Die herrschende Klasse in der Sowjetunion*, Molden, Munich, 1984) agree on this point.

# Conclusion: A Contribution to CPE Theory?

To what extent can the arguments put forward in this book be seen as a contribution to CPE theory?

A theory can be assessed in terms of its consistency (in other words, its logical and explanatory qualities), or again in terms of the kinds of question that the proposed paradigm allows us to ask. Let me conclude with a number of remarks concerning the paradigm proposed in this book.

## Is the System really a system?

Our analysis of the philosophy adopted by the Eastern European Communist parties has shown that 'the System' quite definitely *is* a system. It is not merely a loose collection of phenomena referred to as a system purely for the sake of analysis (examples of this being the 'system of international trade' or the 'Swiss banking system'), but a set of institutions and mechanisms *deliberately created* to fulfil a clearly defined purpose. In this book we have examined the factors that help the System to remain consistent and the principles that determine its operation and economic organization.

The System cannot be seen merely in terms of a single domestic economy, or the economic tissue of any one country, or even the Communist party. It exists in its own right, with its own goals and specific behaviour. This, undoubtedly the most important conclusion to be drawn from our analysis, has extremely far-reaching implications for the future study of CPEs.

## The System versus its environment

Having identified the System as a separate entity, we can clearly
distinguish it from its environment, whereupon the relationship
between the two becomes a matter requiring special study. This
may seem too obvious to need saying; yet a good deal of the
literature on the CPEs disregards this essential fact, and simply
merges the two. In reality, however, a clear distinction can be
made between the domestic environment ('the tissue' or, in a
broader sense, 'the people' or 'society'), which is managed by the
System, and the international environment, which is not.

  The concept of entropy is a not inappropriate way of describing
the relationship between the System and its environment. The
System, in pursuance of its historical mission, attempts to organize
the societies in its charge by reducing entropy locally, while at the
same time opposition or resistance by the environment causes
entropy to increase. This metaphor neatly sums up the conflict
between the System and its environment.

  The economic problems discussed in this book confirm this
analysis, since they all arise out of the unending confrontation
between the System and its environment. The System's constant—but largely fruitless—attempts to tighten its grip on the
tissue, the problem of social discontent (which is essentially a
struggle to determine how best to distribute what the economy
produces), and the System's confrontation with the market economies (whether directly, through the arms race, or indirectly,
through trade) all essentially boil down to the issue of appropriation of wealth. Any economic analysis of CPEs that fails to take
account of the confrontation between the System and its environment is bound to be irrelevant. For this reason, the paradigm
proposed in this book may be referred to as the *confrontational
paradigm*.

## The importance of both macroeconomics and microeconomics

In the confrontational paradigm, macroeconomic and microeconomic analysis are equally important. The essential factor in

the confrontation between the System and its environment is the behaviour of microeconomic agents, which no serious analysis can afford to ignore. János Kornai[1] was the first to alert Western analysts to the importance of microeconomic behaviour and attitudes—something that Eastern European economists, and above all Eastern European managers, had long been aware of.

Nevertheless, Kornai's book still fails to give a true account of the economic problems in Eastern Europe, since he entirely disregards their macroeconomic features. Since the System is only identifiable at the macroeconomic (or even macropolitical) level, its economic role must be perceived from that point of view. Thus, in CPEs, economic performance is determined by the confrontation between a purely macroeconomic force—the System—and the behaviour of microeconomic agents, which is subject to the simultaneous influence of the System and the tissue. Most economic analyses of the Eastern European countries fail to recognize how vital it is to take both macroeconomic and microeconomic factors into account. In this respect, the confrontational paradigm is unique.

## The limitations of economic theory

Economic theory is rooted—one might say trapped—in the idealized patterns of the market economy, in which conflicts of economic interest are resolved one way or the other by means of compromises expressed in terms of prices and quantities. Market forces—an extremely sophisticated mechanism for reconciling incompatible aspirations—are taken for granted in economic theory, which therefore simply overlooks situations in which market forces cannot operate. In CPEs, the confrontation between the System and the tissue, which takes place on several different levels at once, cannot possibly be reduced to a simple two-dimensional price–quantity model. Nevertheless, this confrontation is an eminently economic one, since it revolves around the appropriation of resources.

Most of the tools of economic theory are incapable of analysing a confrontation that takes place in the absence of market forces. The confrontational paradigm, on the other hand, gives economic theory a chance to break free from two centuries of market-economy bias and to begin taking account of social systems in which economic problems are determined by factors other than adjustments of prices and quantities.

The confrontational paradigm attempts to tackle the problems of epistemology and methodology that are raised by the study of the Eastern European economies. This gives it an added dimension when compared with the great majority of writings on the subject, which are caught in a methodological void that is even more disturbing—not to say dangerous—than the strict orthodoxy of prevailing economic theory.

## The consistency of the System

Our analysis of the System and its relationship with its environment has helped to reveal its essential characteristics, which determine how it is organized and how it operates. Economically speaking, the essence of the System lies in the powers invested in it by the Creed. These powers are used by the System in order to control its environment—and in particular the economic tissue—for the sole purpose of getting to grips with material reality and shaping it to its own ends.

This is the basis for the organizational structure of the System. Its self-justifying ability constantly regenerates the powers provided by the Creed, while its self-organizing and self-targeting abilities enable it to handle the confrontation with the tissue. Together, these abilities provide the System with its requisitioning powers, undoubtedly the most important economic feature of the System.

This interdependence between the various elements of the System's organizational structure limits the effectiveness of economic reform. Every social system, and especially the one prevailing in Eastern Europe, is a coherent whole that does not take kindly to being tinkered with. Not only do quite different rules of consistency exist, but they cannot be infringed without threatening the very survival of the System. The appearance of independent economic agents or of a homogeneous monetary system would seriously interfere with the System's requisitioning powers, which is sufficient reason to suppose that the System *will never allow anything of the kind to occur*. Were the System to lose its requisitioning powers, it would cease to exist and would then become—politically speaking—just another totalitarian regime.

These conclusions run counter to the 'constructivist myth', according to which socio-economic systems can be constructed on the basis of predetermined plans, the economic tissue being assumed to be perfectly obedient. Believers in the constructivist myth are particularly numerous in Eastern European countries, which are constantly launching new reform projects.

The analysis contained in this book implicitly demonstrates the limitations inherent in any attempt at economic reform in Eastern Europe. Since the chief purpose of reform is to help the System survive, it will never turn enterprises into fully fledged economic agents or allow money to function homogeneously; for either of these measures would *reduce the System's grip on the economy, and thus curtail its requisitioning powers.*

In short, economic reform—with all due respect to its advocates, Eastern and Western—cannot provide the System with a lasting solution to its problems of survival, since all it can do is release the few reserves that still remain in the Eastern European economies and involve them in the production process—for example, by expanding private production. In other words, what passes for 'economic reform' is merely a stopgap measure, not a long-term solution that will enable the System to withstand the pressures from its environment for any length of time.

## The link between economic reform and economic policy

In the three chapters dealing with the external dilemmas, we saw that the peculiar characteristics of the System limit the efficiency of its economic response. The System has no tools of economic policy that are comparable with those regularly used by the governments of market economies, such as monetary policy, fiscal policy, foreign exchange controls, or trade tariffs.

Our analysis has indicated the reasons for this state of affairs, which may at first appear surprising. The System has complete control over monetary flows within the economy; it has no need of sophisticated instruments to influence them, since it can intervene via the monobank. However, such influence on flows of value is purely academic, since the latter have no effect whatsoever on physical flows, which are what matter when it comes to coping with environmental constraints. The tissue weakens the System's control over flows of value at the level where goods actually circulate. Nevertheless, the only economic policy that the System is really equipped to carry out and that could have any effect at all in controlling its environment is allocation policy.

The limitations of this policy have appeared throughout our study of the System's external dilemmas. As soon as the volume of requisitioning is insufficient to cope with the constraints on the System, allocation policy becomes meaningless and the failings of the System—in particular, its inability to allocate resources efficiently—are revealed. Since allocation policy cannot have any significant effect upon the volume of goods produced by the economy, the System is forced to try and perfect itself, by means of 'economic reform'.

There is thus a kind of continuum between the tools of economic policy available to the System and the various alternative kinds of economic reform. However, the more drastic the reform, the more it is likely to affect the nature of the System, by forcing it to deviate from the Creed.

In other words, we need to know whether the desire for economic efficiency or the need to preserve the System is currently uppermost in Eastern Europe. For the time being we do not have sufficient data to answer this question, for current reforms indicate that the System is desperately searching for a compromise that will enable it to survive but still ensure an acceptable degree of efficiency. The confrontational paradigm allows us to assess the chances of this search succeeding, and shows how the various conflicting constraints on the System are likely to prevent such a compromise from ever being achieved.

## Note

1. János Kornai, *Economics of Shortage*, North-Holland Publishing Company, Amsterdam, New York, and Oxford, 1980.

# SHORT BIBLIOGRAPHY

This bibliography makes no claim to be exhaustive. Detailed, specialized bibliographies will be found in a number of the books listed, all of which are relatively recent and are written in readily accessible languages.

Articles are not included; full references to the most important ones are given in footnotes throughout the book.

## Problems of methodology and paradigm

BOCHENSKI, I. M. (1965), *The Methods of Contemporary Thought*, Reidel, Dordrecht.

GUITTON, H. (1979), *De l'imperfection en économie*, Calmann-Lévy, Paris.

HICKS, J. (1979), *Causality in Ecomonics*, Basil Blackwell, Oxford. 'La Logique et la science économique', *Économies et sociétés*, Cahiers de ISMEA, ser. M, nos. 30 and 31, 1982 and 1983, Paris.

MIGNAT, A., SALMON, P., and WOLFELSPERGER, A. (1985), *Méthodologie économique*, PUF, coll. 'Thémis', Paris.

SCHMIDT, CH. (1985), *La Sémantique économique en question*, Calmann-Lévy, Paris.

SHACKLE, G. (1975), *Epistemics and Economics: A Critique of Economic Doctrines*, Cambridge University Press, London.

## The Creed and the basis of the System

BOCHENSKI, I. (1969), *The Soviet Russian Dialectical Materialism*, Reidel, Dordrecht.

DENIS, H. (1980), *L'Économie de Marx: L'Histoire d'un échec*, PUF, Paris.

DOGNIN, P.-D. (1970), *Initiation à Karl Marx*, Le Cerf, Paris.

—— (1977), *Les 'Sentiers escarpés' de Karl Marx* (2 vols.), Le Cerf, Paris.

LANGE, O. (1963), *Political Economy*, 1, *General Problems*, Macmillan, New York and Warsaw.

NOVE, A. (1983), *Le Socialisme sans Marx*, Économica, Paris.

236     SHORT BIBLIOGRAPHY

*The survival mechanism and the operation of the System*

ARON, R. (1962), *Paix et guerre entre les nations*, Calmann-Lévy, Paris.
BACZKO, B (1978), *Les Lumières de l'utopie*, Payot, Paris.
—— (1984), *Les Imaginaires sociaux: Mémoires et espoirs collectifs*, Payot, Paris.
BESANÇON, A. (1981), *Anatomie d'un spectre: L'Économie politique du socialisme réel*, Calmann-Lévy, Paris.
BRUS, W. (1975), *Social Ownership and Political System*, Routledge & Kegan Paul, London.
DUPUY, J.-P. (1982), *Ordre et désordre: Recherche d'un nouveau paradigme*, Le Seuil, Paris.
HELLER, M., and NEKRICH, A. (1982), *L'Utopie au pouvoir: Histoire de l'URSS de 1917 à nos jours*, Calmann-Lévy, Paris.
'Le Débat sur la nature de l'URSS', special number of *Problèmes politiques et sociaux*, La Documentation française, no. 550, Dec. 1986.
LE MOIGNE, J.-L. (1984), *La Théorie du système général, théorie de la modélisation*, PUF, Paris.


*Internal or organizational dilemmas*

ASLUND, A. (1985), *Private Enterprise in Eastern Europe*, Macmillan, London.
BRUS, W. (1968), *Problèmes généraux de fonctionnement de l'économie socialiste*, Maspero, Paris.
CRUMP, TH. (1981), *The Phenomenon of Money*, Routledge & Kegan Paul, London.
GALBRAITH, J. K. (1985), *The Anatomy of Power*, Corgi, London.
GARVY, G. (1977), *Money, Financial Flows and Credit in the Soviet Union*, NBER, Ballinger, Cambridge (Mass.).
GRANICK, D. (1975), *Enterprise Guidance in Eastern Europe: A Comparison of Four Socialist Economies*, Princeton University Press.
HAFFNER, F. (1978), *Systemkonträre Beziehungen in der sowjetischen Planwirtschaft: Ein Beitrag zur Theorie der mixed Economy*, Dumcker und Humbolt, Berlin.
JANSEN, P. (1982), *Die Inflationsprobleme in der Zentralverwaltungwirtschaft*, G. Fischer, Stuttgart.
KORNAI, J. (1980), *The Economics of Shortage*, North-Holland, Amsterdam, New York, and Oxford.
SIGG, H. (1981), *Grundzüge des sowjetischen Bankwesens*, Verlag P. Haupt, Berne and Stuttgart.

SPULBER, N. (1979), *Organizational Alternatives in Soviet-Type Economies*, Cambridge University Press, Cambridge and New York.

TRAIMOND, P. (1979), *Le Rouble: Monnaie passive et monnaie active*, Cujas, Paris.

TRZECIAKOWSKI, W. (1978), *Indirect Management in a Centrally Planned Economy: System Construction in Foreign Trade*, PWN and North-Holland, Warsaw and Oxford.

WILES, P. (1979), *Economic Institutions Compared*, Basil Blackwell, Oxford.

ZALESKI, E. (1980), *Stalinist Planning for Economic Growth 1933–1952*, University of North Carolina Press, Chapel Hill, NC.

## External or environmental dilemmas

ADAM, J. (1979), *Wage Control and Inflation in Soviet Bloc Countries*, Macmillan, London.

BIALER, S. (1986), *The Soviet Paradox: External Expansion, Internal Decline*, A. Knopf, New York.

BRUS, W. (1987), *Economic History of Eastern Europe, 1919–75*, iii. *Institutional Change within a Planned Economy*, Oxford University Press, Oxford.

CARON, F. (1985), *Le Résistible Déclin des sociétés industrielles*, Perrin, Paris.

DEMBINSKI, P. H. (1984), *L'Endettement de la Pologne ou les limites d'un système*, Anthropos, Paris.

LAVIGNE, M. (1985), *L'Économie internationale des pays socialistes* Armand Colin, Paris.

POPOVSKI, M. (1979), *La Science manipulée*, Mazarine, Paris.

SEUROT, F. (1983), *Inflation et emploi dans les économies socialistes*, PUF, coll. 'Libre-échange', Paris.

SLATER, J., and WEINERT, H. (1986), *Transfert de technologie entre l'Est et l'Ouest: Les Aspects économiques et commerciaux*, OECD, Paris.

SOKOLOFF, G. (1983), *L'Économie de la détente? L'URSS et le capital occidental*, Presses de la Fondation nationale des sciences politiques, Paris.

US CONGRESS (1985), *East European Economies: Slow Growth in the 1980s*, compendium of papers submitted to the Joint Economic Committee, Washington DC, Government Printing Office (these papers appear every three years).

ZALESKI, E., and WEINERT, H. (1980), *Transfert de techniques entre l'Est et l'Ouest*, OECD, Paris.

## Periodicals

There are two particularly useful sources of unprocessed information: *Radio Free Europe Research* and *Radio Liberty Research* (news-sheets published by teams of researchers based in Munich).

The weekly press review on the economies of the Communist countries, published by the NATO Directorate of Economic Affairs, is another essential source.

While it is impossible to provide an exhaustive list, the following scientific periodicals deserve special mention:

*Les Cahiers des Pays de l'Est*, La Documentation française, Paris.
*Revue d'études comparatives Est–Ouest*, CNRS, Paris.
*Journal of Comparative Economics*, Arizona University.
*Osteuropa Wirtschaft*, Osteuropa Institut, Munich.

# INDEX

absenteeism 161, 207, 208
abundance 26–7, 84, 195, 198, 222
accounting 127, 130, 142–4 *passim*,
   146, 192, 214
   consistency in 134
   *khozraschet* 107–8
   method of 100, 126, 160, 195,
     222–3; altering 98–9
   microeconomic 135
   national income/consumption
     values of 159
accounts
   balancing 102, 103, 136, 215;
     release from 124, 137, 168,
     193–4
   System forced to keep 96–7
accumulation 129, 131, 156–8,
   166–7, 173
Adam, J. 178 n., 227 n.
agents, economic 91, 99–100, 140,
   218, 222, 233
   economic relationships and 120,
     124–5, 130
   enterprises as 101–3, 106, 137,
     171, 205, 215
   interdependence of 211
   market forces and 68
   pseudo- 103–5, 109, 124, 148,
     214–15, 216
   System's control over 76, 80
   valuations by 143
agriculture 71, 92, 132, 219
Alexeev, M. 178 n.
Aliber, R. 148 n.
alienation 13, 28
allocation of resources 22, 27, 68–9,
   70, 111–12

class consciousness and 200
informational input and 196
rationing 155, 158, 160, 172, 173
System's apparent inability in 203,
   226, 234
welfare expenditure 184
Althusser, L. 12
Amman, R. 201 n.
Andreff, W. 177 n., 201 n.
arbitrageurs 214
Arendt, Hannah 16, 33 n., 89 n.
arms race 53–4, 179–90, 199, 230
Arnold, A. Z. 34 n.
Aron, Raymond 12, 33 n., 38, 57 n.,
   · 58 n.
Aslund, A. S. 116 n.
assets 100, 103
autarky 71, 204, 213–14, 216–21, 224
autonomy 104

Bacchetta, M. 227 n.
Baczko, Bronislaw 33 n., 34 n.
balance of payments 224
balance of power 43
banking 131–4
Barone, Enrico 68
Basic Law (1924) 30
Bauchet, P. 88 n.
Bauer, Tamas 89 n.
Bautier, Roger 57 n.
Becker, A. S. 183, 201 n.
Beksiak, Janusz 113, 114
benefits 99, 102, 129, 162, 172
Besançon, Alain 1, 5 n., 38, 57 n.
Bialer, S. 228 n.
black market 146, 218
Bochenski, I. M. 33 n.

banking structure and 133
fungibility 140
universal 147
United States 181, 182, 185, 190,
    196, 197
unrest, *see* discontent, social
USSR, *see* Soviet Union

valuations 121, 123, 124, 126, 143,
    194–7
value 73, 99, 101–2, 134, 167, 196
    accounting 96, 97, 142, 144
    flows of 234
    income 158, 172, 174
    labour 23–6, 69, 96, 98, 143, 159
    market 213, 215
    purchase 163, 171
    standard of 121, 122, 125, 126,
        133
    wastage of 69–70
Voslensky, Michael 117 n., 228 n.

wages 95, 97–9 *passim*, 102, 130–2
    *passim*, 169
    determining 159, 160, 211
    expansion in 207

levels of 122
linked to production 208
market economies and 156, 184
productivity and 139, 159, 211,
    212, 220
sterilization and 173, 174
Warsaw 103, 113
Warsaw Pact 187, 189
wastage 74, 83, 109, 166, 167, 194
    value 69–70
wealth, store of 121, 123–6 *passim*,
    133, 139, 145, 170
weather 71, 82
welfare 172, 184, 185, 186, 188
Wienert, H. 228 n.
Winiecki, J. 228 n.
Wittgenstein, Ludwig 88 n.

Young, D. 228 n.
Yvert-Jalu, H. 227 n.

Zaleski, Eugène 88 n., 228 n.
zeal 208, 210, 211
Zielinski, Janusz 52
Zinoviev, Alexander 48, 49